Canadian Circumpolar Institute Press
Northern Hunter-Gatherers Research Series, Volume 5

EVENKI ECONOMY IN THE CENTRAL SIBERIAN TAIGA
at the Turn of the 20th Century
Principles of Land Use

Mikhail G. Turov

*English edition prepared by Andrzej W. Weber
and Ksenia Maryniak*

Edmonton
2010

English translation, with added preface and glossary, of *Khoziaistvo evenkov taezhnoi zony Srednei Sibiri v kontse XIX–nachale XX v.: Printsipy osvoeniia ugodii*. Irkutsk: Izd-vo Irkutskogo univ., Irkutsk, 1990. (ISBN 5-7430-0136-7)

CCI Press, Canadian Circumpolar Institute, Edmonton

English edition © 2010 by CCI Press and the Baikal Archaeology Project,
  University of Alberta
Cover photo © 2001 by Mikhail G. Turov
All rights reserved. Published 2010 – Printed in Canada
15 14 13 12 11 10   1 2 3 4 5

Assistance from the Canadian Federation for the Humanities and Social Sciences' Aid to Scholarly Publications Programme is gratefully acknowledged.

ISSN 1707-522X   Northern Hunter-Gatherers Research Series
                     Andrzej W. Weber, Editor
                     Hugh G. McKenzie, Assistant Editor
                     Ksenia L. Maryniak, Assistant Editor

Library and Archives Canada Cataloguing in Publication

Turov, M. G. (Mikhail Grigorevich)
  Evenki economy in the central Siberian taiga at
the turn of the 20th century : principles of land use / Mikhail
G. Turov. -- English ed. / prepared by Andrzej W. Weber
and Ksenia Maryniak.

(Northern hunter-gatherers research series, 1707-522X ; v. 5)
Translation of: Khoziaistvo evenkov taezhnoi zony Srednei
  Sibiri v kontse XIX-nachale XX v.: Printsipy osvoeniia ugodii.
Copublished by: Baikal Archaeology Project.
Includes bibliographical references.
ISBN 978-1-896445-50-2

  1. Siberia (Russia)--Economic conditions. 2. Evenki (Asian people)--Economic conditions. 3. Subsistence economy--Russia (Federation)--Siberia. I. Weber, Andrzej II. Maryniak, Ksenia III. Baikal Archaeology Project IV. Title. V. Series: Northern hunter-gatherers research series v. 5

HC340.12.Z7S53813 2010   338.957   C2010-902996-8

Printed by Art Design Printing Inc.
Edmonton, Alberta, Canada

Contents

Table of contents iii
List of Figures iv
List of Tables iv
List of Photos iv
Preface to the English edition vi
    Editor's note on the English edition vii
    Note on transliteration and the rendering of languages viii
Author's foreword to the Russian edition 1
Chapter 1. Introduction to the research subject 9
    1.1 First period (17th–18th centuries) 9
    1.2 Second period (19th–early 20th centuries) 11
    1.3 Third period (1920s–1960s) 13
    1.4 Fourth period (from the early 1940s till the present [1990]) ... 15
Chapter 2. Traditional Evenki subsistence activities and their role in the
    land use system 18
    2.1 Subsistence hunting 23
    2.2 Fur hunting for trade 39
    2.3 Hunting equipment 44
    2.4 Fishing 48
    2.5 Summary 54
Chapter 3. Transport-reindeer husbandry in the Evenki economy 57
    3.1 Evenki and Orochen subtypes of reindeer husbandry 57
    3.2 Reindeer husbandry and development of the fur hunt 61
    3.3 Reindeer husbandry and the squirrel hunt 65
    3.4 Reindeer husbandry and large game hunting (moose) 67
    3.5 Reindeer calving 68
    3.6 Other aspects of Evenki and Orochon reindeer husbandry
        subtypes 70
    3.7 Winter: free-ranging 72
    3.8 Spring: calving and the start of the annual round 76
    3.9 Summer: nomadizing, smudges, and pasturing 80
    3.10 Autumn: the rut and preparation for the fur hunt 83
    3.11 Summary 87
Chapter 4. Economic territory, rhythm, and general principles governing
    the exploitation of taiga resources 89
    4.1 The traditional Evenki calendar 90
    4.2 Land use [*osvoeniia ugodii*] 93
    4.3 Selection of camp location 96
    4.4 Camp layout and structures 97

4.5 The Evenki mobile lifestyle 111
Conclusions 116
Glossary 118
References 124
Appendix: Selected photographs 139

Figures

Figure 1. Range of mobile Evenkis and types of reindeer husbandry
    in Central Siberia at the turn of the 20th century 6
Figure 2. The *ukikit* fishing enclosure 50
Figure 3. Types of Evenki caches 69
Figure 4. The *kel'che* toboggan 86
Figure 5. The *irivun* hand-pulled hunting sledge 87
Figure 6. The *urikit* short-term summer camp 97
Figure 7. The *khigolorkit* fall camp, adjacent to the spring *nengnerkit* ... 103
Figure 8. Types of dwelling and household structures of Central
    Siberian Evenkis 106

Tables

Table 1. Diet of Evenkis in the Central Siberian taiga throughout the year 53

Photos

Photo 1. Family of the Evenkis V. P. Kaplin (Pangarakai clan) and
    his wife, M. P. Egorchenok 139
Photo 2. E. I. Rukosueva (Ovodyl clan) of the Chuna Evenki group 140
Photo 3. Permanent *noku-delken* food cache at an autumn base camp 140
Photo 4. Permanent *noku-delken* food cache or *labaz* 141
Photo 5. Reindeer in smudges at a summer stop-over camp 141
Photo 6. Milking reindeer cows in a smudge 142
Photo 7. Starting point in the process of erecting a *chum* 142
Photo 8. Next stage of erecting the *chum* 143

Photo 9. The '*chum diu*' dwelling is ready 143

Photo 10. **Iumgulo** ground-level cache or *labaz* 144

Photo 11. **Noku dzeptyleruk** 'food cache' on three posts 145

Photo 12. Cache or *labaz* made of hewn planks and a pitched roof 146

Photo 13. Cache (*labaz*) on six posts. Katanga Evenkis............................ 147

Photo 14. Reindeer loaded with packs in preparation for migration 148

Photo 15. Permanent cache for storing winter clothing and equipment 148

Photo 16. **Delken** food cache at the autumn base camp of V. P. Kaplin 149

Photo 17. Old cache on one of the travel routes of the Kaplin family....... 149

Photo 18. Evenki woman E. I. Rukosueva beside an old **ugdama-diu**
bark *chum*, or **golomo** lodge.. 150

Photo 19. **Ugdama** cache for a small volume of food stores 151

Photo 20. **Gobchik** log mortuary structure on a shaman's grave.............. 152

Photo 21. Unusual construction of a cache or *labaz*................................. 152

Photo 22. Food cache on two posts up to 3 m tall 153

Photo 23. Crushing trap for wolverines 154

Photo 24. Hunter's snow-shoes/skis 155

Photo 25. Panorama of autumn base camp.. 156

Photo 26. Gateway for reindeer, facing the trail from the previous camp. 157

Photo 27. Churning the cream from reindeer milk 157

Photo 28. Preliminary processing of moose hide into **rovduga** suede....... 158

Photo 29. **Diugani** summer camp... 158

Photo 30. Reindeer in smudges at a summer camp 159

Photo 31. L. P. Sichegir, master of the camp. Katanga Evenkis 159

Photo 32. Early autumn: chum in an autumn reindeer pasture 160

Photo 33. Part of an autumn pasture enclosure.. 161

Photo 34. Close-up of fastening for autumn pasture enclosure 161

Photo 35. **Guluvun** fire for cooking food 162

Photo 36. An ancient method for keeping reindeer close to base camp 162

Preface to the English edition

Prof. Andrzej Weber
Principal Investigator, Baikal Archaeology Project
Editor, Northern Hunter-Gatherers Research Series

Mikhail G. Turov is an Associate Professor and Senior Research Scholar in the Department of Archaeology and Ethnography at Irkutsk State University. His monograph *Khoziaistvo evenkov taezhnoi zony Srednei Sibiri v kontse XIX–nachale XX v.: Printsipy osvoeniia ugodii*, published by Irkutsk University Press in 1990, is essentially the first ethnography produced by a Russian scholar that focused on the cultural-economic adaptations of Evenkis in the Central Siberian taiga. This work is based on the author's extensive field research, as well as on a broad examination of published and archival sources. It differs substantially from the mainstream Russian ethnographic research of the time in its focus, which shifts away from the traditional interests in ethnic history and origins and from static descriptions of material culture, social and political organization, rituals, and religious life or snapshot accounts of various economic activities. Turov's book provides a very comprehensive analysis of the three most important aspects of subsistence activity (moose hunting, reindeer husbandry, and fur hunting) for an Evenki group.

Furthermore, this work will be of considerable interest to Western readers due to its approach, which is as close to cultural ecology as it gets in Russian ethnographic scholarship. While in the West the culture-ecological school was a major breakthrough in hunter-gatherer studies, it never, despite the huge potential, took hold among Soviet ethnographers mostly because of their political and intellectual isolation. With the collapse of the Soviet Union, preceded by a rather lengthy economic crisis, the indigenous peoples of Siberia were faced with a number of new challenges, and these immediately became the focus of contemporary ethnographic work.

Thus, M. G. Turov's monograph retains its status of a very rare ethnography employing an approach akin to the culture-ecological school. For this reason, it should be of great interest to ethnographers and archaeologists working with northern hunter-gatherers past and present.

As for the citation in his text of "Marxist-Leninist classics," the author himself admitted to me during the production of this translation of his work:

> "… in those years, [citation of such works] was indeed one of the mandatory conditions not only for the preparation and submission of publications, but also for the defense of dissertations, conference papers, etc." At the same time, says Turov, "I cannot agree that the inclusion in the text of citations of these authors' works is explained *only* by the strict requirements of that epoch […] I do not consider myself to be a staunch supporter of the so-called 'Soviet regime,' and a fair while ago I was aware of all its pluses and minuses, especially in the final years (1980–90). For me, and even for

a rather significant number of foreign scholars, including historians, social scientists, and economists, the works of Marx and Engels on the economic issues and social organization of prehistoric 'traditionalist' societies, to this day have remained an unsurpassed and fundamental theoretical legacy."

The author would also like to add:

"It is another matter entirely that in the years since the publication of my monograph, a rather large body of ethnographic data has been collected on the economy and material culture of Evenkis that in certain details really does represent a correction to my previous views on the methods and principles of the organization of the economic system and overall subsistence of this people. Nevertheless, my fundamental views on the economic activity of Evenkis around the turn of the 20th century have remained the same, and I would venture to assert that they have been supported by a majority of Russian ethnographers—particularly A. A. Sirina, whom you know well."

Mikhail Grigorevich is referring to Anna Sirina, whose 2002 monograph on Katanga Evenkis was also published in English translation by the Baikal Archaeology Project (Sirina 2006). Sirina credits Turov with encouraging her interest in Evenki ethnography, and we are pleased to add the present volume to the English-language literature on Evenkis in Central Siberia as a testimony to his valuable, inspiring, and, most importantly, enduring contribution to the scholarship on this subject.

Apropos, we are delighted to inform our readers of M. G. Turov's latest monograph on Evenki people, which focuses on fundamental issues of their ethnogenesis and ethnic history (Turov 2008).

Editor's note on the English edition

The original translation from Russian was emendated by the Baikal Archaeology Project's production editor, Ksenia Maryniak, who also did the layout of this English edition and designed the cover. Andrzej Weber carried out a scrupulous and comprehensive revision of the entire translation, as well as a final read-through of the manuscript.

Footnote 5 of this English edition was actually the sole footnote in the original Russian monograph; all the others have been added for clarification purposes. For the same reason, some of the paragraphing has been modified, and we have added paragraph indention for direct quotes, as well as numbered subheadings.

A glossary of selected Evenki and Russian terms has also been included in this English edition, following the Conclusions. It complements and is partly based on a glossary compiled by David Anderson and Ksenia Maryniak for volume 2 of the Northern Hunter-Gatherers Research Series (Sirina 2006). In cases where they differ from Turov's Cyrillic renditions of Evenki terms, the English transliterations of Sirina's renditions are also added. As there is, in fact, only a little overlap between Turov and Sirina's Evenki nomenclature, scholars interested in Evenki terminology would benefit from also obtaining the Baikal Archaeology Project's English translation of Sirina's monograph, *Katanga Evenkis in the 20th Century and the Ordering of their Life-world* (Sirina 2006).

Note on transliteration and the rendering of languages

Cyrillic Evenki and Russian terms in the original are transliterated following the US Library of Congress romanization standard, but without ligatures. The standard for hard and soft signs is respected in italicized text. Evenki words very rarely have an iotized *e*, and thus readers should expect that the romanized character *e* actually represents an э in Evenki or in Evenki-derived Russian words. This applies in particular to the names of the capital of Katanga raion, Erbogachen, and of Evenki people themselves; they are not pronounced as *Yerbogachen* or *Yevenki*. On the other hand, the Enisei River is correctly pronounced as *Yenisei*.

Russian terms are indicated in ordinary italics, e.g., *kormozashchitnaia stantsiia, iagel'nik, gnus*. Evenki terms are indicated in italicised bold type, e.g., **guluvun, meneien, noku-delken** (alternate versions supplied by the author in the text have been moved to the Glossary). Russian plural forms are transliterated, as are Evenki plural forms, which are sometimes consistent with Russian grammar. Note that some Evenki words have become so widely used by local Russians that they have entered their everyday lexicon, e.g., *chum, iasak, labaz, rovduga*. Indeed, Evenki words such as **choom, keta, pika,** and **shaman** have actually become part of the English language.

Author's foreword to the Russian edition

Among the small peoples[1] of Siberia, Evenkis comprise the largest ethnic community (Dolgikh 1960; Gurvich and Dolgikh 1970; Vasilevich 1969: 7). Evenkis (historical name: Tunguses) are the only people that managed in the past to populate and inhabit a vast territory, from the Enisei [Yenisei] to the Pacific shore and from the forest-tundra line in the north to the southern borders of the taiga. From its earliest stages until the present, the ethnic history of Evenkis is replete with evidence of cultural interaction with other Siberian peoples, (Gurvich 1977; Kreinovich 1973; Okladnikov 1950, 1968: 25–42; Simchenko 1976; Vasilevich 1969: 3–7). It follows, then, that since the appearance of the first accounts on Siberia and the native peoples living there, Evenki culture has been one of the traditional objects of Russian ethnographic research. Furthermore, from the point of view of popular, scholarly, and general theoretical significance, the research materials themselves have invariably been highly relevant.

Achievements in the field of Tungus studies [*tungusovedenie*] are well known, and overall encompass a rich store of collected and analyzed documents, artifacts, and census data. The last hundred years of research on Evenki culture have been especially productive, starting from the very beginnings of ethnography as an independent historical discipline. The comparatively large numbers of Tungus ethnographers have not only focused on specific Evenki issues, they have also amassed factual materials that contributed to the development of Soviet ethnographic method and theory as a whole.

As one of the branches of [Russian/Soviet] ethnography, Tungus studies generally progressed from the amateur "collection of antiquities" to systematic investigations with methodological and theoretical foundations, dedicated terminology, and fieldwork methods. As of the mid-1980s, research on Evenki culture has generally focused on reconstructing the ethnogenesis and ethnic history of Evenkis, but also on identifying the place of the traditional culture of these hunter–reindeer herders in the economic and cultural typology of "pre-class societies" (Anisimov 1936; Okladnikov 1950; Stepanov 1939; Tugolukov 1970, 1980; Vasilevich 1969).

Primarily, these results have been applied to a number of issues concerning Evenki social organization, as well as to the structure of their ideological views and religious, everyday, and occupational customs and rituals. However, the study of Evenki economy and material culture is significantly lacking in proper systematic research. Regardless of the actual abundance of information, it could be stated that general research and theoretical synthesis of data in this area of Tungus studies have to date remained only at a very superficial level of description and classification of their individual components. Important relationships between various such components have not been

---

1. The typical terms in Russian are *malye narody* 'small peoples' or *malochislennye narody* 'numerically small peoples'. —*Ed.*

identified, and neither have these components, e.g., the foraging economy [*khoziaistvo prisvaivaiushchego tipa*], been conceptualized within a coherent theoretical framework. While it is essential to relate and to place the Evenki cultural-economic complex within the broader family of advanced hunter-fishers, this kind of typological exercise fails to reveal to any great extent the substance of the specific dynamics of Evenki economy, or the main principles of its functioning. Neither can a generalized typological classification of the subsistence economy account for existing regional particularities and variability in the economic practices of territorially and economically separate and independent Evenki groups of the Siberian taiga. Thus, the originality of the present research lies with the dissemination of a large body of new ethnographic data and with the freshness of the research objective—to examine the traditional Evenki economy and consider it as a relatively closed system within their ethnic *hunting and gathering* culture.

Resolutions of the [Soviet Communist government] dated February 7 and May 20, 1980 "On the further socio-cultural development of small peoples of the Far North and similar districts of Siberia" assigned top priority to accelerated development and integration of the traditional branches of the economy of Siberian peoples into the economic and social structure of Soviet society. These resolutions—along with increasing rates of industrial and agricultural development in Siberia, concomitant environmental issues, the problem of selecting optimal locations for industrial and agricultural centres, and the need to increase employment among the local indigenous population—pose a number of urgent challenges for current ethnographic research. Of central importance among them is the task of studying and extrapolating historical knowledge about the economic development of Siberia by its resident peoples, and by Evenkis in particular. The importance of this research is underscored by the present task of reviving the role of traditional hunting, fishing, and reindeer husbandry branches of the economy of indigenous populations in order to implement the [State] Food Program in recently developed regions of Siberia (Alekseenko 1986; Gracheva 1986; Karelov 1979; Kriuchkov 1979; Lukina 1986; Okladnikov and Alekseev 1981; Rakita 1983).

Achievements in ethnographic theory and in the history of early societies during the last three decades—including fundamentally new approaches to the ethnos theory and theory of culture, development of the theory of cultural economy and of the field of ethnic historiography, as well as recent specific studies dedicated to the economies of pre-class societies—all suggest at least three main reasons emphasizing the need for research on traditional economies of Siberian peoples as a whole, and of Evenkis in particular.

The first reason is *ethno-ecological*, which emphasizes the importance of this kind work from the global historical perspective. Of equal importance is the need to enhance our understanding of the relationship between community and the environment (Alimurzaev 1981; Bromlei 1981a; Chesnov 1982; Gromov 1981; Its 1982; Kim and Danilova 1981; Kozlov 1971, 1983; Kozlov and Pokshishevskii 1973; *Problemy istorii...* 1968; Zhekulin 1982).

The second reason is *general-ethnographic*, which emphasizes the importance of studying ethnic ways of land use[2] as one of the elements ensuring integrity of the ethnos and contributing to intergenerational transformation of cultural traditions. Of further importance is examining the essence of various mechanisms that ethnoses use to adapt to specific environmental conditions (Arutiunov 1981; Bromlei 1973, 1981b, 1983; Krupnik 1977; Markarian 1981a, 1981b).

And the third reason is *Tungus-specific*, emphasizing the importance of studying the Evenki system of cultural economy, both in the worldwide context of cultural economy systems of other peoples and in seeking to explain those aspects of the subsistence hunting model that remain poorly understood to this day. Such phenomena include the distinct territoriality of neighbouring Evenki groups, the institution of military and economic leaders, and patriarchal (domestic) slavery (Anisimov 1936; Markov 1979; Okladnikov 1950; Stepanov 1961; Vasilevich 1972).

This research aims to describe the economic principles that characterize the dynamics and main forms of interaction between Evenki hunting groups and the environment, and ultimately to identify subsistence strategies employed within the inhabited territories. Achieving these goals involves addressing the following general questions:

- How do ecological conditions governing Evenki lifeways, exploitation of natural resources, and overall sustainability of the taiga environment affect the technology and organization of their main economic and production activities?

- To what extent do the main Evenki subsistence activities align with the given environmental conditions?

- What are the general principles governing the organization and regulation of land use for hunting, fishing, and reindeer husbandry?

- What is the relationship between any given approach to land use and the particulars of Evenki nomadic life [*kochevoi byt*]?

- Where does this model of subsistence economy fit within the general typology of cultural economies of Siberian peoples, and what is the applied relevance of these research materials?

---

2. The Russian subtitle of this book includes the concept *osvoenie ugodii* 'lit. 'mastering the land, mastering resources', a term that implies usage and is usually translated as 'land development' (also as 'land tenure' or 'land occupancy', even 'assimilation of territory'). In fact, the mobile and organic approach of Evenkis to land use is incompatible with, and indeed inimical to, the settlement, advancement, and expansion implied in the term 'land development'. Here, we shall translate *osvoenie ugodii* as 'land use', 'resource use', or 'resource exploitation', which are consistent with the culture-ecological school of thought and familiar to English-language ethnographic readers. —*Ed.*

This research is based on field data collected by the author during regular expeditions carried out by the Laboratory of Archaeology and Ethnography at Irkutsk State University on the topic "Ancient History of Peoples in the South of Eastern Siberia." This fieldwork aimed to collect new materials on the ethnic characteristics of Evenki culture and its historical connections with other Paleo-Asiatic cultures. Another goal was to search for and interpret materials regarding the structural links between and within the general system of Evenki economy and material and spiritual culture that had been missing from the existing literature. Expeditions were conducted in 1970–78, 1981, and 1986 in Chuna and Katanga districts of Irkutsk oblast, where, until recently, part of the Evenki population had maintained their connections to tribal territories. Moreover, their economic activities still carried a traditional aspect, known to have existed at least as far back as the mid-19th century. This study also makes use of materials from the Archives of the Leningrad Branch of the Institute of Ethnography of the USSR Academy of Sciences [ALIE], the State Archives of Irkutsk Oblast [GAIO], the Katanga District Archive of the [Erbogachen Village Council] (AKRA), and various Evenki ethnographies from this region published in the past. Materials were selected from the relatively narrow category of *hunting groups*, identified in the literature as *peshie* 'on-foot' or *brodiachie* 'mobile'.[3] Such Evenki groups maintained small herds of domesticated reindeer [caribou] for transportation. In some cases, the ethnographic materials are supplemented with fairly extensive information on geography, the biology of game animals, and human ecology. Although such information is not directly related to customary ethnographic topics, it is nevertheless useful in reconstructing the subsistence strategies employed by Evenki hunters.

Field research showed that the regions under study were inhabited by independent neighbouring groups, formerly documented (in the 17th–19th centuries) as belonging to the Mendezin-Kursk administrative clan in the basin of the Chuna River (Oiedyl-Ovodyl and Chapagir families) and to the Pangarakai, Mongo, and Gole clans that were part of the Erbogachen group of Evenkis occupying the middle course of the Lower Tunguska River (Vasilevich 1969: 274, 277–8; Turov field notes 1974, 1987). During eight field seasons (2–4 months per year), the author was able to participate directly in the mobile life of Evenkis and observe their contemporary system of land use. During each fieldwork season, a distance of 150–200 km or more was covered along [human] footpaths and reindeer/horse trails. These routes existed already in the [19th] century and some have been used to this day in traditional Evenki migration and when camping. Over forty permanent and temporary base camps [*stoibishcha*] and other camps [*stoianki*] were studied and documented in field notes, photos, and sketches. Interviews were conducted with 35 informants, both Evenkis and Russians who for various reasons had

---

3. While 'wandering' is the most literal translation of the Russian adjective *brodiachie*, the more up-to-date term 'mobile' will be used here, which is consistent with the English edition of A. A. Sirina's treatise on Katanga Evenkis (Sirina 2006). —*Ed.*

extensive contacts with the Evenki population in the given region. In part, the interview data provide information about traditional elements of Evenki economic and material culture that are already lost but can still be reconstructed in the memory of the older generation. The single most significant source of information on the Chuna Evenki group was the Rukosueva sisters, Elena Illarionovna and Nadezhda Illarionovna (b. 1914 and 1910, respectively, and both Evenkis on their father's side); Elena Rukosueva, a tenured hunter at the Chuna State Hunting Enterprise until 1972 [Photo 2], began hunting when she was 14 years old. Additional information was obtained from Nadezhda Rukosueva's husband, Petr Filimonovich Burmakin (raised until the age of 16 by an Evenki family of the Chuna group) and from the following residents of the village of Vydrino: V. F. Apokin, N. G. Grigorev, K. M. Smolin, V. Konovalov, and L. Rukosuev. The majority of information on the Erbogachen Evenki group was gathered from V. P. Kaplin (Pangarakai clan), M. P. Egorchenok, N. V. Kaplin, V. P. Veretenov [Veretnov], I. D. Kaplin, V. D. Kaplin (preceding four of the Pangarakai clan), L. P. Sychegir [Sychogir, Sichogir; Photo 31], and I. S. Mongo.

The results of fieldwork and preliminary interpretations (Turov 1974, 1975, 1979, 1982) not only justified the merits of the regional approach to examining the Evenki economy but also demonstrated the benefit of reconstructing the general principles of land use by Evenki groups in the taiga region of Central Siberia at the turn of the 20th century.

As the title implies, this research analyzed materials concerning several comparatively small, localized Evenki groups that historically had lived within the boundaries of a single physiographical area. In limiting the spatial boundaries of the research data, primary consideration was given to the fact that the system of natural, climatic, and landscape conditions specific to Central Siberia, as well as the prevailing types of fauna and flora used for subsistence, make this region a separate, delineated ecological zone, significantly different from several neighbouring zones in Eastern Siberia.

Following the generally accepted physiographical boundaries, we defined the territory of our interest as comprising two taiga "provinces," Tunguska and Angara (Fig. 1). The first covers a major portion of the Podkamennaia and Lower Tunguska river basins. The second province includes almost the entire basin of the Angara River and its left-bank tributaries, except the mouth of the Enisei River (GUGK 1962; Gvozdetskii and Mikhailov 1978). In general, the western boundaries of these provinces follow the Enisei, while the eastern boundaries follow the Lena River until its confluence with the Viliui River. The northern boundaries follow the middle course of the Lower Tunguska, and the southern boundaries follow the Uda-Chuna, a left-bank tributary of the Angara. From a geomorphological point of view, this territory lies within the massif of the Central Siberian plateau, whose elevations generally do not exceed 600 m above sea level. This entire territory is characterized by continuous and rather homogenous forest, dominated by larch, pine, and birch, interspersed with Siberian pine [*kedr*] groves, as well as brushland

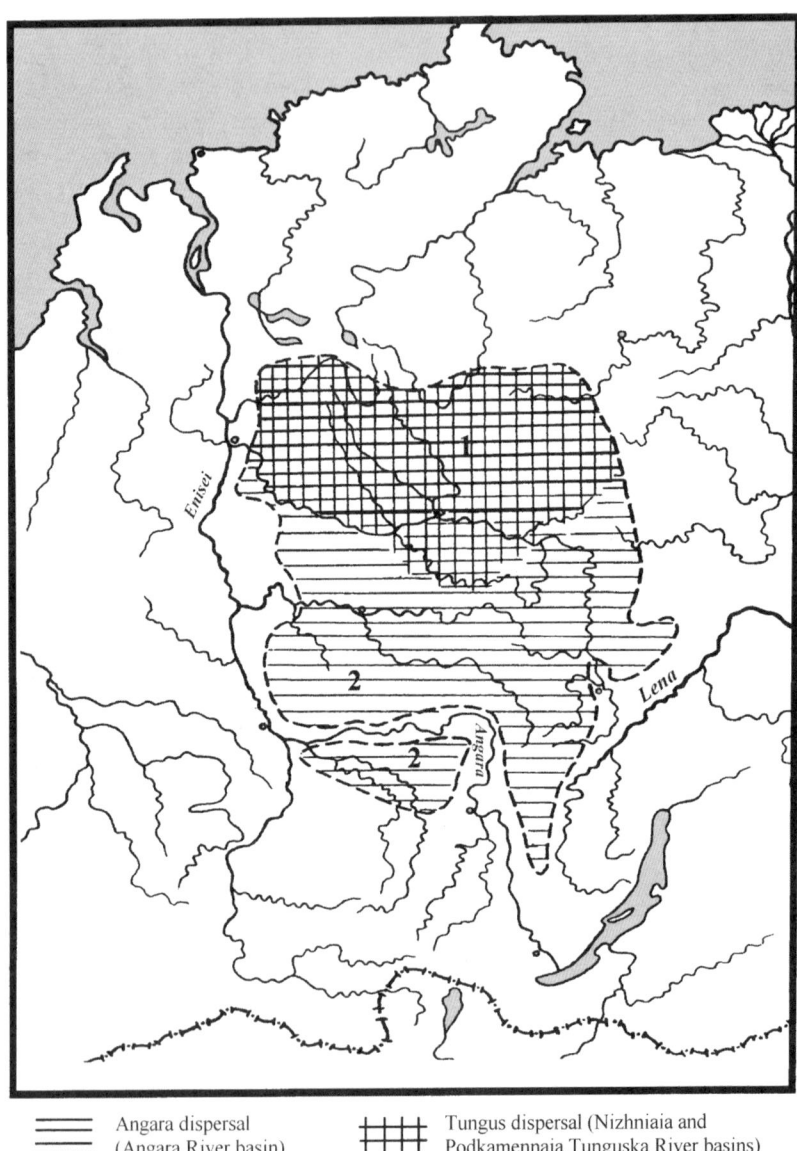

Figure 1. Range of mobile Evenkis and types of reindeer husbandry in Central Siberia at the turn of the 20th century.

and patches of dark-needled spruce taiga along the rivers and other bodies of water. Practically the entire territory features extensive pastures of reindeer moss [*iagel'*],[4] the area and relative density of which increase significantly

---

4. Here the terms *iagel'* or *olenii mokh* 'reindeer moss' seem to include both *Cetraria* 'reindeer moss' and *Cladonia* 'Iceland moss'. —*Ed.*

in the Podkamennaia and Lower Tunguska basins. According to informants, reindeer moss was much more plentiful in the Angara basin in the past than today. Game birds and animals such as moose [European elk], reindeer [caribou], bear, hazel-hen, black grouse, wood grouse, and waterfowl are found throughout the territory. In the past, the following types of fish were very important as food sources: *taimen'*, whitefish, pike, grayling, *lenok*, and burbot. It is also worth mentioning that the population size and density of moose in Central Siberia has always been much higher than in neighbouring regions. In our opinion, the specific ecological conditions for survival and subsistence have played a significant role in defining the distinctive Evenki lifestyle and their subsistence activities in this region, and were conducive to the formation of resource exploitation strategies adapted to the taiga environment.

The specific chronological focus of this research (late 19th to early 20th century) was chosen for three reasons. First, according to the existing literature, of significant importance was the fact that by the end of the 19th century the population of Central Siberia had a stable composition, with well established hunting and exploitation territories. Second, it would be somewhat easier to reconstruct the "traditional system" of the Evenki economy based on materials from the turn of the 20th century thanks to the great volume of research data available for this period; moreover, missing information could still be recovered by interviewing older people, who remembered the traditional system as operating practically without change until the end of the 1930s. Third, this research was mainly interested in the taiga land use system that existed before the Evenki hunting economy was collectivized. Our interest resulted from the specific combination of the main branches of Evenki economic activities during the relevant period, which allowed the most comprehensive exploitation of the taiga's natural resources. Trade and subsistence were the two key branches of this system.

Apart from the classic works in Marxist theory, which in their time described the general character of the economy of pre-class societies as well as their interactions with the environment (Engels n.d., n.d.-a), the methodological basis of this research and the principles governing my approach to the subject matter originate from a theoretical synthesis of numerous works concerned with the history of early societies and with ethnography (Danilov 1968, 1981, 1981; Kabo 1968, 1981; Kozodoev 1977; Lashuk 1970; Semenov 1976, 1973, 1979; Tolstov 1931, 1946, 1961).

The working method for this research consisted of direct observation of the traditional elements of hunting, reindeer husbandry, fishing, nomadizing and mobile life, and other aspects, all of which still exist in Evenki culture today. To some extent, the contemporary nomadic Evenki economy in Central Siberia is still based on longstanding ethnic traditions. As in all ethnographic research, the comparative-historical method was used as a means to identify possible common characteristics between land use within the study area and overall Evenki systems, and to classify the Evenki land use system within the category of *upper foraging type* [*vysshii prisvaivaiushchii tip*] (Markov 1979).

With utmost respect and gratitude, the author dedicates this work to his informants, E. I. and N. I. Rukosueva, P. F. Burmakin, V. P. Kaplin, and M. P. Egorchenok. The author also expresses profound gratitude to the participants in the field expeditions (G. I. Medvedev, A. G. Generalov, and N. A. Savel'ev), as well as the staff of the Department of General [World] History at Irkutsk State University (ISU) and the Laboratory of Palaeoecology at ISU, whose support and participation were invaluable.

Chapter 1. Introduction to the research subject

As mentioned in the foreword, the multifaceted Evenki system of land use of inhabited taiga territories is an essentially new and practically unresearched topic in [Soviet/Russian] ethnography. At the same time, the formulation of our research goal was of course stimulated by prior studies of Evenki culture as well as new developments in ethnographic theory and methods, and also by the increasing amount of ethnographic data. In this sense, it is obviously worthwhile to provide even a very general historiographic overview and assessment of the growth of knowledge on the subject. Overall, four chronologically significant and relatively independent periods can be identified [in the development of ethnographic research on Evenki people].

1.1 First period (17th–18th centuries)

The first period corresponds to the time when the [Imperial] government began overseeing the [Russian] settlement of selected districts in Western Siberia and around Lake Baikal. At that time, the first information about Siberia and its peoples started to appear on a relatively consistent basis. Strictly speaking, ethnographic research did not yet exist, and most materials came from the notes and reports of various travellers, members of diplomatic missions, and government-hired trappers. Travelling through Siberia, in addition to providing descriptions of the routes they followed and of the nature and geography they encountered, these people supplied information on the economy, language, lifeways, and anthropological and social characteristics of the various peoples of Siberia. This ethnographic material displayed a fairly high degree of accuracy for that time, and was usually gathered firsthand or constituted a retelling of information obtained from interviews with the local population, military personnel [*sluzhilye*], local administrators, and other *znatkie liudi* 'important people'.

For example, [upon his return from exile in Siberia (1661–71)] the Polish war prisoner Adam Kamieński-Dłużyk recorded a very interesting description of certain aspects of the lifeways of the Angara and Iakut [Yakut river] Tunguses. He was impressed with the way Angara Tunguses adapted their clothing to the harsh taiga conditions, their marvellous artistry with the bow and arrow, and their friendliness and hospitality. Kamieński wrote:

> "Those *Tunguzy* are an easygoing people... In winter and summer they travel from river to river to feed themselves. They have large herds of reindeer, maybe a thousand or more... they travel from Eniseisk [in Krasnoiarsk Krai] on sledges... and transport loads with teams of four dogs. When there is a wind, the sledges move under sail" (Polevoi 1965: 125).

Kamieński also documented Tungus reindeer-herders on the lower Lena River, noting that they used domesticated reindeer as lures in hunting wild reindeer.

A wealth of material on Evenkis can be found in the reports of the Russian missions to China undertaken in 1675–8 by N. Spafarii and in 1695 by I. Ides and A. Brand. Data from Spafarii's report were published later (1882) in the form of a travel diary, and include notes about numerous Tungus camps along the Angara River. Ides obtained information mainly from interviews with people who knew Siberia and with eyewitnesses to various events. Using these sources, he provided the most extensive and detailed contemporary descriptions of the economy and lifeways of the Angara Evenkis, and also of Evenki groups that lived on the Lower Tunguska and Podkamennaia Tunguska rivers (Zinner 1968). The documents of Ides and Brand, which have been used since by many researchers, can rightfully be considered the first collection of ethnographic materials on Evenki culture (Ivanov 1978: 17–20; Vasilevich 1969: 20).

A great amount of early information gathered by Russian and foreign scholars about Siberian peoples, including Evenkis, was summarized in Nicolaas Witsen's book *Noord en Oost Tartaryen*, published in 1705 [2nd edn.].[5] Summarizing materials from the works of Ides, Brand, Spafarii, and others (Zinner 1968: 12), Witsen undertook the enormous task of compiling all the information available at the time about the geography, ethnography, and history of Siberia, along with various ethnographic and linguistic materials about the Tungus people. Of this body of data, we have been chiefly interested in the remarks about reindeer husbandry [*olenevodstvo*], hunting and fishing, nutrition, and other details of Evenki lifeways. It is particularly worth mentioning that Witsen was probably the first researcher specializing in Siberia to categorize Evenkis into groups according to the animals they employed for transportation: *olennye* 'reindeer-using', *konnye* 'horse-using', and *sobach'i* 'dog-using'.

During the 18th century, the reforms of Peter I, the drive to acquire new lands for the [Imperial Russian] government, and the consequent expansion of Russian migration into Siberia resulted in many new expeditions. Among the various materials compiled by their participants, the most interesting were those published by G. F. Miller and I. G. Georgi. The relevance of these two studies from the perspective of this research is uneven. For example, most of Miller's *Istoriia Sibiri* (1937, 1941) is dedicated to the historical events that resulted in Siberia being incorporated into the Russian Empire. Without analyzing his sources, Miller provides general information about the "forest Tunguses," who lived in the mountains and forests of Central Siberia

---

5. The chapter on Siberia from [the 1705 edition of] Witsen's book, including a section on "Tunguziia and Adjacent Districts," was translated from the Dutch [into Russian] by V. G. Trisman. The manuscript of the translation is stored at the archive of the Leningrad Branch of the USSR Academy of Sciences' Institute of Ethnography [ALIE K-V/1/139–42].

and used domesticated reindeer for transport. Far more valuable is the work by Georgi, who participated in an expedition led by P. S. Pallas. Georgi summarized not only the reports of the members of the expedition, but also the materials of previous authors, including Miller, F. Stralenberg, and I. Gmelin. Georgi's book, *Opisanie vsiekh obitaiushchikh v Rossiiskom gosudarstvie narodov* (1799), essentially sums up the first period of gathering data on the traditional culture of Siberian peoples as a whole, and of Evenkis in particular. The significance of this book lies not only in giving us what was, at that time, quite a detailed comparative-historical description of Evenkis, but also in the fact that Georgi used linguistic and folkloric data to identify Evenkis as a distinct group. Georgi was also the first to classify Evenkis based on subsistence criteria (reindeer or livestock herding, game hunting, and fishing) and modes of transportation (horses, reindeer, and dogs).

As for other 18th-century publications relevant to our subject, one worth mentioning is a sketch of Barguzin and Udin Evenkis written by a Governor-general Brill of Irkutsk [gubernia]; it was published over 100 years later (Kalachev 1871). The author described Tunguses as living a comparatively mobile life, "… settling during summer and then, during winter, travelling with their reindeer herds into the mountains, living in yurts." The author also remarked that these Evenki groups ate predominantly fish, and that their yurts were covered not only with animal skins but also with "fish skins" (Kalachev 1871: 43).

Thus, by the beginning of the 19th century Georgi had produced a summary of the first period of research on Evenki economy and material culture. Overall, the gathering of ethnographic material during this period coincided with collecting information on Siberian regional studies.[6] As a government-sponsored enterprise, the study of local populations was subordinate to the tasks of general state interest such as administering *iasak* 'tribute' and promoting trade between fur hunters, the government, and private merchants. At the end of the 18th century, the research undertaken during that stage resulted in a rich body of factual data available for subsequent dedicated ethnographic research on Siberian peoples, including Evenkis.

1.2 Second period (19th–early 20th centuries)

From the end of the 18th century until the last quarter of the 19th century, the discovery of promising iron ore and gold deposits within the boundaries of Evenki territories along the upper Lena and Lower Tunguska rivers, as well as in the Trans-Baikal and Cis-Amur regions, prompted an overall shift in the geographic focus of regional studies research [*kraevedcheskie issledovaniia*]

---

6. "Local lore" is the term typically used by Russians as an English translation of *kraevedenie* 'regional studies', which in Central and Eastern Europe is a specific scholarly field that includes the natural history and folklore of a given territory. —Ed.

toward the northern and eastern parts of Siberia now undergoing development. For the emerging field of Tungus studies, which organizationally and thematically continued to be connected to regional studies, these circumstances resulted in a large number of Evenki groups living in the huge expanses of Central Siberian taiga being more or less completely overlooked by scholars. This probably explains why the amount of research activity in Tungus studies seemed to decrease in the first half of the 19th century. This trend continued until the establishment of the Eastern Siberian Branch of the [Imperial] Russian Geographic Society[7] (1851) in Irkutsk, which became an important centre for ethnographic research in Siberia. Among the limited number of studies from that period, only a few relate to our topic. The most informative and comprehensive contributions, published by governors-general I. Pestov and A. Stepanov, focused on the Evenkis in Enisei okrug. Of particular interest are their descriptions of reindeer husbandry, the nature of the nomadic economy [*kochevoe khoziaistvo*], seasonal migration [*perekochevki*], and hunting and fishing methods (Pestov 1833: 179–83; Stepanov 1835: 42–4, 73–4). Notable among the publications of data resulting from scholarly fieldwork of that time was the report on expeditions led by A. F. Middendorf (1843–4), who visited the districts inhabited by the Ilimpeia group of Evenkis. Middendorf (1869–77) recorded interesting information about wild reindeer hunting methods, reindeer husbandry in the tundra, and means of transportation.

The establishment of the Russian Geographic Society (RGO) in 1845 and of its Eastern Siberian branch (VSORGO) in 1851 marked a qualitative shift in [Russian] ethnography that allowed Tungus studies to grow in a number of new directions, independently from regional studies.

The common interest of Russian ethnography and Tungus studies in the historical development of primordial [*pervobytnye*] societies prompted the first compilations and generalizations [at that time] of material about social organization, family and marital relations, production-trade relations, and productive forces within a given community. Information about Evenki economy and material culture that had been accumulated while researching general questions on the Evenki ethnos was classified and summarized under the theoretical framework of the "development of productive forces in a primitive economy," and within the theoretical models of primordial societies developed by L. Morgan, K. Marx, F. Engels, N. Ziber, and other proponents of various competing ideological directions. The antagonism between the emerging Marxist and [existing] bourgeois ideologies not only influenced the theoretical and methodological development of [Soviet] ethnography for many decades, but also determined to a great degree its general objectives and specific research tasks.

In Siberian ethnographic studies published during the second half of the 19th century, the topic of our interest was further elaborated with regard to

---

7. VSORGO or VSOIRGO (Vostochno-Sibirskii otdel [Imperatorskogo] Russkogo geograficheskogo obshchestva). In fact, the Siberian branch was not named "Eastern" until 1877, after the establishment of the Western Siberian branch in Omsk. —*Ed.*

economic and geographic aspects of Siberian peoples, their culture and lifestyle. Materials gathered by members of the [Imperial] Russian Geographic Society included publications about Central Siberia, among them an account of the North Baikal Evenkis and Baunt Evenkis (Radde 1858), the observations of a lieutenant Orlov who took part in an 1857 VSORGO Siberian expedition, and notes about the voyage of P. Clark to visit the Ocheul-Tutura Tunguses in the Upper Lena okrug of Irkutsk gubernia (Clark 1863).

Far more extensive and diverse information on Evenkis was published about a series of trips to Enisei okrug and in Turukhansk Krai undertaken by N. Kostrov (1857), N. Tretiakov (1869), and M. F. Krivoshapkin. In 1873–75, the [Imperial Russian] Geographic Society organized the Olenek Expedition, under the leadership of the geologist A. Czekanowski. Another participant in this expedition, F. F. Miller, later published materials about the economy and lifeways of Evenkis of the Erbogachen and Nakanno groups on the Lower Tunguska River (1895). In 1888, N. Grigorovskii travelled to the Upper Angara River and provided a very interesting account of passive fishing methods, using fences placed in the river (1890). Thus, toward the end of the 19th century, the accumulation of a extensive and diverse body of data resulting from research expeditions and personal travel facilitated the establishment of ethnography as an independent specialized field of research, separate from general Siberian regional studies.

There seems to be a hiatus in Tungus studies in Central Siberia that lasted from the end of the 19th century until the late 1920s, i.e., before the establishment of the Soviet school of ethnography. The main activities of VSORGO focused on studying the economy and lifeways of eastern, northern, and Trans-Baikal Evenki groups, outside the region of our interest. The only studies of Central Siberian Evenkis during this period were conducted by K. M. Rychkov, who collected ethnographic artifacts from the Ilimpeia and Sym Evenki groups. Rychkov wrote a series of articles about those travels, which were later incorporated into a research monograph (1917). Rychkov's employment of somewhat imprecise terminology does not diminish the overall importance of this work, which contains valuable accounts of subsistence activities, mobile lifestyle, reindeer husbandry, cooking methods, and seasonal changes in diet.

1.3 Third period (1920s–1960s)

The formation of a Soviet school of ethnographers specializing in Tungus studies sparked renewed interest in carrying out research on traditional forms of Evenki economy and material culture. Early on, this research was based on the previous paradigm of *geographic ethnography*. This was most clearly to be seen in the work of V. G. Bogoraz, whose idea of "ethnogeography" had a marked influence on both the subsequent development of a corresponding branch of Soviet ethnography and on the topic of our research. Apart from overall questions addressed by Bogoraz on the origin and dispersion of [Evenki] culture, most interesting for us are the issues he raised about traditional methods of utilizing reindeer in the economy of Siberian peoples, and about the origins of reindeer husbandry itself (Bogoraz-Tan 1928, 1933). Bogoraz's attempt to connect the cultural particulars of various ethnic groups with the particulars of their natural habitat was an unquestionably positive and indeed significant development. In fact, Bogoraz was the first to justify the discipline of *ethnogeography* and the value of carrying out comprehensive ethnogeographic research on "traditional" cultures (Bogoraz-Tan 1928: 65–6). Other studies from that period, notably by A. N. Maksimov (1928) and M. Plotnikov (1924), focused on theoretical issues pertaining to the origin of reindeer husbandry and future prospects.

The late 1920s and the 1930s witnessed an upsurge in ethnographic research on Siberian and Far North/East Asian indigenous peoples. This was accompanied by significant changes in the objectives and topics, as well as in the theory and methods, of ethnographic research. Influenced by the overall intellectual climate of Soviet ethnography, two parallel and relatively independent directions emerged in Tungus studies.

The first direction was defined thematically by the goals of [Soviet] applied ethnographic research, which focused on finding the most optimal ways of incorporating the indigenous peoples of Siberia, [who were regarded as] socially and economically backward, into the new structure of a "socialist economy." Thus, a whole series of descriptive summaries appeared that included interesting information about traditional elements of Evenki subsistence along with more general data on their economy (Dorogostaiskii 1925; Kharuzina 1928; Kopylov 1928; Koviazin 1936; Sokolov 1925). Among the publications specially dedicated to Evenki hunting and reindeer husbandry, articles by I. M. Suslov (1927, 1930), B. E. Petri (1930), and P. G. Poltoradnev (1932) are worthy of mention. Their attempt not only to record as fully as possible the entire body of information on the Evenki fur trade and on reindeer husbandry, nomadizing, and technological foundations of their subsistence economy, but also to describe land use in the taiga and the overall system of the traditional Evenki economy, make these studies stand out from the rest. Moreover, these works (especially the article by Petri) refer to locally specific variants of the economic system, which are not wholly discernible in the overall economy of Evenki groups throughout the Central Siberian taiga.

In general, the publications of the 1920s and first half of the 1930s could be labelled as *folkloric [narodovedcheskie]*; they included not only ethnographic articles but also archaeological, geographic-economic, anthropological, and other natural history studies. However, for the most part the scholars of that period followed the regional approach to investigating the culture of Siberian ethnoses, which was the dominant type of research prior to the [1917 Bolshevik] Revolution. Tungus studies had not yet disengaged themselves from the influence of evolutionist, chronological, and other tendencies; meanwhile, the Marxist approach was often vulgarized and misinterpreted. In spite of all that, we can hardly fail to notice a positive feature of these "ethnological" works, including their comprehensive approach to examining the ethnic history of Siberian peoples, as well as their emphasis on detailed and systematic collection and assessment of ethnographic data.

The formation of the second, *purely ethnographic* direction in Tungus studies probably took place after the final establishment of ethnography [as an independent scholarly discipline]. It was stimulated by the growing debate during the 1930s on the periodization of primordial society. One of the consequences of this early discussion was that ethnographers apparently abandoned the topic of interaction of ethnic groups with the natural environment as the main research goal, and turned their attention to cultural superstructure. Thus, until the [Second World] War, Evenki ethnographic studies were dominated by topics such as language, folklore, social organization, beliefs, and anthropology, with a focus on examining early stages of the ethnogenesis and ethnic history of Paleosiberian peoples. The most important Tungus studies of this period include contributions by G. M. Vasilevich, A. F. Anisimov, M. G. Levin, and N. N. Stepanov. However, the materials published in those studies most frequently relate to the early economic and social strata of Evenki society (Anisimov 1936; Vasilevich 1936), and only partially characterize individual elements of the Evenki economy or the land use system as a whole (Levin 1936; Stepanov 1939).

1.4 Fourth period (from the early 1940s till the present [1990])

In Soviet history, attention to national identity issues increased sharply during the years of the [Second World] War, and especially during the three decades that followed. This impelled Soviet ethnographers to engage in more detailed studies and theoretical reflection on questions of the ethnogenesis and ethnic history of Soviet peoples, and to identify *ethno-differentiating* and *ethno-integrating* elements and qualities in these cultures. The materials accumulated via this research were summarized in several monographs (Dolgikh 1960; Levin and Potapov 1956, 1961) that provided both macroscopic and microscopic viewpoints on the ethnic and cultural history of Siberia. Study by geographic area [*areal'nye issledovaniia*] prompted the creation of the theory of cultural economy and ethnic historiography (Levin and Cheboksarov 1955). Similarities in form of economic and material culture in genetically distinct ethnoses were explained in terms of similar environmental conditions. In turn, this explanation stimulated interest in the interaction between a given ethnos and the environment, as well as in the indirect influence of geographic factors on the development of productive forces.

The dominant role of the focus on ethnic origins [*etnogenez*] in Evenki studies left its mark on research programs related to Evenki material and spiritual culture, and it also defined the strategic objectives of the data gathering expeditions undertaken during this period (Okladnikov 1950, 1968; Stepanov 1961; Tugolukov 1962, 1969, 1970; Vasilevich 1949, 1961, 1962, 1964, 1966, 1969; Vasilevich and Levin 1951). Fieldwork goals and thematic selection of empirical materials for publication were likely defined in such a way as to examine how one or another component of the economy or material culture of a given ethnos determined its overall cultural specificity. By the end of the 1960s, Tungus studies had accumulated a very large body of factual data regarding the subject matter of our interest. However, the empirical information summarized in the monographs allowed for only a very general assessment of individual ethnic characteristics and particulars of the Evenki economy. While this material permitted scholars to identify how the Evenki economy differed from a series of typologically similar economic systems of other Siberian peoples, information was lacking on the specific components of their economy and material culture that defined the internal-structural links between relevant culture-forming elements. Such components are not themselves explicit carriers of Evenki ethnic characteristics, but are indispensable to the reconstruction of their land use system. Nevertheless, even at this high level of generalization, this economic data displayed regional particulars with regard to hunting and reindeer herding as well as overall economy and lifeways in every territorially distinct group (Vasilevich 1969: 45–51, 75–7).

During the 1970s and 1980s, data on the Evenki economy were accumulated and interpreted against the background of an overall increased interest on the part of ethnographers and historians in the processes of class formation, the origins of early class-based state entities, and the investigation of the theory of ethnos and culture, including its differentiating and ethno-integrating characteristics. Close attention was given to researching the adaptations to nature of every cultural subgroup of a particular ethnos. Interesting new hypotheses emerged from the discussion of historical correlations between maternal and paternal clan, and assessment of the transition from a matrilineal to a patrilineal form of community/clan structure (Semenov, Lashuk, Kozlov, and others). More specifically, it was postulated that an earlier than previously thought transition to the paternal-kin structure was made possible by a combination of environmental and social factors (Averkieva 1974; Bakhta and Seniuta 1972; Butinov 1977; Kozodoev 1977; Markov 1979; Semenov 1976; Vasilevich 1972). In consequence of this discussion, ethnographers and historians of primordial societies became interested once again in subsistence and production economies. Research in this direction promoted the further accumulation of knowledge about the development of productive forces in pre-class societies, as well as the general identification of regional ethnic variability in culture-historical processes.

Publications of research data on subsistence economies (e.g., Kabo 1979, 1982; Masson 1971; Shnirel'man 1980) discussed the development of productive forces in fisher-hunter-gatherer societies from the position of new empirical data, and also revived some of the older theoretical concepts at a qualitatively new level. Several papers dedicated to general questions of ethnography and history of pre-capitalist societies emphasized the need for ethnogeographic and ethnoecological research that would make it possible to summarize the history of the relationship between humans and their environment (e.g., Bromlei 1981b, 1983; Kim 1981; Kozlov 1983; Semenov 1982; Zhekulin 1982).

From our point of view, despite the growing general interest in ethnographic theory, the field of Tungus or Evenki studies is by no means fully established, particularly as regards economy, material culture, and traditions. Only a few dedicated works by V. A. Tugolukov (1962, 1969, 1970, 1974) and one by V. V. Karlov (1982) are worthy of mention. In the context of the relevant subject matter, the latter study, in which Evenki economy is addressed in a separate section, is especially valuable. For our work, of particular interest are Karlov's various accounts of subsistence hunting, trapping fur-bearing animals, fishing, and reindeer transportation, and assessments of their place in Evenki economy. However, he does not venture far beyond brief descriptions of the main ethnic characteristics of Evenki economy, provided mostly as a background to the main topic of his study, namely, changes in the social sphere of Evenki culture taking place in response to the integration of goods and capital from Tsarist Russia into their traditional economy. Moreover, Evenki land use methods are not described in Karlov's monograph.

Thus, it may be considered that up to the present time, research on our topic of interest was limited to the compilation of empirical data by G. M. Vasilevich, subsequently detailed and presented in more concrete terms by V. A. Tugolukov and V. V. Karlov. These materials, as before, demonstrate only the place of the Evenki economy within the typological classification of hunter-gatherers and fishers. All this justifies the need and timeliness of taking a new approach to the examination and reconstruction of local variants of land use patterns in different groups of hunter–reindeer herders that inhabited a geographically and ecologically homogeneous region during the period of our research.

Chapter 2. Traditional Evenki subsistence activities and their role in the land use system

Considered together, the traditional economic production activities of mobile Evenkis that survived to the early 20th century, i.e., hunting, fishing, and gathering, represent an example of a subsistence economy. This type of hunting–reindeer herding economy in Central Siberia has historically manifested as an interrelationship between methods of "appropriating" natural resources, along with a specific set of corresponding means of appropriation [*prisvoeniia*], and the ecology of the given environment. Researchers have long been interested in human ecology, and to date a great number of theoretical as well as highly specialized papers have been dedicated to such issues. Although the majority of ethnographic studies [in Russia] is conducted on the economies of ethnic groups that are often typologically remote from Evenkis, the main conclusions of such research, and statements characterizing the dialectical connection of societies with nature, may be considered wholly applicable to our topic of interest.

1. "Labour is, in the first place, a process in which both man and Nature participate, and in which man of his own accord starts, regulates, and controls the [exchange of goods] between himself and Nature..." (Marx 1960: 188). As concerns core subsistence issues, the way human means of subsistence are produced "... depends first of all on the nature of the actual means of subsistence they find in existence and have to reproduce." For humans, this mode of production is a definite "mode of life on their part" (Marx and Engels n.d.: 19).

2. "The degree of development of productive forces defines the degree of human power over nature... The development itself of forces of production is defined by the characteristics of man's geographic environment" (Plekhanov 1923: 244).

3. "One of the most important features, common to all contemporary hunter-gatherers... is the dependency of their population size, relative mobility, and their whole way of life on ecological conditions and on the focus [*napravlenie*] of their economic activity" (Kabo 1979: 92).

4. "Being a less specialized type of activity than agriculture, hunting and gathering create a more flexible structure and allow a society to manoeuvre and adapt more easily to the changing external environment" (Shnirel'man 1986: 265).

5. "There is ... ample evidence to show that in the long centuries of so-called tribal society men acquired a vague but adequate appreciation of the relation between their terrain, their customary food standards, and the size of their population" ([F. Le Gros Clark, quoted in] Weiner 1979: 588).

Thus, we may imagine that the production and lifestyle spheres of the traditional culture of mobile hunting and reindeer herding Evenki groups of Central Siberia were adapted, to a certain extent, to the ecological conditions of production. Accordingly, in this chapter we seek to provide comprehensive answers to the following fundamental questions:

- What was the main focus of Evenki economic production activities in Central Siberia at the turn of the 20th century?
- How did the natural environment and tools used in material production influence the nature and methods of said activities?
- How did each type of economic production activity influence the overall way of life of hunting groups?

It is well known that the incorporation of Siberia into the Russian state—and, subsequently, the gradual integration of the economy of the indigenous Siberian population into the general Russian economy—did not in practice change the traditional structure and orientation of the economy of the Siberian population. This is particularly true for the economy of taiga hunters, which did not really change beyond its traditional nature until the 1930s.

The problem of the interrelationships between the developed economy of the Russian state and the economies of hunting societies—which were predominantly at the stage of disintegration of their primordial clan-based social system—is a separate research topic with no direct relevance to our subject. Nevertheless, we should try, if possible, at least to sketch out some reasons why the "natural economy" still formed the foundation of subsistence for Evenkis in Central Siberia at the turn of the 20th century (Anisimov 1936; Gurvich and Dolgikh 1970; Popov 1926; Rychkov 1917; Vasilevich 1969).

From the beginning, economic relations between central regions of the Russian state and its Siberian periphery were constructed in a very distinctive way. They were actually quite different from relations in corresponding parts of North America and Canada. For example, for the Inupiaq [эскимосы] living in continental Alaska, development of the fur trade—and of the accompanying *commodity relations*[8]—was stimulated by regular large deliveries of a very wide assortment of food and commercial goods to the local indigenous markets, including such "top necessity" items as canned meat, bread, fat, firearms, and ammunition. Consequently, these goods, which were the ones Alaskans traded their furs for, soon became the main source of provisions. Thus, the fur trade virtually eliminated the traditional hunting of migrating caribou herds from the [indigenous] economy. The process of reorienting this economy toward a *commodity basis* obviously went too far. The [Inupiaq] population became almost completely dependent on the vagaries of the fur trade, and was doomed to death by starvation when demand for furs decreased (Averkieva 1974; Helm and Leacock 1978; Mowat 1981; Veltfish 1978).

---

8. A Marxist term (Russ. *tovarnye otnosheniia*), which today might be rendered as 'market relations'. —*Ed.*

In contrast to what was experienced in corresponding parts of Northern America, the *iasak* 'tribute' exacted from the indigenous Siberian population by the [Imperial Russian] administration created conditions that only to a minimal degree facilitated the development of new commodity relations in the Evenki economy. The exchange of goods between hunters delivering furs and the *iasak* collectors representing the Russian administration was [not intentionally designed to increase demand but] implemented by force. In essence, the payment of *iasak* was merely an additional burden for hunters that allowed them "once a year... to exchange pelts for rifles, hunting supplies, and food, without which most could manage in the taiga" (Vasilevich 1969: 69). The commodities exchanged by Evenkis through the "treasury" were mostly metal goods, the demand for which had shrunken significantly on the local market as far back as the beginning of the 17th century. According to N. N. Stepanov, often the *iasak* collectors had to nearly force the hunters to take the goods provided for exchange (Stepanov 1961: 223, 238, 240). Since the hunters were not actually interested in expanding trade or increasing the volume of furs delivered to the market, the necessary conditions for transformation of the hunting economy into a commodity economy based on the fur trade did not exist and, thus, such a transformation could not take place.

Obviously, because Russia was industrially poorly developed—its agricultural and manufacturing centres far away from Central Siberia, and regular transportation routes between the nomadizing territories of the hunters and the fur trading posts extremely underdeveloped—an increase in the profitability of the fur trade, and a consequent reorientation of the Evenki economy to focus more on trade, could not have happened earlier than at the beginning of the 19th century. More favourable conditions for intensification of the fur trade, and accelerated development of a commodity focus among Evenki hunting groups, started to emerge at the end of the 18th century but consolidated only after the mid-19th century with the growth of industrial and trade centres and large private corporations in Eastern Siberia (Karlov 1982: 103–9). During this period, demand increased for firearms and ammunition, flour, groats, salt, sugar, matches, and miscellaneous light industry items, and provided a stimulus for intensive development of the fur trade. Hunters obtained ammunition and firearms mainly through the "treasury," while other goods were procured from private fur dealers who also engaged in petty trade with Russian peasants who lived nearby the nomadic hunting lands and traded their farm produce for furs. Archival data from the Alien Upravas [*Inorodnye upravy*] and the administration of the former Irkutsk gubernia include complaints filed by hunters about the lawlessness of the fur dealers, and orders of the central gubernial administration that aimed to regulate trade with hunters.

In spite of clearly unsatisfactory dealer payments to Evenkis for their furs, it is perfectly obvious that by the end of the 19th century the welfare of every Evenki family was to a significant degree, if not fully, tied to a successful trade of furs for goods from dealers' stores and the "treasury." The lack of accurate data makes it difficult today to establish the volume of commodity trade between individual hunting families and various fur dealers, or to calculate the profitability of the fur trade in quantitative terms. The reports of dealers who had a monopoly on trade with hunters during the period under study contained, as a rule, extremely varied data on both prices for goods that hunters were interested in and revenues from trading with the *inorodtsy* 'aliens' (GAIO 161/2/907). Records on *iasak* collection do not provide any accurate data, either (GAIO 26/3/8, 26/3/59; 32/4/245), nor do the reports of the Irkutsk Gubernia Administration's Rural Department (GAIO 32/34/31; 461/2/1, 461/2/7) or the Irkutsk Treasury Department.

Nonetheless, intensification of the fur trade can in fact be partly demonstrated on the basis of increased revenues to the treasury from the sale of Eastern Siberian furs (Dulov 1983: 74–9); this, in our opinion, was encouraged by [several] factors. First, hunters needed firearms and twice-yearly replenishments of ammunition. Since by the beginning of the 19th century the use of firearms completely forced out the bow and arrow from Evenki hunting practice (Gurvich and Dolgikh 1970: 53; Vasilevich 1969: 54, 62), replenishing ammunition was of the utmost importance for hunters. Second, the complete arbitrariness of fur pricing very quickly led to a situation in which every hunting family was in various degrees of debt to a number of dealers. More often than not, a hunter setting out to "market" his furs would obtain the goods he needed not for the offered furs but on credit, by mortgaging his future harvest. Third, by that time non-local provisions had already attained an important place in the Evenki diet. This is confirmed partly by the reminiscences of old people, who recall above all else the shortages of gunpowder, lead, flour, salt, and tea. Thus, we can be quite certain that in the second half of the 19th century, the Evenki economy was quite closely affected by fluctuations in the fur market (Karlov 1982).

Moreover, increased demand for furs and profitability of the fur trade for Evenkis was obviously temporary. The increase in numbers of animal pelts harvested by every hunting family, growth of purchasing power, and expansion of the commercial aspect of their economy could not continue indefinitely. Already by the mid-18th century, the supply of sable, the most profitable item in the fur trade, had sharply diminished. Toward the end of the 19th century, sable became so rare that catching one was considered by hunters to be an extraordinary instance of good luck. This is demonstrated partly in reports on the Siberian fur fairs, where only a few sable pelts are recorded (GAIO 26/3/8; 150/1/27; 461/2/1). Under such circumstances, the Evenki fur trade became oriented toward squirrel and other fur-bearing animals; the latter may have been more highly valued on the market but were not caught in such large numbers [as squirrel]. According to the same archival documents, it was very rare for Evenki hunters to procure pelts from fox, wolverine, wolf, bear, moose, or reindeer.

The continuously shifting nature of squirrel hunting territories also led to a significant decrease in the average yearly supply of this animal. As a whole, the profitability of the fur trade and the corresponding ability of hunters to provide for their families depended to a great degree on the squirrel "harvest capacity," which peaked every four years. Therefore, a hunter could count on the fur hunt to ensure his welfare only once every four years. Furthermore, the unpredictability of income from the fur trade led some Evenki groups to engage in fur farming.

The absence of a developed network for the government monopoly on fur procurement, and the replacement of this monopoly with private enterprises, also contributed to the overall decrease in profitability of the fur trade. Very often, the *miagkaia rukhliad'* 'soft stuff' was purchased from Evenkis at prices far below those established by the government. Moreover, being dependent on the market, fur prices were quite volatile. Some indication of fur prices duringthe relevant period can be obtained from the archival collections "Alien Upravas," "Irkutsk Treasury Chamber," and "Irkutsk Gubernial Statistical Commission" (GAIO collections 26, 32, 148, 461). For example, during the last decade of the 19th century and the beginning of the 20th century, prices [per pelt] ranged as follows: 6 to 20 kopeks for squirrel; 4 to 35 roubles for sable; and 1.5 to 12 roubles for fox. At the same time, prices for the main foodstuffs purchased by Evenkis were much more stable: 1.4 to 2.5 roubles per pood (16 kg) of rye flour; 3.2 to 5 roubles per pood of buckwheat groats; 30 to 40 kopeks per pound of salt; and 25 to 40 kopeks [per litre of] vegetable oil.

According to [the Lithuanian-born explorer and ethnologist] Waldemar Jochelson, "Owning the rifle was only half the matter for hunters; the second half was to obtain gunpowder and lead, which for the nomadic aliens was not an easy task... A petty dealer's take for a *para* 'pair' (according to Jochelson, a pair was 1 pound of gunpowder and 2 pounds of lead—*Auth.*) was at least 3 roubles, or 20 squirrels. The *para* produced 100–150 charges, with some lead left over" (Jochelson 1898: 23). A flintlock was even more expensive, with dealers asking up to 300–400 squirrels for it, or up to 30 reindeer. Food items were also quite expensive: "a brick of [loose] tea from the dealer costs 20–30 squirrels, 1 pound of tobacco [costs] 10–16... for one otter [one could purchase] 1 pound of tea, 1 pound of sugar, 6 arshins [4.3 m] of calico, and 1¾ [pounds] of tobacco... [while] three red foxes and three silver foxes (*sivodushki*) paid for 1 copper tea-kettle, 1 axe, 1 pound of tobacco, 1 brick of tea, and 1 tea cup with saucer" (Jochelson 1898: 126).

All this considered together was hardly an incentive for hunters to increase their fur harvest. Due to its low profitability during the time period under research, the fur trade in the Evenki economy maintained its high levels only as a consequence of the obligatory *iasak*, the constant and growing dependence of Evenki families on fur dealers, and the fact that fur barter was the only source of critical supplies of lead and gunpowder. Under these circumstances, game continued toremain a necessary and stable source of food for Evenkis, as well as of raw materials to make clothing and some household items. As a result, by the turn of the 20th century a balance of sorts was established in the Evenki economy between the hunt for fur and the hunt for meat; rather than hindering each other, they complemented one another, ensuring the welfare of the family. The traditional subsistence branches of the Evenki economy and the new commodity branch evolved together into a rhythm of economic production and societal lifeways as one whole that did not favour either but had positive effects on the overall Evenki economy in Central Siberia.

The economic activity of the Evenkis, based predominantly on traditional foraging approaches, was regulated by the environment and climate of the inhabited areas, as well as by the biological characteristics of the procured animals. Practical knowledge of the taiga environment, accumulated over many generations by its residents, formed the foundations for developing and refining the most suitable technology and rhythm for their economic production activities. In this context, it is clear that the Evenkis' empirical knowledge, which defined the dynamics and techniques of hunting and fishing, also included the ecology and behaviour of game animals. All available evidence shows that Evenki hunters were well aware of the size and relative density of the animal population, their seasonal feeding ranges and behavioural characteristics, and the nature of and reasons for animal migrations and the distances covered, as well as the optimal hunting times and harvesting capacities of wild animals. At the same time, given that commercial hunting depended overall quite rigidly on the game species' ability to regenerate their population size, the quotas for commercial and subsistence hunting differed substantially. The [latter] remained stable as long as the hunters' demand for food and hides was stable. [On the other hand,] the commercial fur hunting quotas were dictated by unpredictable private and government markets. Thus, the scale and intensity of commercial and subsistence hunting were often unrelated, and their impact on hunting conditions and hunters' way of life differed, as well.

2.1 Subsistence hunting

The traditional Evenki production economy was based on an almost year-round hunt for moose (***moty*** 'tree eater', ***sektakaty*** 'willow eater') and, occasionally, for reindeer (***bagdaka***). Various types of forest birds and waterfowl were caught incidentally along with the ungulates, and served as a supplement to the game meat; together with the fish catch, these met [most of] the daily food needs of Evenki families during summer, less so in winter.

There is evidence to suppose that the dominant place of moose in the hunt for meat is comparatively recent. While there is no exact testimony supporting this, Evenki accounts show that starting from the middle of the [19th] century, the reindeer population in the taiga gradually fell, and the southern border of reindeer territory across Central Siberia moved to approximately 58–60° latitude north (Kopylov et al. 1940: 119–20). Moose prevalence increased concomitantly in the same northerly direction, with some moose now being found even in the tundra. According to our informants, in the mid-19th century wild reindeer were hunted fairly frequently in the northern part of the region, whereas moose hunting was rarer due to their limited numbers. For example, V. P. Kaplin recalled that about one hundred years previously ("My grandfather was still a boy") there was such a sharp decrease in reindeer population in the area of the Lower Tunguska River that hunters were forced into the theretofore unfamiliar practice of hunting moose. At first, "when there were fewer wild [reindeer], we'd see moose more often. Our people wondered what kind of animal it was; we thought it was no good to eat. But then the Katanga Evenkis (Podkamennaia Tunguska Evenkis—*Auth.*) started teaching us. They said: hunt this animal, it is good to eat."

It seems likely that the above-noted decline in reindeer population was caused primarily by the shrinking of natural feeding ranges, probably the result of some kind of climate change in Central Siberia, but also due to anthropogenic factors. According to informants, we know that at the turn of the 20th century northern flora were being partially replaced by more thermophilic species, among which the most widespread were birch and alder, with smaller numbers of Siberian pine, various willows, and shrubbery. Experts in ungulate biology have noted that agricultural development, clearance logging, and tillage of huge tracts of taiga land in Central Siberia, especially the parts covered by pine and Siberian pine, which were the richest in reindeer moss, created favourable conditions for growth and expansion of the moose population, on the one hand, and precipitated the movement of wild reindeer herds into remote taiga regions not occupied by the rural [human] population, on the other. As recorded toward the end of the 18th century, the increased numbers of domesticated reindeer in the Evenki economy evidently also played a role in the reduction of wild reindeer habitats. It is known that herds of domesticated reindeer feeding on natural pastures in the northern taiga constituted serious competition for wild reindeer, due to the fact that the sharp increase in population size of domesticated reindeer altered the natural balance between reindeer population [size and density] and available browse. At that stage of reindeer husbandry, when food requirements of the domesticated and wild reindeer were very similar, competition between the two was intense. Thus, during the period covered in our work, moose became the main subsistence resource for Evenkis, while wild reindeer hunting, though it did not disappear, became secondary in importance.

According to current estimates, the average size of the moose population in Central Siberia is about 30,000–40,000 head, with an average density of about 0.7 head per 1,000 ha [10 sq. km] of habitat (Kaletskii 1978: 87–128; Karelov 1979: 91). Judging from interviews, and taking into account pressure on the moose population from legal hunting as well as poaching, these data are unlikely to differ greatly from [the 1940s] data. The area populated by moose covers 75–80% of the taiga in Central Siberia, and their population size and density are lower only in areas directly adjacent to industrial or agricultural centres. However, it should be mentioned that the calculated average population density of the species paints only a relative picture of moose habitat, as it indicates the probable overall proportion of the moose population to the size of the area they occupy. Hunters themselves tell us that in the past, moose were more evenly distributed and could be encountered all over the territory inhabited by Evenki groups. Even during the 1950s, moose numbers were still high throughout Central Siberia, while in his time, A. F. Middendorf had written: "In Siberia, moose are found up to the zone of low-growing trees. In 1812, it was rare to meet a hunter who did not capture around 6 of these animals per year" (Middendorf 1869–77).

The average density of the moose population varies with the seasons. During summer, it can decrease to 0.1–0.2 head per 1,000 ha [10 sq. km], and in autumn, during the pre-rut period, it can increase up to 6 head per 1,000 ha (Bannikov 1964: 10; Popov 1977: 383–5). Seasonal changes in moose distribution have not yet been fully researched. In a number of specialized studies dedicated to the ecology and behaviour of this species, the data on moose population size depending on quality and quantity of food available, and on the relationship between moose distribution range and changes in environmental and climatic conditions, are often contradictory. Nevertheless, it is obvious that the high ecological resilience of this species, including its flexibility regarding food requirements, allows moose to live off the most varied kinds of land (Iurgenson 1964; Kaletskii 1978: 96–7). It has been observed that most of the moose populating the area around a *kormozashchitnaia stantsiia* 'sheltered foraging site'[9] exhibit a year-round sedentary way of life (Kaletskii 1978: 98–9, 116–17; Vereshchagin and Rusakov 1979: 202). Hunters were well aware that birthing moose cows and cows with calves are less mobile, as are yearlings and bulls weakened after the autumn mating season and not being able to regain enough fitness during winter food shortages for extensive migration (Sokolov 1979: 101). Moreover, throughout the entire summer they hardly move away from the autumn pre-rut gathering places. With the appearance of *gnus* 'gnats and mosquitoes' this portion of the entire moose population moves around constantly during the daytime, and congregates around water sources (taiga streams, bogs) or stays in the taiga bogs, surrounded by dense underbrush. The wind blowing over the bogs protects the moose from the insects, and the underbrush shelters them from the heat.

At the end of April and beginning of May the remaining, smaller portion of moose territorial population—adult bulls that did not participate in the rut, three-year-old bulls and heifers, and barren females—leaves the winter habitation ranges one at a time, and gradually moves from the taiga watersheds toward the valleys of the big rivers. At the beginning of June, after the ice

---

9. Soviet-Russian scientific nomenclature often implies a greater constructivist framework than exists in reality. What in fact is being spoken of is no more than a known, sizeable lichen patch in the taiga brush that affords good protection from the elements. —*Ed.*

breaks up on the rivers, both settled and migrating segments of the moose population come to the riverbanks, where they browse on the young spring shoots and stay in the water during the hottest midday hours (Kaletskii 1978: 98–9). By the beginning of July, the moose are dispersed over practically every part of the taiga, reaching a population density of about 0.1 head per 1,000 ha [10 sq. km]. This time also marks the start of reverse movement by the migrating segment of the moose population, as far away as 150–200 km from their wintering sites to tracts in closer proximity to their autumn/winter sites, with plenty of slash and thin, dried-out pine forest that allow the wind to blow through, thus providing protection from annoying gnats and mosquitoes during the daytime.

It should be mentioned that moose have weak thermoregulation and poor overall endurance; thus, their behaviour is usually rather phlegmatic. Most of the time, these animals move around very little and get up from their lairs only to forage. Only rare individuals cover the maximum migration distances, such extreme movement generally being prompted by overpopulation in a given area. The number of moose within favourable habitats remains stable during much of the year, i.e., from April until mid-October (Kaletskii 1978: 116; Starikovich 1982: 89–91).

In September, the density of the moose population increases locally with the start of the mating period, peaking from the end of September through the first half of October (6–10 head per 1,000 ha). During this time they gain the most weight [of the year], with adult bulls and cows reaching 400–450 kg, and 3–4-year-olds weighing 350–400 kg (Popov 1977: 385). According to hunters, during this time the animals remain close to patches of burnt-out forest and unmixed pine and Siberian pine forests. Often, several young 3–4-year-old bulls would join a (bull and cow) pair; this occasionally provided the opportunity for experienced hunters to capture 3–4 animals at a time. One of the features of moose behaviour is its attraction to mating locations in the taiga that are used over and over for decades. These mating grounds tend to be located at the watersheds of adjacent rivers. It has also been observed that during the mating period moose become so aggressive that they lose all caution, allowing hunters to approach to the distance of a sure shot, i.e., 50–60 steps (Vereshchagin and Rusakov 1979: 193–4).

At the end of October, after the rut and a brief fattening period [*zhirovka*], the moose concentrate in relatively small areas of the autumn/winter sheltered feeding sites and move around during most of the day (Evenkis would say, "Game is walking a lot, lots of tracks everywhere" and "Moose hunt is very good during the *zhirovka*"). Then the moose migrate to the wintering sites, where they remain relatively stationary. With the first snowfall, the animals form herds of 30–40 head. When there is a lot of snow, they do not move around much in search of food, only about 5–6 km per day. During winters with little snowfall, when the cover is no deeper than 50 cm, the moose can live a practically settled lifestyle as long as their population density is low. In these cases, the maximum distance moved during the whole snowy period might not exceed 25–40 km (Kaletskii 1978: 117–18; Vereshchagin and Rusakov 1979: 195).

The great ecological flexibility of moose and their ability to adapt to various feeding and climatic conditions are the reasons not only for their decidedly sedentary life within relatively small areas but also for the stability of their population size. No less important for stability of moose population is their capacity, under favourable conditions, to recover quickly from population loss, even after a sharp decline (Kaletskii 1978: 95). Under extremely unfavourable conditions—very snowy winters and periods of limited forage availability—the balance and stability of the moose population is maintained by migration of part of the herd into new regions; thus, its distribution range increases [during difficult times]. According to informants and expert assessments, during the last 100–150 years the size of the moose population of Central Siberia has remained practically unchanged. Moreover, with the increase in conservation measures introduced recently [1960s–1980s], the moose population has actually grown slightly (Bannikov and Teplov 1964: 8–11; Turov 1974, 1978).

All these circumstances evidently provided Evenkis living the turn of the 20th century with stable food resources. Evidently, the common perception of frequent famines has little to do with the periodic fluctuations in availability of game animals. However, a few isolated occurrences of game shortage that could have taken place over 150 years ago might still have remained in people's memory. For example, according to the Evenki woman E. I. Rukosueva, "Our grandmother was still a girl when all the animals left to fight their wars." Another reason for famine could have been irregular supply of the goods that Evenkis obtained from dealers, especially ammunition.

According to informants, despite the decrease in population size mentioned above, wild reindeer continued to be a major natural source of both meat and hides for Evenkis. But reindeer hunting was infrequent, occurring usually after sightings within the Evenki nomadizing territory of fresh evidence of feeding at a reindeer moss patch [*iagel'nik*], or when herd tracks were found. Hunters did not deliberately embark on reindeer hunts. To an extent, Evenki hunters from the Lower Tunguska River territory were an exception to that rule, because the reindeer density there was considerably higher than elsewhere in the Central Siberian taiga. Specialized research usually distinguishes between *tundra, highlands-taiga,* and *woodland* subspecies of reindeer, each of them having their own specific characteristics. While the highlands-taiga and tundra subspecies have some features in common, the woodland subspecies differs from the other two with regard to herd size, degree of sedentism, and seasonal distribution and behaviour.

During the period under research, the population size of wild woodland reindeer was slightly higher than today. According to expert and informant estimates, the total head count [in the Central Siberian taiga] was 20,000–25,000, with an average density of 0.4–0.6 head per 1,000 ha [10 sq. km] of habitat (Semenov-Tian-Shanskii 1977: 12–13). Up until the 1940s, the natural habitat of wild woodland reindeer was predominantly in the taiga zone bordering the tundra, but small herds sometimes migrated as far south as 46° north latitude, practically overlapping in distribution with the montane subspecies during seasonal movements (Kopylov et al. 1940: 121–4).

The average slaughter weight of wild reindeer is slightly higher than that of domesticated reindeer, reaching a maximum of 150–200 kg (just before the annual rut). Wild reindeer populations tend to be highly sedentary, with mostly localized herds, some members of which migrate no farther than 100–150 km. Fertile cows and young 1–3-year-old remain sedentary within the boundaries of small year-round pastures, including permanent locations for calving and mating (Baskin 1970; Popov 1977: 392; Semenov-Tian-Shanskii 1977: 12; Sokolov 1979: 105). In spite of some differences in the timing of calving and mating, related primarily to latitudinal microclimatic conditions, the calving period of all wild woodland reindeer populations occurs one month before the start of the [vegetation] growing season, and the mating period begins when the larch shed their needles (Baskin 1970: 184; Turov unpubl. material).

For the most part, the distribution area of wild woodland reindeer is characterized by gently undulating relief. Summer ranges are normally found in the sparse pine and larch stands near the bottoms of river valleys. Winter ranges are located in the snow-covered valleys of watersheds, where trees provide shelter from the wind. Here, the snow cover is slightly deeper than in the open spaces, but the snow itself remains loose for most of the winter, which makes the lichen beneath it accessible. During the summer, the sedentary part of a territorial group of reindeer breaks up into small, amorphous herds of 6–12 head. They group and disperse easily, and the animals spend most of their time alone, remaining within eyesight of one another. Hunters believe that such dispersal of animals within a herd provides the best defence from both predators and biting insects. Unlike the tundra reindeer populations, woodland reindeer scatter in different directions at the first sign of danger, using their speed to escape pursuit.

In mid-September, approximately three weeks before the rut starts, the reindeer form large herds in which the bulls engage in battles. In mid-October and the beginning of November, with the start of the mating period, the herds break up into separate "harem families" consisting of several cows, yearlings, a bull sire, and several bulls that are contenders for herd leader. The overall number in a "harem family" is 20–25 head, and remains the same after the rut until spring. During winter, after the snow has set in, the herds congregate in areas with the least snow cover (Semenov-Tian-Shanskii 1977: 20).

Within the overall species-specific distribution area, the population of wild woodland reindeer is typically characterized by an uneven density, depending on the location of pastures. Permanent and more-or-less sedentary groups of these animals settle in rather small areas, while large tracts of land in between remain uninhabited, even during summer when the herds move around the most (Semenov-Tian-Shanskii 1977: 40). During the mating period, [wild] bulls typically do not react to people or dogs nearby, and are not startled by shouting or gunshots; they frequently charge right into herds of domesticated reindeer. This considerably simplified the autumn hunt of wild reindeer, especially when [domesticated] reindeer decoys were used (Semenov-Tian-Shanskii 1977: 37).

A comparison of moose and reindeer ecology and behaviour reveals common as well as distinctive characteristics. Among the commonalities are a sedentary mode of life for much of the overall regional population, an altitudinal direction of seasonal migrations (i.e., from the highest points of watersheds to the lower parts of river valleys), permanence of mating locations, and small size of wintering ranges. Both reindeer and moose are able to recover their numbers relatively easily after epizootic diseases or losses that occur due to lack of forage, natural predation, or commercial hunting (Baskin 1978: 184). Differences between reindeer and moose include the generally patchy dispersal of reindeer within their distribution range, greater mobility of reindeer within a feeding range, greater stability of reindeer herd size and distribution, and different reactions in response to danger. Another important differentiating characteristic is the reindeer's endurance and vitality. Evenki hunters were clearly very aware of all the abovementioned characteristics, as well as many others related to the biology and behaviour of these two ungulate species. Given their paramount importance as game animals, the long-term experience of Evenki hunters watching reindeer and moose resulted in the accumulation of a large body of practical knowledge about these species, knowledge which was used by them to ensure successful hunting.

In our opinion, it does not seem likely that the natural decline of woodland reindeer population or the shrinking of its habitat were the main cause of moose gradually becoming everywhere the principal species of subsistence hunting. The well-known "primordial" rationality of Evenki hunters could hardly fail to take into consideration that the biological and physical characteristics of moose produced greater yields than those of wild reindeer for the same amount of time and energy expended in the hunt. The average slaughter weight of a moose is 350–400 kg, while for a reindeer it is only 100–150 kg. According to wildlife experts, "The muscle and fat tissue and edible organs of a killed game animal make up 60–65% of its live weight. More than 30 kg of internal and subcutaneous fat can be obtained from a well-fed moose… moose meat contains about 18.5–19.0% proteins. As little as 100 g of moose meat provides enough vitamins to meet human daily requirements" (Kaletskii 1978: 122–3). Clearly, from the Evenki perspective, these indicators demonstrate high productivity of moose hunting. Under these circumstances, occasional reindeer hunting (which occurred only after spotting fresh tracks) remained a secondary means of obtaining meat, as well as hides for bedding, clothing, and footwear.

The amount of game meat harvested was directly related to the needs of each Evenki family. For our calculations, we assumed that the average Evenki family in Central Siberia consisted of five people. The average daily energy requirement of such a family is about 50,190 calories. In order to fulfill the daily requirement of the adult human organism for proteins, fats, vitamins, and micronutrients, it is sufficient to consume 1 kg of meat (Gal'perin 1977: 198–9; Weiner 1979: 502). In reality, based on our observations, the average daily consumption of adult Evenkis is somewhat higher than the calculated amount, provided there are sufficient quantities of meat products available. The usual meal frequency is five per day. During the morning tea (5 or 6 a.m. during summer), two adults (most often the head couple of the family, who watch for the reindeer to come to the smudges) eat about 0.2 kg [each] of dried meat, or about 0.5 kg cooked, along with some bread. During the second breakfast, at about 9 or 10 a.m., all the family members eat about 1 kg [each] of dried meat (1.5–2 kg if cooked). In the winter, rendered moose fat and copious amounts of tea complement the dried meat or bread served during breakfast.

During lunch (1 or 2 p.m.), the whole family consumes a broth containing up to 3 kg of cooked meat. When there is no fresh meat, the soup is cooked with 1–1.5 kg of dried meat. For the evening tea (essentially the supper), the family consumes 1.5–2 kg of cooked meat or 1 kg of dried meat. Thus, a family's daily meat consumption amounted to approximately 6.5–7 kg of fresh or 4 kg of dried meat. However, Evenkis usually served such portions only during the first few days after a kill, when there was a sufficient supply of dried meat, or when other food products used by Evenkis as meat substitutes were scarce. Overall, our calculations and the reports of our informants showed that the yearly requirement of meat products was achieved by taking eight moose, given an average slaughter weight of about 350 kg per animal.

Taking into account the average moose population density at various seasonal feeding ranges, its generally sedentary mode of life, its uniform distribution within a given area (0.5 head per 1,000 ha of habitat), and assuming the minimum biologically sustainable cull quota of 10% of the entire population (Bannikov 1965: 4; Kriuchkov 1979; Vereshchagin and Rusakov 1979: 261), the size of territory covered by Evenki hunters would have to be around 75,000 ha. This corresponds to a tract of land measuring 10×75 km (750 sq. km). In reality, according to informants, during the first half of summer alone nomadizing families migrated about 150–200 km from their winter base camps, thus covering a territory 2–3 times that size. This discrepancy is not unexpected, because our calculations were based on parameters relevant only to ungulate hunting. Obviously, the extensive travel [lit. 'vagabondage'] of the Evenkis and the large territories they covered are not explicable only in terms of "the hunters' never-ending pursuit of food," but must also take into account overall economic links of the hunting community with the inhabited territory, and the interdependence between specific economic production activities and number of people in the hunting group (Gromov 1981: 322; Kabo 1979: 92).

Interestingly, the estimated size of territory required for game hunting coincides with the size of territory exploited by Palaeolithic (750 sq. km) and Neolithic peoples (500 sq. km) that hunted woodland reindeer (Masson 1971: 31–2). This concordance is even more interesting given that, according to V. A. Shnirel'man, Neolithic hunters almost invariably lived in more or less sedentary communities. In fact, Shnirel'man defines sedentism not as "permanent habitation at one hamlet for many years," but rather as use of land far smaller in size but far more intensively than previously (Shnirel'man 1986: 239; emphasis mine—*Auth.*). Thus, there is evidence to suggest that a territory of 150,000–200,000 ha [1,500–2,000 sq. km] should have been sufficient for a group of 20–30 people practicing a combination of hunting and fishing economy, assuming a rather intensive use of the entire area.

When using the term *miasnaia okhota* [lit. 'meat hunt'] (meat being a major source of nutrition for most of the year), we are referring to more than just ungulate hunting and to other types of hunting besides active hunting. Like any other type of economic activity, the harvesting of meat by Evenkis in Central Siberia was directly related to the recurring bio-cycles of the game animals, seasonal changes in local conditions, and opportunities for intensive land use (Kabo 1979: 93–4). Regardless of its fundamentally dominant position, game hunting could be pushed back in priority, depending on the specific season, and replaced by harvesting forest birds and waterfowl, fishing, or (to some extent) [plant food] gathering.

With regard to "meat hunting," four periods could be identified that, on the whole, mirror the four seasons of the year (autumn, winter, spring, and summer). Year-round ungulate hunting, primarily of moose, peaked during the autumn months and slowed down sharply from the end of May to the first half of August (only 1–2 animals per summer). There are a number of reasons for such a significant decrease in the number of moose captured during summer. According to informants, the main reason is rate of return. With the onset of the "mosquito season" and the increasing effects of various biting insects on animals, moose have a tendency to remain alone and travel extensively (as much as 30 km per day) within the boundaries of a local range. Thus, the moose population is at its lowest density in summer ranges: 0.1–0.2 head per 1,000 ha of habitat. Essentially, all the animals harvested during summer are taken either at the beginning of June, when large numbers come out to browse on young shoots and water plants on the banks of taiga rivers and lakes, or at the end of August, prior to the rut, when moose congregate in burnt-out forests and scattered pineries.

During the rest of the season, according to Evenkis,

> "… moose walk all day, and startle very easily. In summer, Evenkis do not see meat for a month or more. They find very fresh moose tracks, they let the dogs out; even one hour ago the animal passed by, makes no sense to tire a dog, it won't catch up to the animal anyway" [Turov field notes].

Ungulates, particularly moose with their poor adaptability to extreme temperatures, do not tolerate heat very well at all. The moose's great mobility and its ability to forage during the short daybreak hours when gnats and mosquitoes are at their lowest, as well as its poor thermoregulation and substantial weight loss due to high daytime temperatures, are the main reasons for the low slaughter weight of the animal and, thus, the low food value and low return rates of hunting moose during [summer]. Environmental conditions for moose become even more difficult in the second half of June and in July, when gadflies appear. Evenkis say:

> "During summer, moose gets scrawny; skin looks like it's been fired at by a shotgun, all in wormholes (gadfly larvae—*Auth.*)." For this reason, moose hunting is least profitable during summer and occurs very rarely, Evenkis say, only "when you really hanker for fresh meat." On such occasions, moose was hunted in the morning hours or, rarely, in the evening, [by floating in] birch-bark boats to a location where moose tracks were spotted. An animal soaking in the water would be an easy catch for the hunter. "In the evening, you can hear a long way along the river. Float quietly, barely moving the paddles, and you can hear his champing (i.e., moose feeding in the water—*Auth.*), but he can't hear anybody at all, allows us to come close" [Turov field notes].

Evidently, the low subsistence value of summer moose was not the only reason for limiting the hunt to 1–2 opportunistically taken animals during the entire summer. While not exaggerating Evenkis' commitment to observing environmental conservation measures to protect animal herds from complete depletion (Jochelson 1898: 151; Turov 1974), it is worth noting that poaching game was unknown to them. Rather, there is ample evidence that Evenkis consistently took measures aimed at resource conservation (or protection). For example, all informants told us that it used to be strictly forbidden between June and mid-August to take pregnant moose cows or cows with suckling calves. Moreover, this ban also extended to the harvest of moulting forest birds, and of nesting wood grouse and black grouse. According to informants, during the nesting season hunting dogs were kept on a leash, "lest they destroy the nests." It would be unreasonable to think that in times of pressing need, hunters did not breach their own rules, as long as their reasons for doing so were sanctioned by their community. But it is also obvious that such incidents were rare. If we take into consideration that in summer any animals that hunters caught sight of were only the most vulnerable individuals—old or sick bulls weakened from hunger during the second half of winter and therefore often left behind on the small permanent ranges—it becomes clear that the summer hunt could not be considered crucial given its low intensity, efficiency, and resulting nutritional value. According to Evenkis, "lots of food in summer everywhere, anyway."

All ungulates, including moose, have the useful characteristic of achieving optimum body condition in a very short time. Starting in the second half of August, with mushrooms appearing and biting insects on the wane (the

Evenki term is *irkin* "fattening time for animals, because there are few mosquitoes"), the weight lost because of insects and heat is regained by reindeer and moose literally within a few days. Moose hunting gradually picks up the pace in the last ten days of August and peaks around the start of the mating period in the second half of September or beginning of October. As mentioned above, at this time the animals increase their mobility, moving toward the permanent mating locations and forming pairs or small herds of 4–6 head.

During this period, hunters leave camp with a one- or two-day supply of food and set out in search of moose, usually alone but sometimes in teams of 2–3 people. The decisive factor here is to bring along a well-trained *laika* [husky] that is capable of quickly finding moose tracks and cornering the animal. About 1.5–2 km from camp, the hunter lets the dog off the leash and then walks in a wide arc through the area where large numbers of fresh tracks were found (no more than a day old). The last part of the search route usually ends at his family's next stop-over camp, the location of which was agreed upon before he set out. Because moose sharply increase their mobility before the mating season, the success of the hunt depends almost entirely on the hunter's skill in finding fresh animal tracks. Evenkis described the process as follows:

> "We look for morning tracks. Find yesterday's tracks, makes no sense to let the dogs loose. He [the moose] walked far overnight. Today's dogs are no good for some reason, they scent yesterday's tracks and run. Don't even see the moose yet, they're hollering (i.e., baying) already. Used to be, a good dog followed tracks silently, spotted the animal, and only then bayed non-stop. But the smartest ones would lead the animal toward you to meet it upwind" [Turov field notes].

Indeed, it is important for hunters not only to have a clever husky, but also to understand the situation, that the prey would try to break away from the dog and run with the wind in a circle, trying, as Evenkis say, "to check on his old tracks." Regardless, the importance of a good dog, capable of cornering a strong and aggressive animal, is obvious. At first glance, it might look as if the hunter is simply following the husky, which is leading him after the tracks. In reality, as hunters explained to us,

> "A good dog never runs aimlessly; listens to its master even from far away. Walks on one side, then the other, keeps an eye on the hunter all the time, doesn't run away too far. It's not the dog who leads but the master and his path who lead the dog" [Turov field notes].

When scouting the target areas beforehand, where the "moose left lots of tracks," the hunter deliberately traverses the possible paths of the animal, thus finding the freshest tracks one way or another. If, after a long time, hunters still did not come upon areas with clear signs of a high concentration of moose, they continued the search for 2–3 days, bringing 2–3 young dogs with them in addition to an older experienced dog. "They keep an old dog nearby;

indeed, she doesn't run far, hovers around within eyesight, nose is poor, legs weak, needs to rely more on the younger dogs." In this case, the young dogs searching farther away would usually find fresh tracks, and their faint baying marked the route along which they were pursuing the animal. The old dog would naturally hear the baying of the questing dogs better than the hunter; she either made the hunter stop and listen or, pulling on the leash, led him directly to the prey.

Usually, while searching for moose, the hunter moved slowly, carefully looking at the tracks and listening for the dogs baying. During summer days with no wind, a baying dog could be heard at a distance of up to 5 km, and up to 10 km in the evening, but this distance sharply decreased in windy weather. We observed on more than one occasion that a hunter, after hearing the dogs baying, was not only able to choose the correct direction to move but also, thanks to his excellent orientation after several hunting seasons in a familiar area, he could determine with impressive accuracy the spot where the dogs "placed" the prey, the relief and the best approach, using hiding spots so as not to be seen by the moose before coming within a distance of 40–50 steps. In order to prevent human scent being carried toward the animal, to determine wind direction even in practically windless conditions, the hunter simply rubbed dry lichen or tree bark between his fingers.

Usually, after turning the dogs loose and not seeing them for half an hour, the hunter tried to walk in approximately the same direction that he last saw the huskies running. He walked for 2–3 hours in that direction, stopping every 500–1,000 m to listen [for baying], and tried to choose a path that allowed him to stop on top of elevated places, where he could listen in two or three directions at once.

If the dogs did not come back for a long time, or if the hunter could not hear them after 2–3 hours of walking, he would stop and wait for them. More often than not, having pursued the animal too far and then not sensing the master approaching, the dogs would drop the quest. Once the dogs returned, the hunter continued his search, either turning toward the next camp or walking in the same direction in order to overnight on a river or some other body of water. Usually, the dogs would return late in the evening, *potemnu* 'in the dark', but hunters have told us about occasions when an "impetuous" husky would pursue the prey for 2–3 days. The unhurried movement of the hunter during the search and the many stops to "listen for the dogs" explain why the average daily route, setting off before the dew disappeared ("on the dew, animal scent stays longer") and ending 2–3 hours before dark, covered no more than 10–15 km. At the same time, both the hunters and their families were moving toward the sites of their permanent winter base camps (**meneien**); therefore, searching for game for 2–3 days in a row from the same camp was rare. Most often, if hunters did not capture any game, they preferred to move with their family to another area along the general nomadic route but not far from the reindeer caravan trail (Petri 1930: 35–6; Turov unpubl. material).

This way, moving gradually toward winter base camp, where clothing and ammunition necessary for the autumn fur hunt were stored in *labazy* 'platform caches' (***noku-delken***), by mid-October hunters often stocked up on sufficient amounts of meat to last through winter and the squirrel hunting season. (Food storage methods will be described below in greater detail.) If meat stores were clearly insufficient, then after arriving in the area of the winter base camp, Evenkis continued moose hunting, setting out on one-day trips. One way or another, by mid-October a minimum of 2–3 moose per family was stored, either dried or frozen (after below-freezing temperatures set in). Later in winter, during the fur-hunting season, moose hunting was an opportunistic activity, according to informants, taking advantage when spotting fresh moose tracks near the stop-over camp.

At this time [i.e., autumn], moose activity sharply decreases, and with snowfall they become practically sedentary within small sheltered feeding ranges and wander around only about 4–5 km per day. Knowing this seasonal characteristic of moose behaviour and their usual feeding locations, hunters did not need to take much time away from the fur hunt in order to pursue moose when the opportunity arose. When the snowfall was very deep the fur hunt would end, and hunters, after returning to the ***meneien*** base camp, would engage in moose hunting, as a rule, only when there was not enough meat stored up in autumn to last until the spring hunt. According to our observations, after big snowfalls, which greatly reduced moose mobility, flocks of up to 20 moose often congregated in areas not far from the permanent Evenki winter base camps. Therefore, Evenkis could replenish their meat supplies any time "at home nearby" by taking the biggest individuals. However, during especially snowy winters and extreme sub-zero temperatures, which limited the mobility of Evenki families, and also at times when there were no sedentary reindeer near camp, the meat supplies stored in autumn were generally completely consumed by the end of winter. Usually, however, those meat stores were saved as a reserve until the beginning of the hunt on the snow crust and the spring fur hunt, while the bulk of the diet consisted of *svezhenina* 'fresh meat', harvested near the ***meneien***.

From the second half of February to the beginning of the calving season of domesticated reindeer (second half of April, or May), a time in the Evenki calendar referred to as ***giraun-ektenkire*** 'time of snow crust, of snow melting', the hunting was done by pursuing animals *po nastu* 'over the snow crust'. All ethnographers and travellers studying Evenki life have described this type of hunting. They have noted that hunting moose and reindeer over the snow crust was an important source of food and raw materials for Evenkis during the long, settled period of winter life (Bannikov and Teplov 1964; Dorogostaiskii 1925; Jochelson 1898: 150–3; Kopylov et al. 1940: 119–21; Petri 1930: 54–5; Suslov 1927: 44–9; Vasilevich 1969). However, these accounts create a somewhat misleading impression of both the role of this type of hunting in the overall structure of the Evenki economy and of its scale and technology, as well as of the corresponding mobility of hunting groups.

Generally, the hunt on snow crust involved groups of 2–3 hunters setting out on one- or two-day trips, each with a small supply of food lashed to a board-frame backpack [***ponage,*** Russified as *poniaga*]. It appears that the pursuit probably did not require as much time and effort as was described by G. M. Vasilevich (1969: 53). First, differences in moose and reindeer biology effected certain differences in hunting technique. According to Evenkis, "Moose is easier to pursue, gets exhausted quickly," while, on the other hand, "Reindeer is easier to stalk, it's completely blind, with poor hearing." Taking advantage of this, hunters stalked reindeer upwind, at a short distance, on skis covered with hare skins. It was particularly easy to do this when reindeer were feeding ("It's completely ***kuiki*** 'deaf'; come up close and it still can't hear a thing"). Moose cannot tolerate long pursuits at all and usually, even after a short and fast run, quickly start to stagger; therefore, pursuing them over the snow crust for several days makes no sense. As Evenkis say, "Don't chase moose too fast, the meat turns to soap; even the dogs won't eat it. If you're really hungry, cook the meat a long time, then it's edible, but still smells bad."

For Evenkis, hunting during the snow crust period, when moose and reindeer were significantly limited in freedom of movement, was easy and particularly productive. The employment of dogs, which could run easily over hard snow crust and were capable of cornering game quickly, required more than simple endurance for the hunter to pursue the animal for several days on skis [Photo 24]. Rather, it took a special skill to locate the prey and approach it quietly, within a reasonably close distance,

> "... so the moose didn't see the man. Even a wounded moose, seeing or smelling a man, runs away and runs very fast till complete exhaustion... even the dogs are left far behind... A slightly wounded [moose] startled by a clumsy hunter can run away so far that it's impossible to catch up to it or find it" (Petri 1930: 55).

Thus, during the snow crust period a sufficiently experienced hunter would spend most time and effort on searching for the prey, and this is actually how the phrase that the game was "chased sometimes for several days" should be interpreted. It seems that neither the searched area nor the time involved were in fact all that significant.

In the taiga, the deep snow cover remained until approximately the end of March, and moose stayed within their winter ranges. Consequently, hunters required literally only a few days to replenish dwindling food supplies and to stock up on spring hides used for making light summer clothing and footwear. Given that the simultaneous intensive hunting of squirrel and sable, which took up most of a hunter's workday, was still in progress, the hunt on snow crust was limited to only 1–2 weeks. The area covered by hunting parties was not very extensive because the hunters, together with their entire families and herds of domesticated reindeer, had to move to the permanent calving locations before the beginning of the calving season. An Evenki family of 5–6 people would stock up 3–4 moose during this time, which is a little more than during the autumn hunting season because the moose had to supply the family not only with food but also with materials for making clothing. For clothes alone, one adult required 2–3 reindeer hides or 1.5 moose hides for the summer period (Popova 1981: 85).

It is important to mention that for Evenkis, as for all other cultures in which hunting was the main source of subsistence, the spring hunt on snow crust never turned into a massive, uncontrolled slaughter of practically defenceless animals. First, hunting on snow crust was always selective, just as it is in modern-day licensed hunting. And second, as in summer, it was forbidden to take pregnant cows. Among the most frequently culled animals were young bulls, barren cows, and old bucks. Following the accepted principle of "what's enough is enough" (Lukina 1986: 121), the extent of the hunt on crust, its main purpose being replenishment of necessary stocks of cured meat and hides, did not go beyond ecologically sustainable quotas and thus did not compromise the reproductive viability of game animals. Even with Evenkis not being conscious of it, this principle, together with the prohibition against harvesting certain protected individuals, ensured the protection of the reproductively active core of the moose population within any given territory.

Assessing the overall size of Evenki territory and the degree of their mobility, both clearly dependent on the capacity to store of large food provisions, we may suggest that these two variables approach closely the corresponding [cultural] markers of a semi-settled way of life. The extended period of summer travel by nomadic Evenki groups can be considered the exception. However, as mentioned above, the size of Evenki territory and their mobility are not explicable only in terms of the conditions and character of ungulate hunting. The spring supply of dried meat, stored in special caches along the summer travel routes but mostly transported along with the [travelling] families, granted Evenkis a significant amount of autonomy, eliminating any pressing need to hunt ungulates during summer.

Naturally, once the supply of regularly purchased market goods such as flour, tea, vegetable oil, etc. was stabilized, an Evenki family could, as mentioned above, rely entirely on these foodstuffs during summer. Given the almost total absence of price controls on the main food staples and, especially, on ammunition, which was the largest expense against the *miagkoe zoloto* 'soft gold [i.e., furs]' used as tender, the fur hunt was only marginally profitable in the Evenki economy, if at all. The practice of exchanging goods in kind and the lack of a clear understanding by Evenkis of the real market value of their furs resulted in hunters obtaining only small, non-equivalent quantities of goods [in exchange for their furs]. Nevertheless, we are not inclined to overdramatize the situation. Rather, it is likely that during some years, especially those with good fur harvests, hunters were able to accumulate many pelts before the start of the trading season, particularly the highly valued sable, silver fox, and muskrat. During such years, foodstuffs purchased in summer could play a role in addressing food problems experienced by

Evenki families. We also believe that despite their arbitrary pricing practices, long-term fur dealers had to maintain a certain minimum supply of goods if they wanted to continue business with hunters. Based on our data, we know that foodstuffs purchased in some years were stored as a reserve in special caches along the summer travel routes, together with the dried meat.

Forest birds and waterfowl are an additional source of food in summer not to be overlooked [in this examination]. One might think that procurement of this kind did not have a significant effect on the nomadizing lifestyle characteristic of the Evenkis. *Active hunting* with rifles, employed in the vicinity of regular base camps during spring and early autumn, had low returns and usually was not carried out by the main productive members of the hunting group. In summer, bird and waterfowl hunting was assisted by the dogs. Active bird hunting was conducted virtually concurrently with other economic activities, and did not take up a lot of time. During the most settled period of family life around the winter base camp, Evenkis engaged only in *passive hunting* of forest birds and waterfowl, using non-portable and portable traps (snares, nooses). This type of hunting coincided with the autumn moose hunt, and therefore only old members of the hunting group took part.

On the whole, among Evenkis and other peoples of Siberia the passive hunting of birds, and other small animals too, made a somewhat substantial contribution to large-scale food storage efforts only when the majority of the group lived a relatively settled lifestyle (ALIE 14/1/167 ff 304–7; Turov field notes 1974, 1986). Bird hunting was generally ruled out in summer, at least for June and July (the most mobile period for Evenkis), because harvesting wood grouse and duck was prohibited during these months. The taboo against bird hunting during moulting and nesting was observed by members of all Evenki age groups. During the remainder of the year, this type of hunting provided a significant contribution to family food supplies, as mentioned on numerous occasions in the ethnographic literature (e.g., Krivoshapkin 1863; Popov 1926; Rychkov 1917; Vasilevich 1969).

The materials described above can be summarized as follows. Implementation of all active methods of food procurement related to tracking and hunting animals (i.e., involving travel by the hunters themselves as well as by their families) was spatially limited to relatively small territories. Furthermore, intensity of food procurement activities by Evenkis reached its peak as they approached the winter base camps, or continued in their direct vicinity once the families had already settled in and the hunters could set out on short-term hunting expeditions. According to our data, the routes covered while hunting ungulates rarely exceeded 60–80 km [per trip], and the overall maximum time spent was about 30–40 days [per year]. In any case, we do not have sufficient evidence to associate Evenki mobility, i.e., continued long-distance travel of a group, with the kind of subsistence hunting characteristic of Evenkis in Central Siberia at the turn of the 20th century. On the other hand, the particular approach of Evenkis to fur hunting provides a slightly better justification for their mobile lifestyle. Specifically, fur hunting is related to the season in Evenki life—the so-called *bol'shoe shaganie* 'long walk'—that extends over an interval of 4–5 months in the 7-month-long autumn/winter half-year in the Evenki calendar (Vasilevich 1969: 44–52).

2.2 Fur hunting for trade

As mentioned above, toward the end of the 19th century fur hunting likely did not play a significant role in supplying Evenkis with foodstuffs obtained via the fur trade, but it was in fact the only means of supporting vital domestic and subsistence activities with necessities such as rifles, ammunition, and various other items of hunting gear.

Evenkis harvested mainly squirrel and sable. Even when they did not set out purposefully in search of it, on account of the sable's high market value (since it fetched at least 6 roubles per pelt, one sable was worth as much as 30–40 squirrels) hunters would not pass up any opportunity to take sable when tracks were discovered, and they were willing to pursue the little critter indefinitely.

In spite of the high auction value of moose, reindeer, wolverine, wolf, bear, and fox pelts, however, Evenkis rarely offered them for trade. This is explained by the fact that the skins of the first two [moose and reindeer] were used entirely by the Evenkis themselves for clothing, footwear, bedding, and tent coverings [Photo 28]. Hunting of bear and wolf was marginal due to the special place these animals occupied in Evenki religious beliefs. For example, we frequently heard from old people the following general explanation of their attitude toward wolves: "Why should I kill him? The wolf is a hunter, same as me. The wolf has his own trail, and I have mine." It should not be ruled out that a practical understanding of the role this predator played in maintaining nature's balance influenced the shaping of the Evenki attitude toward wolves. For example, the Saami people [explicitly] linked the health and stability of the reindeer population with the positive "sanitary" role of the wolf (Chernolusskii 1972: 102). Finally, fox hunting not only required specialized skills, which Evenkis did not have, but also special dogs for burrowing and pursuit; furthermore, it did not produce any significant quantities of skins. From this, we may conclude that in order to assess the profitability and intensity of the fur hunt, as well as its impact on the overall lifestyle of Evenki hunters and their families, we should focus mainly on the conditions and technology of procuring squirrel and, to a lesser extent, sable.

According to recent estimates, which naturally differ from the data pertaining to the researched period, the density of the sable population is 0.2–0.5 head per 1,000 ha [10 sq. km] of taiga. [Wildlife] experts note that sable is highly adaptable to various forage and shelter conditions in different environments; this, together with its ability to adapt to a wide range of landscapes and climatic zones, predicates the little animal's largely sedentary way of life.

The radius of sable's foraging range usually does not exceed 10–15 km. Only extreme circumstances (for example, high population density in a given area) would force sable to forage farther (Dorogostaiskii 1925: 4–5; Kopylov et al. 1940: 33; Sokolov 1925: 14–27). Therefore, Evenkis (and other hunters) distinguished between "local" and "transitory" sable groups, with the former consisting of older, mature males and females that have inhabited the territory for several years and are the most valuable for hunters. The somewhat greater mobility of females searching for food, observed especially before the birthing period, does not change the general opinion of the wildlife experts that sable is one of the most sedentary game animals in Siberia (Popov 1977: 330–7; Sokolov 1979: 52, 174).

By the beginning of the 19th century sable had almost completely disappeared from most of the Central Siberian taiga, which seems to justify the decision not to consider the effects of the sable hunt on the formation of the Evenki mobile lifestyle. However, the high market price of sable and the possibility of obtaining a significant volume of goods for a single pelt must have enticed hunters to expand their hunting ranges as well as extend the duration of their search quests for sable. Without possession of any accurate data about the scale of such travels, we can only assume, based on hunter accounts, that these distances were significantly greater than those involved in hunting ungulates.

As stated above, a sharply decreased sable supply resulted in squirrel taking the top spot in the Evenki fur trade. Unlike sable, squirrel is rather fastidious regarding its food preferences in terms of composition, quality, and annual availability of forage in any given area (Kopylov et al. 1940: 20, 77, 82; Voilochnikov 1977: 179–82). Our own observations and the stories of old hunters correspond well with the opinion of wildlife biologists that squirrel is a unique species due to its characteristic periodically undertaken mass migrations. Moreover, there are two kinds of migration: one involving a small area and the other encompassing a much greater territory. The first type of migration consists of the usual movement of the population within the boundaries of a seasonal foraging range. In this case, the migration is connected to seasonal availability of forage and the search for shelter from the elements. This species [squirrel] consistently inhabits dark-needled spruce and Siberian pine forests, where the trees have relatively dense, closed crowns. In pineries and larch forests, even in years with a good crop of pine cones, squirrel will not stay around after the establishment of a stable snow cover because the sparse [albeit] sunlit stands of pine do not provide enough shelter for the little animals from cold winds, nor do they provide reliable concealment. Approximately at the beginning of November, the squirrel move to more remote tracts of spruce and silver-fir, confined to boggy and marshy sections of taiga creeks and streams. They make their nests (*gaino*) in the dense crowns of spruce and silver-fir trees, where they wait out the frigid winter, rarely leaving their nests. On extremely cold and windy days the squirrel may stay in their nests for several days at a time, descending infrequently to forage near the *gaino* and search for food under the snow cover (last year's "sour" pine cones), or feeding right "on the porch of their house" during years with a good crop of spruce cones.

In Central Siberia, stands of Siberian pine [*Pinus sibirica,* which the Russians call *kedr* 'cedar'—*Ed.*] are encountered only as small islands within the large expanses of pine, spruce, and larch forests. Thus, in the majority of Evenki hunting territories, permanent squirrel habitats are found within spruce and silver spruce stands. On these forest floors, most spruce cones survive for 4–5 years, serving as an important source of food for the species during poor years and in winter (Kopylov et al. 1940: 83; Voilochnikov 1977: 180). On relatively warm pre-winter days and at the beginning of spring when the weather is calm, squirrel raid nearby pineries. In autumn, they forage for mushrooms, and once the snow falls they feed on pinecones, as long as they are plentiful. In spring the sparse, sun-warmed pine stands serve as mating grounds. On the whole, then, according to informants and biologists, squirrel numbers in larch and pine forests are 4–5 times lower than in dark-needle forests, especially in stands of Siberian pine. The size of the squirrel population, as well as the distance and direction of migration between foraging sites, depends directly on availability of the main food, Siberian pine and spruce [cones]. Severe shortages of this forage lead to the development of epizootics, a decline in the overall viability of the species, reduced fertility, and sharp decreases in local population size.

A periodic fluctuation in squirrel population size occurs every 3–6 years. During years of abundant Siberian pine forage, squirrel populations reach their maximum size. However, the animals inhabit relatively small tracts of taiga, and their density per square kilometre is extremely high. Slightly lower densities are observed in years abounding in spruce cones, because their nutritional value is significantly lower, which forces squirrel to spread out over larger foraging territories. Evenkis still consider such squirrel to be "local," because sufficient numbers of them can be harvested within the nearby hunting territories. Then, in the year following an abundant forage year, there is a surplus of squirrel in their habitats, with demand for forage exceeding supply. The number of local squirrel remains quite high, but even before the Evenki fur hunt starts, the majority of "excess" squirrel leave to look for unoccupied land. In subsequent years, the squirrel population gradually decreases as they move farther and farther away from previously inhabited places. In the worst years for forage supply, the numbers of migrating squirrel and distances covered reach their peak. In such years, squirrel migrations can reach distances of 600–800 km. The little animals withdraw almost completely from most of the hunting territories covered by pineries and larch forests, and move to the expanses of Siberian pine forest—a rarity in Central Siberia—that are found in the foothills of the Sayan Mountains along the Enisei [Yenisei] and upper Lena rivers, as well as the upper reaches of the Podkamennaia and Lower Tunguska rivers (Kolosov 1980: 33–4; Kopylov et al. 1940: 82; Popov 1977: 143; Sokolov 1979: 160). Such instances of widespread disappearance of squirrel were reported by our informants and Russian hunters as having taken place on the Angara River and its left tributaries, along the entire middle course of the Lower Tunguska, and throughout the Angara river basin during the 1974, 1978, and 1986 fieldwork seasons, respectively. In most cases, a hunter would take no more than 50 squirrels per year while hunting close to his permanent *zimov'ie* 'winter base camp', usually 15–20 during each of the autumn and spring seasons of the [fur] hunt.

The rather marked periodical fluctuations in squirrel population size and their perpetual migrations also led to consistently high Evenki mobility during the fur hunt, and the [equally] perpetual travel of hunters' families for significant distances (up to 400 km). This, in turn, resulted in an increased size of squirrel hunting territories compared to that of [ungulate] hunting, and periodic exploration by hunters of unfamiliar new taiga regions (Petri 1930: 5–6; Suslov 1927: 47–9). However, it should be noted that the high Evenki mobility did not last for the entire duration of the hunt. Its peak came during late autumn and beginning of winter, when hunters strove to reach the most remote parts of the hunting area that were otherwise inaccessible in winter due to deep snow. During this time, the hunter's entire family participated in the hunt, constituting a hunting artel. The pace of movement of an artel was high, averaging 12–15 km per day. However, Evenki preferred to hunt squirrel close to their *chum* 'conical tent, tipi' [aka 'choom'], where food supplies were kept. In the morning, hunters left their camp *na legke* 'with light loads' and surveyed the tracts of mixed spruce and pine forest that were closest to their nomadic routes and which served the squirrel simultaneously as foraging ranges and reliable shelter from predators and the approaching sub-zero temperatures (Suslov 1927: 45).

Hunting was usually done on foot, using huskies to sniff out squirrel tracks. The typical hunting gear consisted of a rifle (***pykteraun***), a *pal'ma* 'bear spear' (***koto***), a hunting knife (***purto***), and a board-frame backpack (***ponage***), to which the hunter fastened a small food ration and the carcasses of taken animals. In some regions (for example, the Podkamennaia Tunguska watershed and the region inhabited by Preobrazhenka and Erbogachen Evenki groups along the Lower Tunguska river), tying food rations and harvested animals to the rifle case (***nagaliska***) was broadly practiced. Interestingly, even in the 1940s and 1950s, when domesticated reindeer became the usual means of transportation not only for the elderly, women, and children but also for hunters, most of fur and ungulate hunting was done on foot. This is best explained by the specific conditions of hunting in the taiga (Tugolukov 1969: 22). In general, assessing the mobility of hunting artels during the first half of the fur-hunting season, it is possible to suggest that travel remained at a consistently high level regardless of the distribution of squirrel foraging ranges or the size of the "local" squirrel population.

In years abundant in "local" (i.e., sedentary) congregations of squirrel, Evenkis tried to harvest as many pelts as possible in areas close to winter camp during autumn and winter hunting expeditions, leaving only a negligible "quota" for the spring. Hence, fluctuations in squirrel population size and migration range influenced the degree of mobility and travelling distances of the hunting artels mainly during autumn. Our data allow the assertion that these characteristics [of the squirrel hunt] varied with the periodic changes in squirrel population size and distribution (the staple game animal in the 19th and early 20th centuries); this, in turn, entirely depended on the availability of forage. For example, during the first two years after abundant forage in areas adjacent to a permanent Evenki winter base camp, a hunting artel required minimal travel in order to hunt around those areas and collect a substantial fur crop, thus ensuring sufficiently high revenues from trade. In the following 2–3 years, decreasing size of the "local" squirrel population and its migration to distant areas with more forage resulted in a corresponding increase in the scale of Evenki movement and general mobility of the hunting artel. Moreover, during the second half of the fur hunt (February–March and even through the first half of April), the length of the routes approached the distances covered by nomadizing Evenki groups in summer.

During the second half of December and first half of January, Evenkis lived a fully settled lifestyle, their fur hunt severely hampered by severe cold and large quantities of snow. Indeed, during the snowiest and coldest weather, it was not possible to use dogs and the fur hunt was temporarily suspended. Moreover, the search area was reduced to a minimum by the short span of daylight hours and by the fact that squirrel spend most of the day in their nests. Thus, from the second half of December until February the squirrel hunt virtually stopped altogether. As an exception, some hunters periodically set out to explore the nearby taiga, but only if the autumnquirrel harvest had been low.

After mid-February, with the formation of a hard snow crust, the fur hunt intensified. Gradually venturing ever farther away from the winter base camp, a hunting artel, consisting usually of a single family and a minimum number of pack reindeer, moved from one camp to another, covering a maximum of 10 km per day on average. One of the family members led the way on skis in front of the caravan, tamping a path for the reindeer. The hunter himself, flanking the main path of the caravan, quested in the adjacent taiga and arrived at dusk at the location of the stop-over camp agreed upon beforehand. The average stay at one camp was not too long, about 2 or 3 days. The family stayed longer in one place if there were large numbers of squirrel at that location, or if a moose feeding site was found [in the vicinity of the stop-over camp]. In the latter case, in order to replenish winter supplies of meat, the adult hunters would set out to search for the moose [*goniat' zveria*], while those who stayed at the camp—youth capable of hunting on their own, as well as women and sometimes old people—hunted squirrel in their nests or tracked them. The length of their stay in one place was also dependent on the capacity to transport the harvest and on the process of drying meat to be stored for spring travel. If the squirrel population in a given area was sufficiently large, the stay could extend to 2–3 weeks. If the squirrel population was small and the autumn hunt not particularly successful, the Evenkis were compelled to abandon that place even if prospects for ungulate hunting were good, and move to a new location where the hunters expected to make up for the shortage of [squirrel] fur.

At the start of April (*ektenkire* 'snow begins to melt'), the soft snow allowed Evenkis to step up the tempo of nomadizing. In years with a poor harvest of "local" squirrel, a hunting artel would move ever farther away from its **meneien** 'winter base camp', constantly increasing the length of daily travel.

Another reason for increased Evenki mobility at this time was the natural drive of domesticated reindeer herds, more specifically its pregnant cows, to reach the permanent spring base camps before the beginning of the calving season. The fur hunt lasted until the first patches of thawed ground appeared on southern slopes warmed by the spring sun; this period was called **turan** 'month when crows return' (April). Animal pelts lose their value at this time and hunters switch to a basically sedentary lifestyle.

2.3 Hunting equipment

The development of fur hunting and resulting expansion of "commodity relations"[10] did not lead to a significant transformation of the technical means employed by Evenkis to facilitate their subsistence and hunting activities. It is likely that the only benefit of commodity relations entering Evenki culture (besides foodstuffs, of course) was the increased assortment and regular supply of firearms and some processing tools. Although this equipment did not completely replace the extensive inventory of bone and stone implements, it nevertheless made the manufacture of clothing, everyday household items, hunting gear, and means of transportation far quicker and easier, without notably changing the technologies themselves. The equipment of primary importance in Evenki life included iron woodworking instruments, steel needles, and knives.

Several researchers (Gurvich and Dolgikh 1970: 53; Vasilevich 1969: 54, 62) have asserted that replacement of the traditional bow and arrow with firearms, which was complete by the beginning of the 19th century, brought about the intensification of the entire game hunting branch of the Evenki economy. In general, we consider this view to be accurate, to the extent that it reflects the potential of employing firearms in order to intensify hunting activity. However, it fails to describe the details of the intensification, or the changes which took place in the Evenki economy as a result of replacing *luchnoi boi* 'bow-and-arrow hunting' [with rifle hunting].

First we should emphasize that even today, Evenkis and most other peoples living in the Siberian taiga still practice traditional active hunting and tracking methods for meat and fur procurement. Use of the traditional

---

10. See page 19, footnote 8.

bow and arrow persisted in the hunter's repertoire of hunting methods long after regular supplies of firearms and ammunition became available to hunters (Pelikh 1981: 87–8; Tugolukov 1969: 25). There are various reasons for this, ranging from the aforementioned high prices for rifles and ammunition to reluctance to spoil valuable pelts with shotgun fire. Furthermore, in some instances rifle shots would scare off groups of reindeer or moose that were being stalked by a hunter, and therefore he might only capture one animal instead of several. All these questions require further dedicated research.

The supreme bow and arrow skill of Evenkis is quite well known from [19th-century] literature. For example, A. P. Okladnikov cites an informant named Maak who asserts that the rate of fire from a bow in the hands of an experienced Evenki hunter could be up to twenty (!) aimed shots per minute. The following account illustrates the accuracy of bow shooting. An Evenki hunter encountered by Maak on the Murozhnaia River (Angara basin) shot an arrow into the air and then aimed to hit this target with the shots that followed. Before the [first] arrow fell to the ground, ten others were released, of which about seven or eight hit the target (Okladnikov 1950: 232).

Obviously, this degree of shooting accuracy (perhaps a little exaggerated in this case) must have been uncommon among Evenkis. However, taking into consideration the well-known Evenki inclination to practice target shooting, encouraged among boys and girls by various bow and arrow games, high shooting accuracy should be considered a skill honed by any self-respecting Evenki hunter. The aforementioned rate of fire from the bow is confirmed by data not only on Evenkis but also with regard to Nganasans, who did not use the bow and arrow to hunt as much as Evenkis did (Polevoi 1965: 125; Popov 1948: 51). In contrast, the maximum rate of fire of a muzzle-loaded smoothbore gun was only one shot every 3–5 minutes (Mavrodin and Mavrodin 1981). According to the informants, this was evidently the reason why hunters had to try to reload their guns on the run after having taken a shot and only wounding their prey. While the low rate of fire of muzzle-loading rifles was not crucial for fur hunting, this disadvantage was more apparent for hunting larger animals. According to Evenkis, in autumn a hunter with a bow and arrow could kill all animals in the group he was stalking without making any noise, but with a rifle the animals would startle and scatter at the first shot before the hunter could reload.

We think that the significance of firearm characteristics such as greater range of the direct shot in comparison with the bow, as well as greater killing power, should be assessed separately for the contexts of fur hunting and procurement of large game. [Firearms] being relatively simple to use and sufficiently reliable in any climatic conditions allowed for the training and involvement of new individuals for the hunt, including youth, the elderly, women, and even adolescents who had not yet participated (Vasilevich 1969: 69). This clearly facilitated the intensification of the fur hunt and improved its productivity. Obviously, the same features also enabled the widespread use of firearms in subsistence hunting. Nevertheless, some indirect data from the literature (Clark 1863; Middendorf 1869; Rychkov 1917; Vasilevich 1969) and our own field observations permit us to state that regardless of the potential for intensification due to the introduction of firearms, the technology of meat hunting, relevant procurement activities, and processing of the harvested products all remained at the subsistence level even after the introduction of firearms.

In all cases observed by us, the fairly dense underbrush limited effective shooting at animals from modern rifles to a distance of 60–80 steps at the most. According to Evenkis themselves, shooting from greater distances was effective only in the open spaces of large bogs, slash, or tundra. Ungulate hunting involves a whole range of techniques whose main purpose is to approach as close to the prey as possible. As for hunting conditions in the taiga, since reindeer and moose spend most of their time not too far from dense forests and piles of burnt and fallen trees (used by the animals for shelter in times of danger), even the most sharp-eyed hunters could not spot an animal from a distance greater than 150–200 m, while shooting is usually done from a distance of 40–50 steps. Thus, in principle, given hunting conditions in the taiga, the purported superiority of early muzzle-loaded guns over the bow and arrow did not produce the effects that might have been expected [from this development].

In our opinion, for Evenki hunters the most important properties of firearms included the greater distance (compared to the bow) and more variable angles from which a direct shot could be taken, as well as the ability to deliver a fatal blow with the first shot. These features led to the widespread use of firearms as the main tool in fur and meat hunting. The increased distance of the direct shot allowed hunters to hit their targets from the maximum stalking distance without having to correct the trajectory of the bullet. (Such correction was necessary when shooting from the bow because the launching speed of an arrow was far slower than that of a bullet.) Hence, hunters who used rifles had the advantage of superior lethal force and greater distance of direct shots, but the disadvantage of rate of fire, which was very slow for the muzzle-loaded guns. The latter was an especially important factor in ungulate hunting, where the rate of fire influences not only the number of animals killed, but also the hunter's own safety. Missing the target using the bow was less dangerous for the hunter than missing with a rifle because the hunter could manage to send a second or third arrow before the prey escaped out of range or charged.

Overall, there can be little doubt that the old-system [muzzle-loaded] firearms could not significantly modify the traditional Evenki hunting techniques, though they certainly increased the efficiency of the hunt itself. Primarily, this was due to the greater numbers of animals killed by the first bullet. Moreover, in the case of highly skilled hunters, it greatly reduced the percentage of wounded prey, thus freeing them from the necessity of pursuing wounded animals, sometimes over considerable distances. The most effective features of firearms, together with the possibility of increasing the number of individuals participating directly in the hunt, are among the factors which facilitated intensification of Evenkis' hunting activities, and therefore increased the output. In addition, it may be suggested that the use of firearms in subsistence hunting led to a decline in the size of the reindeer population, because

> "... the reindeer are shot by hunters while in the herd, and so the shooters have an opportunity to select a bigger target. This unquestionably leads to population degradation... weakening its gene pool, and can become a factor in population decline" (Vereshchagin and Rusakov 1979: 283).

On the other hand, employment of rifles in moose hunting, the bulk of which was carried out using traditional methods involving special dogs, has led to a sort of selection process in which culling weaker individuals promoted, to a certain degree, a healthier and more flourishing moose population.

In general, evaluating the effects of introducing firearms in hunting, we may assert that certain features of the new weapons facilitated intensification, but this effect was fully realized only in the trade-oriented fur hunt. The most obvious results of the intensification of fur hunting included the apparently sharp depletion of the sable population and the introduction of new categories of hunters such as teenagers and young women. In contrast to fur hunting, meat hunting (the main purpose of which, as mentioned above, was to obtain necessary food from natural sources, following strictly defined and well-known norms) remained at the same levels of intensity as in "pre-rifle times." Accordingly, the extent of subsistence hunting territories did not change, either. This was true not only for Evenkis in Central Siberia but also for a number of other peoples living in the Siberian forest zone (Alekseenko 1974: 218–30, 1986: 61, 71; Kreinovich 1973: 146). It is well known today that all hunter-gatherer-fisher societies have a detailed empirical understanding of the necessity and practicality of utilizing natural resources in harmony with their regenerative capacities (Davidson 1975: 47–9; Kabo 1979: 92–3; Weiner 1979: 588).

Examination of the degree of Evenki mobility and the scale of their nomadic exploitation of natural resources, assessed as a function of the subsistence hunt only, and its comparison with the truly high mobility of hunting groups during the commercial fur hunt, contradicts the notion that the Evenki mobile [*brodiachii*] way of life was derived from the entire system of their hunting economy (Orlov 1857: 180–1; Vasilevich 1969: 42, 1972: 166). Our research data show that, given its low overall productivity and the prohibition against taking certain animal species, it is doubtful that game hunting was the actual reason for Evenkis' high summer mobility. During these months, hunting groups consisting of single families or two small families together with their reindeer herds (or at least large parts of them) sometimes covered distances of up to 200 km. Evidently, the reasons for and goals of summer nomadizing should be sought in the ways that other natural resources were utilized in the taiga territories inhabited by Evenkis at the turn of the 20th century.

2.4 Fishing

Another Evenki subsistence activity that influenced their characteristic nomadizing economy to a certain extent during summer was fishing [*rybolovstvo*]. Here, it may be noted that the expression *rybnye promysly* 'fishery, fishing craft' constitutes a better reflection of the nature and actual scale of this activity in the Evenki economy. In our opinion, fishing can be regarded as a separate branch of the economy, or as a branch of overall production activity, only in cases when such fishing leads to extensive storage for future utilitarian use, or when fishing is an element of commercially oriented activity. Regardless, the usual approach in Evenki ethnography is to juxtapose the dominant hunting activity against the subsidiary fishing activity, which has sometimes led researchers to artificially diminish the role of the latter in the traditional Evenki economy.

In the majority of rivers and watersheds of Central Siberia, the biological characteristics of game fish predicate three main types of fishing: during spawning runs, during the fattening time in holes, and during autumn migration to larger rivers and deep lakes. At the turn of the 20th century, fishing equipment was not only capable of obtaining large quantities of fish but it was also meant to be used over the entire summer or even the entire year.

Most taiga rivers break up in May, except for the tributaries of the Lower Tunguska, which break up two weeks later. However, fishing was rare at the beginning of summer, i.e., end of May and beginning of June. The *polaia voda* 'spring run-off' hindered large-scale fishing, and the active fishing season started only when the banks dried out and the water cleared, i.e., at the end of June or a little earlier. After the end of calving season in the domesticated reindeer herd, Evenkis set out for their familiar fishing spots. Three different methods were used to harvest the fish migrating up the tributaries of large rivers.

1. During the day, Evenkis *karaulili* 'watched' for running fish from birch-bark boats called *berestianki* at the upstream ends of riffles, stabbing fish with a ***kiramki*** 'leister'. Usually there were two people fishing in the boat, one holding it against the current and the other, sitting at the bow, spearing the fish in the head ("Don't stab in the tail, the water will fool you.")

2. Harpooning at night was done using birch-bark torches (***taliun***).[11] Night harpooning [*pokolka*], generally taking no more than 1–2

---

11. These were prepared in large quantities beforehand in the spring when the birch sap starts flowing and the bark is easy to strip off. To make the ***taliun***, birch bark was cooked in large pots, the same way as for making tipi covers. Several layers of bark were rolled into cylinders with moss inside ("water seeps up along the moss, cooks all the birch bark from the inside") and were cooked in a pot with water over a fire for a whole day. The cooked layers of birch bark were tightly rolled into torches, which burned for a long time and were conveniently transported to the fish harpooning sites

hours, involved two fishermen floating downstream and trying to stay close to the riffles. They speared any fish that came up to the light. Harpooning fish, especially at night, required a great deal of patience, a sharp eye, and quick reaction. For this reason, apparently, it was usually young hunters who fished, though this type of hunting was not considered an unworthy activity among adult men, either. In fact, the high art of spearing fish with one stab was considered no less an achievement than shooting accurately, and a skillful harpooner enjoyed no less respect than did a skilful hunter. Needless to say, these two skills were often found in one individual. In deft hands, a faultlessly employed **kiramki** could bring in 20–30 kg of fish in a single session, including the largest kinds—*taimen'*, *sig* 'whitefish', *nalim* 'burbot', and pike—with individual specimens weighing as much as 5–6 kg. Evenkis considered harpooning to be no less dangerous an activity than hunting for meat. According to their accounts, certain specimens of *taimen'* and pike could, with a jerk or a blow of the tail, capsize the tippy *berestianka* if an inexperienced fisherman was less than accurate in stabbing the fish with his harpoon. This is probably the reason why old Evenkis preferred harpooning from small bridges thrown across narrow taiga streams.

Among the Evenkis of the Podkamennaia Tunguska and Katanga rivers, the tradition was to greet young fishermen who returned from their first successful harpooning with as much ceremony as they met hunters. During collective nomadizing by several families, all big fish, no matter who caught them, were divided equally among all inhabitants of the base camp, in the same way it was customary to share a moose. Here, too, the successful fisherman kept only the head of the largest fish (Vasilevich 1969: 86).

In Evenki life, this type of fishing lasted briefly, only as long as the fish travelled upstream along the riffles to their spawning locations. With the end of the spawn, the fish went to quiet, deep holes [*plesy*, "*iamy*"].

3. From this period until the end of August, Evenkis fished mainly with the help of wicker traps, known by their Russian names *mordy vershi* 'fish-trap muzzles', *korchagi* 'creels', and others. Similarly constructed traps are called **nalba** in all Tungus-Manchurian languages. In fact, it seems to be a traditional Evenki device that originated independently from similar Russian fishing gear. This trap, usually left for the night in a deep *ulov* (river hole full of fish), produced an average of at least 5 kg of fish per single setup. The trap could be transported in packs for short distances

---

in pack loads. [Author's text, moved to this footnote.—*Ed.*]

from camp to camp. In every good fishing spot (*ukikit*), *nalba* or *kenger* traps were stored by families for several years on special platforms or in trees, easily accessible and ready for use.

With the development of trade, factory-made fishhooks were introduced into the Evenki household inventory, albeit in very limited quantities, and thus they were highly valued. However, with the availability of large quantities of metal following soon afterward, Evenkis quickly learned to make fishhooks themselves from old needles or forged iron. Thus, fishing with lines made of horsehair or strong thread became very popular among youth, women, and the elderly and brought plentiful supplies of fish as everyday fare.

At the end of August Evenkis would arrive in their travels at the mouths of small taiga rivers with many shoals and riffles, where fish started their reverse run toward the big rivers. With the first leaves falling, several families installed *ukikit* weirs (Fig. 2), damming the river at the riffles (Turov 1978; Vasilevich 1962: 106). This was done by driving stakes at some distance from one another in order to set up tripods across the river bottom. The top ends of the tripods, about 40–50 cm above the water, supported heavy cross-poles to which, in turn, the lattice-partitions (*buchivun*), made of willow twigs or larch laths, were attached. The lattices were submerged deep into the water, and secured tightly to the tripods by stakes driven into the bottom. Two or three logs [foot-bridges] were placed across the stream over the tripods, and the ends of the logs were secured to the shore with stakes. At both ends, the *buchivun* had openings that were slightly narrower in width than the

*Figure 2. The **ukikit** fishing enclosure.*

openings created by the *nalba* or *kenger* traps attached to the partitions. One such trap was placed with its opening upstream and another with its opening downstream. During the intensive feeding period, the fish swam actively upstream and downstream from one hole to another looking for food and, moving through the enclosure, they would get caught inside the trap. *Lapnik* (silver-fir or spruce boughs) covered the lower parts of the traps and their tops in order to prevent the fish from escaping. The traps were checked at least twice daily, usually morning and evening. Sometimes the catch was so large that two men could hardly lift the traps. At the time of our fieldwork, the average catch per trap was 6–10 kg of fish.

In late autumn, before the start of the fur-hunting season, all members of the base camp worked together to build a second type of *ukikit* enclosure. This device, with which we became familiar, was practically the same as the one described by G. M. Vasilevich (1969: 84). The only difference was that in contrast to the first type of *ukikit*, the second type was erected in deeper locations, a little downstream. This enclosure was more tightly set, and with wider openings covered with fir boughs that caused a small damming of the water upstream from a riffle. Near one shore, an opening was left in the *buchivun* partition at the level of the raised water. The trap itself, called *uki*, consisted of a large latticed box, made of thick willow switches and opened from the top. The *uki* box was placed on stakes driven into the stream, positioned near an opening in the fence-dam, and with the bottom of the trap barely covered by water ("Do not move the *uki* too quickly in the water, the fish will jump and escape through the top"). According to the Evenkis, so many fish, running in schools to the deep waters of big rivers and lakes, would be caught in the *uki* that "one catch was enough to feed the whole village (i.e., camp— *Auth.*)." However, in spite of some large catches, this method provided fish to eat for only a very short period of time, until the start of the ungulate hunting season, for fish runs of such abundance lasted only a few days.

Today, based on the existing literature it is difficult to say how effective the various fishing methods were in different seasons, and what quantities of supplementary foodstuffs were served daily at the family table (in addition to meat). There is only a general, largely fanciful impression that fish were caught in exact quantities sufficient for a single meal. According to data we obtained from the small Chuna group of Evenkis, we know that ice fishing in winter and spring provided a considerable supplement to the traditional meat fare. In this regard, E. I. Rukosueva reported:

> "The elderly are too weak for squirrel hunting; stay home more than anything. All autumn until the snows, and before the *ukikit* freeze up, they fish with *mordy* 'muzzle traps'. Not a lot of fish, frankly, rarely more than half a pail. But anyhow, in autumn there is no day without fish on the table. In spring, fish start their runs, feeding. They set up rods in the holes using meat as bait, which works well for *nalim* 'burbot'; catch lots" [Turov field notes].

G. M. Vasilevich observed ice fishing in the Ilimpeia group of Evenkis—not with rods but actually with so-called bone spokes, harpooning through holes using *pekar* fish lures (1969: 84–7).

In general, we can be quite certain that in summer the fish catch played a contributing role and added variety to the family diet of all Evenki groups. Moreover, as ungulate hunting during summer was less effective and return rates were low, fishing was an important and full-fledged source of necessary food products for Evenkis.

The importance of fishing in the Evenki economy becomes even clearer when we analyze the use of fish products in the Evenki family diet. The nature of meat consumption by the Evenkis of Central Siberia has already been described above. According to the most significant variables—time spent, volume of meat products, preparation methods, and overall importance of meat in supplying hunters with necessary calories and vitamins—hunting was the priority activity among the Evenkis. However, fishing compensated the possible shortage of meat products, thus creating a certain balance in the summer and winter diets. For instance, the Evenki sisters E. I. and N. I. Rukosueva recounted their grandmother's story:

> "One time, suddenly the game became scarce. Moose and hare, leaving their notches on the aspen (i.e., tooth marks—*Auth.*), maybe took off somewhere for their own war. There was hunger, and there was nothing to wear. Everyone took to fishing, fished a lot. People ate fish and shared fish skins between the tents, wore *taimen'* and pike skins. That's how it was" [Turov field notes].

Disregarding the slightly fanciful explanation for the disappearance of moose and other game animals, the rest of the story quite clearly indicates that under certain unfavourable conditions, fishing not only supplied families with food but also provided raw materials for clothing. Other authors have also written about the former Evenki tradition of using fish skins (Georgi 1799: 40, 43–6; Vasilevich 1969: 86).

Strong evidence that fishing by taiga Evenki groups was a significant source of supplementary food has also been found in records of dietary content and annual diet variability from various years (Krivoshapkin 1863; Popov 1926; Vasilevich 1969; Turov field notes 1972, 1974, 1978).

The data in Table 1 demonstrate that fresh fish was a priority product in the diet of Evenki families from July until September, and even into early October. However, much larger quantities of fish than venison were required to satiate an adult. Dried [game] meat, coming during summer months from spring or even autumn stores, was not sufficient to satisfy people's food requirements. Evenkis themselves said, "Won't survive for long on dried meat; chew on it all day, and still be hungry. Dried meat alone won't keep an Evenki full." Lacking vitamins and micronutrients, unsalted dried meat is not particularly nutritious; it is quickly absorbed, and over a long term does not provide enough calories. Therefore, it is likely that dried meat was always

Table 1. Diet of Evenkis in the Central Siberian taiga throughout the year.

Month	Composition of diet (ordered from continuous to periodic consumption)
December–February	Supplies of frozen and dried venison (autumn stocks), rendered and frozen fat, fresh venison (periodically)
March–April	Fresh meat of ungulates, supplies of dry venison, fresh fat, meat of pine forest game
May–first half of June	Cured and dried venison (periodically fresh venison), fresh fish, reindeer milk
second half of June–August	Fresh fish (always), dried venison (fresh venison very rarely), fresh berries, wild garlic/onions, coral lily bulbs, pine forest game, reindeer milk
September	Fresh fish, fresh venison (more often than in previous period, esp. toward the end of the month), pine forest game, waterfowl, berries (bilberry, red bilberry), reindeer milk (often with berries)
October–November	Fresh venison (always), meat of pine forest game, fresh fish (rarely and only at the beginning of this period)

consumed either together with fat or bread or in a soup with flour-thickened gravy added for satiety.

To what extent were fish products able to replenish the calories expended by humans and supplement the meat in their diet? Today, the lack of documented data makes it difficult to estimate the exact quantities of fish harvested and consumed per family during the period of our interest. Evenkis usually answered our questions on this subject as follows:

> "Lots of fish caught in summer; all summer there was fish, we never lived without it. Before, there was a lot of fish in the streams. In the past, though, people were really foolish, no clue how to cook fish or fry it in oil. Always they grilled it on skewers, ate it like that" [Turov field notes].

According to N. Popov, Evenkis on the Lower Tunguska "do not eat enough fish… the catch is very meagre in summer, probably only 20 poods [~320 kg] per household for the whole summer… but the Tunguses like fish very much, and willingly come to those sections of a river where they can catch a lot" (1926: 23).

At first glance, Popov's account casts doubt on the importance of fish to Evenkis. However, if even 15 poods (i.e., 240 kg) of fish were caught on average per summer per family, then a simple calculation shows that each member of a family consisting of 5–6 people could consume about 0.5 kg of fish every day. Neither should we disregard the fact that Popov estimated the Evenki fishing harvest based only on his observation of groups living along the Lower Tunguska River. He obviously did not include in his calculations the fish caught in numerous taiga streams, as we have now documented, or in oxbows and lakes with flowing water. This is where the majority of local commercial fishes—pike, *kharius* 'grayling', *taimen'*, whitefish, *lenok,* and other species—are concentrated from the second half of June until the beginning of September. As mentioned above, this is characteristic of all taiga water systems in Siberia.

Fish is a nutritious food: 100 g of fish contain up to 20 g of animal proteins and other nutrients necessary for the human organism. This is a substantial amount, given that adults require an average of 165 g of protein daily (Gal'perin 1977: 198–9; Weiner 1979: 504). Moreover, fish is an easily digested food. Given the nutritional requirements of an average adult, more fish needs to be consumed than venison. Regardless, it is evident that fish, caught with traditional but relatively efficient fishing equipment, was not only a supplement to an Evenki diet dominated by venison. Our data demonstrate that, along with dried meat or sometimes fresh venison and wild berries with reindeer milk, fish was the most important food source for mobile Evenki groups during summer.

2.5 Summary

The materials described in this chapter invite a number of conclusions. At one time, A. A. Popov wrote the following—about hunter-fishers in general, to be sure, and not specifically about the Evenkis of Central Siberia: "No single activity… in their complex economy can be considered as subsidiary; each is vitally important" (ALIE 14/1/167 f. 12). It seems that the notion expressed in this quotation is wholly applicable to Evenkis, as well. All the subsistence activities of mobile Evenkis at the turn of the 20th century demonstrated an integrated, comprehensive use of the entire complex of hunting and fishing resources. The dominant place held by game products, particularly ungulate hunting, was relative within any given calendar year. Meat hunting and fur hunting, the major sources of food and raw materials for domestic manufacture, were practiced essentially throughout the entire year. At the same time, they were conditioned by the environment, as were other branches of the Evenki economy. In essence, nature itself determines the seasons and norms for the most efficient exploitation of any given resource, dictating also necessary adjustments of the focus on any particular resource, such as ungulates, ichthyofauna, and forest birds. Hence, for example, [the importance of] ungulate hunting declines during summer, giving way to regular, daily fishing. All economic production activities together follow the principle of comprehensive, continuous, year-round use of the taiga, regulated by nature and reinforced by religious-ethical practices in order to obtain supplies from nature at exactly sustainable levels that would not endanger the capacity of the natural resources to regenerate.

Along with V. A. Tugolukov, we consider the notion that the mobile Evenki lifestyle can be explained exclusively by the requirements and conditions of hunting activity to be a misconception (1969: 16). Of all the described types of Evenki economic production activities, only fur hunting has direct links with the mobile lifestyle. The requirements of fur hunting arise directly from the biological characteristics of the main fur species, and continuous human travel is indeed necessary, sometimes over considerable distances. To be sure, the mobility associated with fur hunting is limited to one season only, albeit a long one. During the rest of the year, the nature of Evenki subsistence activities, including the requirements and scale of movement of hunting parties, should result in a lifestyle of relatively low mobility, basically similar to that of "settled" Evenkis for whom fishing is considered the main branch of subsistence. On the other hand, we cannot agree with K. M. Rychkov (1917: 12), V. Kharuzina (1928: 13–14), or I. Georgi, who maintain that Evenki summer travel is entirely linked to facilitating the "ease of fishing" (1799: 40). The summer diet—which, as described above, consisted of a wide variety of animal and plant foods in addition to fish—allows us to assert that the summer cycle of Evenki migration was related to all subsistence activities in which they engaged during this season.

The materials discussed above can be summarized in the following statements:

1. The procurement branch of the Evenki economy can be divided into two parts: a) the natural consumption part, which comprised activities whose main purpose was to meet the vital needs of Evenki families with regard to food as well as raw materials for domestic manufacturing and processing. Hunting, fishing, and gathering are practiced together in a continuous, year-round process based on the principle of acquiring products made available by nature; and b) the trade-oriented commercial part, which is represented by fur hunting and characterized by well demarcated temporal and territorial production cycles of the main commodities.

2. Considered as an aggregate, the overall rhythm of subsistence activities of Evenki groups, their mobility, and shifts in exploitation intensity of this or that resource define the Evenki nomadic lifestyle. In turn, the nomadic lifestyle should be viewed as the main method by which Evenkis effect a comprehensive and efficient exploitation of the natural resources, including game and fish, available to each group within the territories they inhabit. To a certain degree, the mobile Evenki lifestyle is a form of cultural adaptation to the environmental conditions of their habitat, developed over many generations.

3. According to ethnographic data on Evenkis from the 19th century till the 1950s, the traditional combination of subsistence and commercial branches of their economy was not always, and

not necessarily, accompanied by a mobile way of life, i.e., by the continuous nomadizing of hunting parties over huge tracts of land. The *sidiachie* 'sitting' (*beregovye* 'shoreline' or *lodoshnye* 'boating') Evenkis mentioned above, who lived in Central Siberia on the banks of large bodies of water and who had similar economies to the one described here, developed a semi-settled—or, more accurately, a seasonally settled—lifestyle. This entailed: (a) having two permanent ***meneien*** base camps, one for summer and one for winter (Anisimov 1936); (b) hunting and fishing within a relatively smaller territory than mobile Evenkis; and (c) hunters nomadizing only in conjunction with the fur hunt, leaving their families in permanent base camps and often hunting not for the entire season but setting out on "hunting expeditions" of a sort. These circumstances inclined us to search for additional economic factors which contributed to the extensive nomadizing by Evenkis not only during the fur-hunting season but also during summer, and which provide us with grounds to put forward the idea of a *nomadic method of taiga land use*.

Chapter 3. Transport-reindeer husbandry in the Evenki economy

Questions about the origin and various types of reindeer husbandry [*olenevodstvo*] among the peoples of Northern Eurasia have attracted scholarly interest for more than fifty years. Despite extensive historical research on this topic, however, starting from earlier works dedicated to reindeer husbandry (Bogoraz-Tan 1933; Koviazin 1936; Maksimov 1928) and continuing till present times (Gurvich 1977; Kozmin 1981; Krupnik 1975, 1977; Pomishin 1971; Popov 1948; Simchenko 1976; Vainshtein 1960, 1970, 1971, 1972), these questions remain far from answered (Shnirel'man 1980: 175). One of the main reasons for such persistent attention to this topic is the prevalent assumption that reindeer husbandry is a precondition for the transition from a foraging economy to food producing economy.

Evidently, due to the overall focus of previous research on identifying differentiating ethno-cultural characteristics, the study of Evenki transport-reindeer husbandry has been somewhat one-dimensional in comparison to studies of reindeer husbandry among groups holding large herds, such as the Chukchis, Koriaks, and, to a certain degree, the Nganasans. In fact, even today there is a dearth of comparative and typological research on reindeer husbandry among the different ethnic groups in the taiga. Most of the research has noted only general cultural-typological similarities in reindeer husbandry for transportation purposes among Siberian peoples. Issues that are important from our point of view, such as seasonal methods of reindeer use, feeding and herd maintenance, and traditional disease treatment methods have yet to be thoroughly investigated. In general, it can be asserted that to date there has been no systematic examination of transport-reindeer husbandry as an important component of the production culture of a given ethnos. Therefore, the objective of this chapter is to investigate the following issues in the Evenki economy: organization of reindeer husbandry, herd maintenance, seasonal forms of reindeer use, and the specific place and importance of transport-reindeer husbandry in the economic exploitation of the taiga.

3.1 Evenki and Orochen subtypes of reindeer husbandry

The available ethnographic and cultural-genetic studies view Evenki reindeer husbandry, with its *Evenki* and *Orochen* subtypes, simply as an auxiliary field that facilitated the intensification of hunting activity (Gurvich and Dolgikh 1970: 39–40; Vasilevich 1964, 1969: 72–9; Vasilevich and Levin 1951). It is interesting to note that the nature of this intensification in overall Evenki life has not been studied, nor has the general transformation of Evenki life and economy that took place with the appearance of transport reindeer. Some narrowly specialized studies by I. M. Suslov (1930) and P. G. Poltoradnev (1932) are the only exceptions, in which the importance of transport reindeer in facilitating the fur hunt is analyzed in local Evenki groups on the Podkamennaia Tunguska and Lower Tunguska rivers.

Starting with the works of F. I. Stralenberg and I. G. Georgi, groups of "wandering" hunters that used reindeer [*oleni*] for transportation were assigned the descriptor *olennye* (Georgi 1799: 39–40; Karlov 1982: 9; Stepanov 1961: 211; Vasilevich 1969: 4, 21). With further research on the origin and development of reindeer husbandry among Siberian peoples, and particularly that of transport reindeer among Evenkis, the concept of *olennye* groups was divided into two types in Vasilevich's classification of reindeer herding economies: *Evenki* and *Orochen* (1964: 3–4, 1969: 75–80). According to the Vasilevich typology, the nomadic hunting–reindeer herding groups in Central Siberia belonged to the Evenki type of reindeer herding economy.

We accept this classification in general; however, while it is based on data from various periods within the development of Evenki reindeer husbandry, we should mention that the classification lacks detailed empirical data and specific references to the Evenki economy at the turn of the 20th century. It is also necessary to explain the content and meaning of the criteria which form the basis of the Evenki type of reindeer husbandry specific to the taiga zone of Central Siberia.

As documented, transport-reindeer husbandry among mobile Evenkis served primarily to facilitate the traditional production aspects of their economy. This necessitated a certain subordination of reindeer husbandry relative to hunting and fishing. Does this mean that in order to cater to hunting and fishing, the hunter–reindeer herders had to forego the interests of reindeer husbandry? Some sources maintain that this subordination should not be understood so literally, and that to a certain degree the reindeer husbandry branch of the Evenki economy had its own independent importance. Marking this overall epochal development in the culture of previously *lodoshnye* 'boating' and *sobach'i* 'dog-sledding' hunters, we would agree with V. G. Bogoraz's figurative (albeit somewhat exalted) description that domesticated reindeer "gave wings" to the *peshie* 'on-foot' hunters (Bogoraz-Tan 1933). At the same time, G. M. Vasilevich's response has merit in pointing out that Evenki dispersion over, and use of, vast areas of the taiga probably occurred before the reindeer husbandry period in the Evenki ethnogenesis, or that it occurred during the very first stages of the establishment of transport-reindeer husbandry (Vasilevich 1969; Vasilevich and Levin 1951). Without going into a detailed analysis of the early importance of domesticated reindeer in the economy of taiga hunters, it should be noted that the regular autumn slaughter of reindeer for meat (Vasilevich 1964, 1969), which has been suggested as a characteristic of the Evenki type of reindeer husbandry, should hardly be considered as the main differentiating factor in the development of the Evenki and Orochen types.

Indeed, the documented instances of reindeer slaughter before the start of the fur hunt certainly cannot in themselves be taken literally as one of the reasons that taiga hunters kept domesticated reindeer. Since game hunting was a sufficiently reliable and stable source of food and raw materials for mobile hunters, it is quite obvious why the culling by Evenkis of individuals in their domesticated reindeer herds, which incidentally provided meat for human consumption, was extremely rare. The autumn slaughter of 2–3 reindeer (usually second-rate animals, old barren cows, and calves) was likely intended to maintain optimal herd size for the hunting economy, and also to cull the older riding and pack reindeer, the majority of which would likely have perished anyway under the conditions in which reindeer were kept in winter. In other words, the autumn slaughter of domesticated reindeer by Evenkis should be considered as a kind of preventive measure to ensure suitable hunting operations, not as proof that part of the reindeer herd was kept for the purpose of supplying meat (Shnirel'man 1980: 185–6).

The following statement, recorded on the Lower Tunguska River at the autumn base camp of V. P. Kaplin, supports the idea that the autumn slaughter of a few reindeer could be, from the point of view of the Evenki hunting economy, more or less a way of achieving optimal herd size. The Evenki group to which the Kaplin family [Photo 1] belonged had individual holdings and maintained a communal reindeer herd of 40–50 head. They hunted and nomadized with their reindeer throughout the year within the boundaries of "clan" hunting territories. The statement below was recorded in autumn, during the mating season of the domesticated reindeer herd and before the start of the fur-hunting season. Therefore, it can be considered a reflection of practical Evenki knowledge regarding optimal size of a reindeer herd. M. P. Egorchenok (the *khoziaika* 'head woman' of the base camp), who was watching the reindeer with us, stated:

> "Reindeer are nothing but trouble. Autumn (i.e., during the hunting period) is the worst; need to go hunting, can't gather them together. Loading the females, the bulls come after them to mate (it is the rut period). By the time you've loaded the last one, all the packs are trampled. Reindeer don't get lost easily, survive well—better if I kept only 20 head, that'd be enough. Keep so many only because we worry" [Turov field notes; parenthetical comments by author].

We may also assume that the autumn slaughter of old bulls, barren cows, and weakest calves was a type of selection process that ensured the domesticated reindeer herd maintained good condition (endurance, weight, and overall physical health). One purpose of the culling was to preserve the strongest reproductive members of the herd, bulls and fertile cows, by selecting the strongest, hardiest, and most viable animals for reproduction. From this point of view, the slaughter of old bulls and yearlings doomed to die from lack of forage or from wolf predation during winter should not be considered as evidence that the meat of slaughtered reindeer was a continuous or important source of food for hunter families. It would be more correct to consider this as proof of a conscious action, honed by the practices of generations of hunter–reindeer herders, the purpose of which was to maintain a herd at the optimal size for hunting operations. Then, we could presume that the establishment of an enduring tradition in taiga reindeer husbandry of resolving an autumn meat supply problem by slaughtering part of the domesticated reindeer herd would have occurred only in times of crisis in the traditional ungulate hunt.

However, no evidence of such crises is found in the ethnographic literature of the 19th and early 20th centuries.

The similarities and differences between the Evenki and Orochen types of reindeer husbandry, identified only in a preliminary way by G. M. Vasilevich (1969: 84–7), require further examination. It appears to us that before the time we have focused on in our research, the differences between these two types of reindeer husbandry were [already] becoming blurred, especially under the influence of the developing and expanding fur hunt. Moreover, such aspects of the reindeer herding economy as herd size, treatment of reindeer, and development of traditional maintenance methods became generally standardized. Based on the Vasilevich scheme, until the 19th century the pure *Orochen type* was to be found only in the small Trans-Baikal groups of Evenkis (1964: 3, 1969: 6). On the other hand, the only changes in the *Evenki type* of reindeer husbandry occurred in their attitudes toward domesticated reindeer, including the prohibition against saddling reindeer, probably imposed due to the concern about preserving small herds. In addition, by the 17th century the possession of domesticated reindeer had become an established indicator of prosperity among hunting families, and a motivator for more frequent armed conflict between some Evenki groups. In his time, N. N. Stepanov noted repeatedly that Evenkis without reindeer, whom 16th–17th-century documents classified as *sidiachie* 'settled' or *lodoshnye* 'boating' Evenkis, were not respected by their nomadic kinsmen, who went even so far as to refuse to pay *iasak* 'tribute' on behalf of these **amanat** 'hostages' (1961: 195). In Evenki historical folklore one often finds descriptions of armed conflicts; in these heroic legends and specific clan tales, domesticated reindeer herds are always mentioned as the number-one trophy (Vasilevich 1966: 284–9, 290, 292, 296–7).

Notably, some tribal tales directly attribute the introduction of reindeer into previously non-*olennye* Evenkis to the arrival of the Russians in Siberia, and to the development of commodity relations[12] and fur hunting in Evenki communities (Vasilevich 1966: 290, 296–7). Even more characteristic in this regard are the folkloric texts of the mythological "bear" cycle, widespread among Evenkis and reflecting their common beliefs about the origin of reindeer (ALIE 22/1/37; Vasilevich 1936: 42–3). All these texts explain the origin of domesticated reindeer as resulting from the marriage of an orphan-girl to an **amaka** 'bear' (aka *dedushka* 'grandfather', *starik* 'old man'). The animal's intestines, or, in other accounts, its furs, are transformed into reindeer.

> "The reindeer were created, then became wild. The Supreme Master **amaka** showed Evenkis how to tame reindeer. He urinated on moss to entice the reindeer to eat it. Some of them… began to eat… and the humans captured them. The Supreme Master gave the humans lassos and bridles, and told them: 'Do not kill reindeer. If you do, I'll throw you into the Underworld, onto barren land.' From that time on, humans protected the reindeer" ([ALIE 22/1/37] folio 9).

---

12. See page 19, footnote 8.

This text clearly demonstrates that such ritual beliefs (which can be considered a testimony to the stability of norms and rules of the reindeer husbandry tradition) defined both a general concern for the reindeer herd and the relative antiquity of husbandry methods and usage of domesticated reindeer [e.g., Photo 36].

Obviously, such terms as *maloolennye* 'with a small number of reindeer' (Evenki-type husbandry) and *mnogoolennye* 'with a large number of reindeer' (Orochen-type reindeer husbandry) are somewhat relative, as is the number of reindeer required in a hunting economy. Thus, the notion of optimal herd size varies with changes in the overall orientation of the economy. For example, in the Evenki economy of the 15th–16th centuries, before the advent of commodity fur hunting, a herd of 5–10 reindeer per family was clearly more than enough to meet all possible transportation needs related to hunting and nomadizing. At the same time, a herd of 30 head or more, as mentioned above, could be a serious hindrance for [efficient operation of] a single household, especially during the period of the fur hunt, because a large herd required allocation of labour that could otherwise be used in the hunt. Thus, the data on reindeer husbandry among the Evenkis of Central Siberia reveal the following particular characteristic: The development of fur hunting and commercial relations led to an increase in the size of domesticated reindeer herds in families practicing the Evenki type of reindeer husbandry.

According to the earliest sources from the 17th–18th centuries, the most prosperous Evenki families of "fishers–fur hunters" were considered to be those having reindeer herds of 20–30 head, while most other Evenki families held herds of up to 10 head maximum (Georgi 1799: 39–40; Vitsen 1705). Sources from 19th–20th centuries mention that Evenki families with the least numbers of reindeer had herds of 10–15 head, while the herds of the majority of mobile hunters averaged 25–30 head. There were even a few *bogateï* 'wealthy ones', whose herds of domesticated reindeer sometimes reached 1,000 head and more (Clark 1863: 89; Levin and Potapov 1956: 710; Miller 1895: 280; Pestov 1833: 179; Petri 1930: 35, 96; Radde 1858: 145; Stepanov 1835: 73–4; Tretiakov 1869: 462; Tugolukov 1969: 50; Vasilevich 1964: 4).

3.2 Reindeer husbandry and development of the fur hunt

We suggest that among Evenkis the synchronous links between the development of fur hunting and its gradual transformation toward a commercial basis, on the one hand, and the growing importance of reindeer and increasing size of herds in the economy of mobile hunters, on the other, are not accidental. This association can be explained by the clear dependence of fur-hunting success on having adequate numbers of reindeer. Specifically, they help hunters and their families to access territories quite remote from winter base camp, which is where, prior to the onset of the fur-hunting season, the main supplies of food, gear, and ammunitions were concentrated. Accounts about this relationship can be relatively frequently found in 19th- and early 20th-century literature (Clark 1863: 89; Grigorovskii 1890: 12–14; etc.). Quoting 17th-century sources, N. N. Stepanov wrote the following:

> "In 1653, the Olenek Tunguses reported that they had also eaten their *olenishka* [reindeer] and did not have any to hunt with in order to pay their sovereign's *iasak*" … "… there was a large snowfall in early autumn, and many of their reindeer died during the hunt, and they could no longer hunt sable […] with the reindeer" (Stepanov 1961: 223, 240).

At the beginning of the 1930s, in conjunction with the objectives defined by the Committee of the North[13] regarding the development of the hunting economy and culture of indigenous inhabitants [*korennye zhiteli*] of Siberia and the Far East, specialized research expeditions were carried out among Evenkis, Tofalars, and other hunting peoples of Siberia. In particular, they studied the potential for intensification of the traditional branches of their economies, including fur hunting. During expeditions among the Podkamennaia Tunguska, Angara, and Lower Tunguska Evenki groups, I. M. Suslov and P. G. Poltoradnev established that the greatest fur-hunting output was found in families that kept an average of 20–25 head of transport reindeer (Poltoradnev 1932; Suslov 1930). Contemporary researchers studying the possibility to further intensify the economies of Siberian peoples (particularly hunting) have considered improvements to transport-reindeer husbandry as an indispensable condition for advancements to be made in hunting activity (Karelov 1979: 156; Kriuchkov 1979: 89). Hence, by the mid-19th century, with the development of commercial fur hunting and subsequent depletion of the fur-bearing animal population and resulting expansion of hunting territories, the majority of mobile Evenkis in Central Siberia were indeed forced into more intensive reindeer husbandry (while still maintaining the traditional *peshii* 'on-foot' hunting method) and into using domesticated reindeer more extensively for transportation purposes (Petri 1930: 35, 95; Stepanov 1961: 186; Vasilevich 1969: 42–50). Moreover, according to our field data, the Evenkis' use of domesticated reindeer was considerably more multifaceted, reaching well beyond the transport of gear and foodstuffs during the fur hunt. In fact, the new developments in transport-reindeer husbandry, and the conceivably much earlier reorientation toward a commercial emphasis, would have had an impact on all aspects of Evenki subsistence activities.

The distinguishing feature of the use of reindeer for transportation by groups of mobile hunters was, as a rule, using them to transport people only. This could be regarded as a consequence of the relatively small reindeer herds per hunting group and the particulars of the hunt itself. The whole cycle of transport-reindeer usage can be divided into two periods, summer and autumn/spring, with the winter period in between, during which reindeer were free and "vacationed" in remote forest valleys rich in reindeer moss and sheltered from the cold winter winds.

---

13. A ministry-level Soviet executive government body. —*Ed.*

In order to gain a better sense of the kinds of changes in land use methods that followed the introduction of reindeer-based transportation, we need to compare them with those described in materials on Evenkis without reindeer, who either switched to a completely settled way of life and gave up their reindeer, or who, like the 16th–17th century "sitting-boating" hunters, nomadized between two permanent *meneien* 'winter base camps' within a significantly smaller territory. In this regard, our analysis of data on the economy of various Evenki territorial groups reveals that during the fur-hunting period, Evenki households with no reindeer, or with merely a few (up to 5 head), used only the lands closest to the *meneien*. Being the permanent food supply and ammunition base, hunters were forced to leave their families in the *meneien*. Before the snowfall, the hunters packed a one-day food ration in their *poniaga* 'board-frame backpack' and scouted the adjoining areas rich in "local" squirrel. Usually hunters returned to the *meneien* in the evening of the same day, staying out only on those occasions when the dogs pursued a sable *potemnu* 'in the dark', or when they were lucky and happened to capture a moose (Suslov 1927: 45; Turov field notes 1974, 1976–78).

With the advent of heavy snowfalls, the majority of hunters left their families at the *meneien* for several weeks, organized themselves into hunting parties of several men, and traveled far from their camps, using hand-pulled sledges or *kel'che* 'toboggans' (Russ. *volokushu*). They would return to camp to replenish their food rations, or when hunting in that area was not yielding enough game. On rare occasions (e.g., when the family of a young hunter did not yet have children), the hunter's wife and parents also participated in the hunt. Dogs were sometimes harnessed to sledges to help hunters transport heavy loads, which can be regarded as a relict of the times when dogs were the only transport animal available (Polevoi 1965: 125; Turov field notes 1986; Vasilevich 1962: 105, 1964: 4, 1969: 45, 68, 88).

It is likely that Evenkis with small numbers of reindeer were less successful as fur hunters due to the limited areas accessible to on-foot hunters, as well as the necessity of switching from fur hunting to ungulate hunting in order to replenish the meat supply (Poltoradnev 1932: 10–11). It may be that this, from quite early on, led Evenkis with no reindeer to reorganize their fur hunting toward the use of passive hunting methods, employing devices such as the *plashka* 'billet' and sacks, nets, traps, and *cherkan*-type snares [Photo 23]. This is documented particularly in the data collected by A. A. Popov (ALIE 14/1/167). Considering the distribution area of passive hunting methods among Siberian peoples, including Evenkis, Popov points out that in the late 19th and first quarter of the 20th centuries, these fur- and animal-hunting methods were most widespread among those Evenkis who had become settled, whereas the active hunting methods were more characteristic of the nomadizing groups.

Thus, it is perhaps not accidental that groups of settled and semi-settled Evenkis with no reindeer established the custom quite early of allotting hunting territories to separate families for temporary use, regulated by social contract; this later evolved into a system of inherited rights to control a certain territory and its resources. Within such a territory, each hunter had his own parcel with one or two hunting cabins (*izbushka* or *stanok*). A similar reorganization of fur hunting and the rules of land use took place, for example, among the Chuna Evenkis, who had lost their herds of domesticated reindeer around the mid-1930s. It should be mentioned here that the establishment of family ownership of hunting territories, legalized by common law, is associated again with settled life and the availability of a *zavod* 'arsenal' of trapping equipment for fur hunting (Vasilevich 1972).

The situation changed drastically, however, with the appearance of transport reindeer and, in particular, with the increase of herd size in order to facilitate optimal nomadic land use. It is interesting that B. E. Petri, who specifically studied intensification and sustainable fur hunting among the Ocheul-Tutura Evenkis living a settled existence for most of the year, noted that "... for this semi-nomadic branch of [the Evenkis], the [observed average of] 7.1 riding reindeer per family" should be sufficient to conduct the fur hunt under typical conditions (1930: 32). In the event that a household had at least 15 reindeer, it was possible for the entire family to leave camp [and be mobile] for the duration of the whole autumn season. Not only could they roam for practically unlimited distances, transporting packs with the coverings for autumn and winter *chum*-tents, food supplies, and hunting gear, but they could also control a much larger territory than what would have been possible for hunters with only a few reindeer or none at all. Having a realistic opportunity during the fur hunt to work not just one tract close to the ***meneien*** but several areas of squirrel concentration, some as far away as 150–200 km, such hunting parties provided an example of the most rational and effective use of hunting territories. In other words, for a hunter with a herd of 15–20 head of reindeer, the success of the upcoming fur hunt no longer depended in the least on the expected availability of the main squirrel forage that year, or on how far from the ***meneien*** the squirrel population migrated in search of [adequate] forage before the beginning of the fur hunt. In addition, possessing adequate numbers of transport reindeer allowed the hunter a certain independence from the food supplies stored at the ***meneien***. Although hunters on a hunting trail in search of squirrel would not pass up an opportunity to take a moose wandering close to their route, ungulate hunting in itself did not draw them away from fur hunting, which remained their main task at that time. Reindeer-less hunters would have to interrupt the *belkovka* '[coll.] squirrel hunt' in order to replenish their meat supplies, which would take 1–2 days in the best case. Evenki hunters with reindeer, on the other hand, could use them to transport food supplies, allowing them to devote all their time to the fur hunt. In this regard, Evenkis recount the following:

> "We walk far in autumn, load up all the dried meat. We try to get *svezhenina* 'fresh meat' when we get a chance, but in autumn we don't purposely hunt moose [*sokhatit'*]; rather, we eat what we brought with us from the *labazy* 'caches' or what we dried back in autumn at the *labazy* or what we stored frozen in a ***iumgulo*** (ground-level *labaz*; Fig. 3-[4]), thinking to hunt here

in autumn. On the *chernotropa* 'black trail' (i.e., before snowfall), no time to hunt moose in autumn; got to hunt well [*udalo khodit'*] to get as many squirrel as possible. Take moose only if it's spotted very close to camp (meaning the next stop-over camp while travelling around the exploited territory—*Auth.*)" [Turov field notes; parenthetical comments by author].

Under these conditions, and if squirrel forage was abundant everywhere, nomadizing and hunting began with the arrival of the *vykhodnaia* 'decked-out' squirrel, i.e., starting mid-October, when the *zverok* 'little critter' switched from summer to winter fur, which fetched the maximum price on the fur market.

3.3 Reindeer husbandry and the squirrel hunt

During seasons when squirrel migrated to areas distant from the Evenki winter camps—which, as explained above, depended on forage availability—the use of transport reindeer allowed hunting parties, consisting of the hunters themselves and practically all of their family members, to travel to even the most remote places in quick trips undertaken before the snowfall. Starting there, they hunted in local areas of squirrel concentration, striving to return to their **meneien** before extreme sub-zero temperatures set in (Petri 1930: 6). Thus, squirrel hunting always occurred close to the place where the entire family camped.

> "Leaving for the hunt in early morning, the Tungus returned home to his *chum* the same day by evening" (Suslov 1927: 45). Moving to the new camp, "… the men do not travel with the caravan, but go into the [adjoining] forest and hunt… The *khoziain* (i.e., the head of the hunting party—*Auth.*) tells the *khoziaika* 'the head woman of the camp' where she should arrive with the caravan and where she should wait for him" (Petri 1930: 35).

Having determined the stop-over camp location, the hunter went out hunting after breakfast, his *poniaga* packed with a one-day food supply and all the necessary gear and ammunition, and accompanied by a hunting dog. The remaining family members set out along the route in the afternoon, after gathering the reindeer and loading them with packs.

The loaded reindeer were tied together into [several] teams, each consisting of a few animals, and together these teams made up a caravan. A specially designated "taboo" reindeer (usually white) was placed at the front of the caravan, separate from the rest, carrying bags with the clan's sacred objects such as **sheveki** icons (family protectors) and hunting amulets (Turov 1974, 1978: 167–76). Each team was led by an old cow, thus setting the pace for the entire caravan. Using a halter, each reindeer was tied to the packsaddle of the reindeer walking in front of it. Namely, a **gilbevun**—a V-shaped bracket carved from a reindeer antler—would be tied reindeer to the rear cross-bar (**tolboko**) with *rovduga* 'suede' thongs. The thongs tying up the **gilbevun** with **tolboko** were strung through holes drilled in the lower part of the **gilbevun** bracket.

The reindeer in a team were arranged in such a way that docile animals alternated with restless ones, and sometimes the restless reindeer were tied with a shorter halter. The overall caravan proceeded in a zigzag formation, which allowed the Evenkis, when they turned their heads around, to see all the animals in a team. Thus, the teams walked along a straight route, zigzagging every 100–200 m to one side and then the other. Since the women leading the caravan (or sometimes older males) had to take turns tamping a trail through the snow to make it easier for the reindeer, the usual distance covered per day was small.

Once the snow fell, the hunting parties hastened to arrive as soon as possible at the ***meneien*** permanent winter base camps. At this time, Evenkis watched the snow conditions very carefully, as it was practically impossible for travellers with reindeer to get out of deep snow if they were caught far away from the ***meneien*** (Petri 1930: 36). The danger was that if the hunters found themselves snowbound, they would be cut off from their food supplies and, more importantly, from warm winter clothing and warm dwellings (Mainov 1898: 192–4).

In spring, when the snow cover started to melt and crumble, hunting parties resumed travelling, their reindeer loaded with packs. During this period, reindeer were used mainly for transportation, facilitating the game hunt *po nastu* 'on the snow crust'. During poor squirrel harvest years, when the autumn hunt did not produce enough pelts to trade, at the end of March or beginning of April (***oktankire*** 'snow is melting'), Evenkis gathered whatever reindeer remained at the winter base camp and traveled to places where they expected to find squirrel concentrations. The use of reindeer for transport during this time was the same as in autumn. Since the calving season was not very far away (barely more than 1 month), the travelling speed of hunters and their families was as fast as the snow cover conditions allowed. A great deal of effort was spent tamping the trail; usually a man not participating in the hunt would clear the path, walking in front of the caravan on skis and leading a large, lightly loaded reindeer by the reins. The rest of the hunters flanked the caravan route, harvesting the occasional squirrel. The main hunt, as mentioned above, consisted of one-day trips from temporary camps, where the length of stay was determined by the availability of squirrel in that area.

In years with a poor squirrel harvest, hunting groups were forced to travel maximum distances from the winter ***meneien*** area. Therefore, it is understandable that reindeer played a significant role as the transportation means that allowed hunters to move all the necessary items for hunting and dwelling over long distances (sometimes up to 200 km), including bulky items such as *chum* covers, food supplies for a month, and ammunition. Naturally, hunters with no reindeer were at disadvantage, even when using hand-pulled sledges to transport loads. In particular, such hunters needed to return to the main base camp to replenish supplies and to rest, and were far less mobile than those who used reindeer for transport when hunting.

3.4 Reindeer husbandry and large game hunting (moose)

With the onset of warmer temperatures, along with snow melting or thinning and becoming loose, game animals, as already mentioned, started to migrate away from their winter feeding ranges, spreading out over a broader territory. At this point, nothing remained to limit the use of reindeer in hunting. Hunting parties focused on extensive storage of moose meat and hides, and, to a lesser extent, those of wild reindeer. The base camps split up into families that nomadized separately, and hunting again became an individual endeavour. This seems to be the reason why hunters always left meat at the kill site, and returned to the base camp with light loads, taking with them only as much meat as could be packed on their *poniaga*. Hunters without reindeer, regardless of how far from the stop-over camp their prey was captured, would have to move their whole family to the kill site, where they would stay as long as the meat lasted. Families with transport reindeer, on the other hand, moved to the kill site only if it was near the camp and along the main travel route. Otherwise, the hunter would not be distracted, delegating family members to move the kill, and continued game hunting or searching for squirrel in areas close to camp.

Given that there was little snow left by this time and that game was frequently captured in an open space, the problem of protecting the fresh meat from predators was particularly important; it was addressed in the following manner. Having killed the animal, the hunter followed a specific protocol in dividing the carcass into pieces of roughly equal weight. It seems there is reason to believe that the ritualized carcass butchering procedure, besides resulting from the belief about the subsequent rebirth of the killed animal, served yet another purpose, namely, to ensure transmission of the established method, honed by generations of hunters, of preparing the carcass for transportation from the kill site to the camp. Thus, it seems appropriate at this point to provide a more detailed description of how the animal was dressed out.

The first step was to prepare the site for butchering. According to Evenki descriptions, poles, shrub branches, or birch boughs cut nearby (conifers were not used because the resin would make the meat smell and mess up the hide) were used to build a low platform, large enough to eliminate any contact of the meat with ground or snow. The platform was set up beside the carcass, and the cutting itself was done on the ground. The animal was placed on its back and in order to fix it in this position, a large debarked log [*lesina*] was placed on top of it lengthwise. The hide, removed at this time from both sides, was laid on the platform, and the dressing out began. An incision was made with the sharp end of the knife from sternum ribs to groin, releasing the innards, which were then removed. It should be mentioned that all the internal organs—heart, kidneys, and liver, as well as gullet and windpipe—were removed by hand, with incisions made only lengthwise in the tissue and blood vessels connecting the organs. "Must not cut across, you will cut off your path to happiness," is how the Evenkis explained their actions.

After opening the abdominal cavity and removing the internal organs, the hunter waited for the blood to run down into the abdominal cavity; to this end, two or three lengthwise incisions were cut in the heart, emptying the chambers. Then he cleaned the stomach (which in all ungulates consists of two chambers), cut it into two halves, and collected the blood in these bowl-like vessels, their rims stitched with willow twigs. All the internal organs removed thus far and the blood-filled stomach halves, along with the meat removed from the sternum, were carried by the hunter himself in his *poniaga* back to the base camp.

All of the cutting was done only with a knife. Next, the entire carcass was dismembered into the following parts: head with the neck up to the third vertebra (*dyl*), front legs (*negil'*) with shoulder blades (*kolbikol*), hind legs (*amargil*), neck (*nikomna*) and three sternum ribs (*tukcho*), sternum (*tygdon*), eight ribs from each side (*optyle*), and, lastly, the backbone, broken into two halves, front (*darama*) and back (*duki*). Matched into pairs, each such portion of the carcass, weighing about 15–20 kg (the heaviest were packed individually), made a load for one reindeer.

The hunter stored the meat thus prepared for transportation in a high *labaz* 'platform cache' (*telgokon*) constructed at the kill site (Fig. 3.1; see Turov 1975 for a detailed description of its construction). Possibly leaving behind some of his belongings under the telgokon or making a long-lasting smudge (to keep predators away from the catch), the hunter set out for the base camp, bringing with him the heart, liver, or a cut of the sternum meat ("proof of the kill"). The rest of the stored meat was removed and transported without the hunter's participation, by other members of his family or his game-hunting group.

It normally took 8–12 loaded reindeer to transport the meat of one moose. All the tasks of removal and processing of the meat, curing and drying it on the fire, as well as transporting loads of the dried meat to nearby caches, were women's tasks (Levin and Potapov 1956: 707; Vasilevich 1936: 80–5, 215–24; 1969: 73). Spring stockpiling of dried meat coincided with calving in domesticated reindeer herds, and looking after the calving cows provided enough occupation for almost all members of the spring base camp. Therefore, each household supplied a few reindeer, escorted by female relatives, in order to transport the butchered animal for further processing, preparation for summer storage, and delivery to special caches.

3.5 Reindeer calving

According to our informants, it happened sometimes that ungulates were hunted by individual nomadizing families on their way to the permanent domesticated reindeer calving sites. Pregnant cows about ready to calve would also be used when necessary to transport the meat, particularly in families with small herds.

If a reindeer cow gave birth en route to spring base camp, [an Evenki] carried the calf for the first few hours, with the *olenukha* 'reindeer cow' led by the reins. Once the calf was able to follow the herd it was released, while the cow was still led by the reins until arrival at the camp; there, she was released only

*Figure 3. Types of Evenki caches: 1–temporary **telgokon** at the kill site; 2, 3–permanent **noku** for food and gear; 4–temporary **iumgulo** for storing meat at a camp or in fur hunting territory.*

once the calf was tethered first. However, such cases were quite rare since, as a rule, families arrived at the permanent annual calving sites in advance of the calving season, in spite of the fact that the moose hunt was most intensive at this time, and stayed there until the start of the mosquito season.

During summer nomadizing, which, as mentioned above, was less predicated on hunting than on other types of land use, we can distinguish two periods of reindeer use for transportation. The first period lasted from the beginning of June to the second half of August, when households travelled individually or in groups of 2–3 families, covering half of the summer nomadizing circuit. During this time, the use of domesticated reindeer was mainly restricted to transporting [family] belongings and food supplies, including dried meat prepared during the spring hunt. Occasionally the reindeer were used to transport freshly acquired venison. Typically, this happened only in cases when the animal was captured far from the stop-over camp or on a detour from the main travel route of the nomadizing group. Evenkis were well aware of the sites where moose concentrated in summer and usually set up their camps a few kilometres away from those locations. Therefore, after a hunter bagged a moose or wild reindeer, his family could move as quickly as possible to the kill site and set up a stop-over camp, staying there until all the meat was dried. Starting in the second half of July (the second period), Evenkis embarked on their return routes to winter base camps, where clothing and gear were stored for the autumn fur hunt in long-term *noku-delken* caches (Photo 3). The nature of reindeer usage changed at this time, facilitation of the ungulate hunt becoming the main task. Starting around the end of August, hunters travelled from camp to camp, gradually moving toward the places of autumn/winter base camps and hunting in areas close to the travel routes. As during the autumn fur-hunting season, a hunter decided the location of the stop-over camp before leaving in search of prey, carrying only a light load and delegating the task of leading the caravan to the head woman of the household [*khoziaika*].

When [the hunter] captured a moose, the family moved to the kill site to dry the meat, after which they continued their interrupted travel, usually packing only some of the meat with them; the remaining part of the kill would be transported to the ***noku-delken*** long-term food cache closest to the travel route (Photo 4). According to testimony provided by Evenkis, meat taken to the ***noku*** at this time was cached there to provision the autumn or spring fur hunt that would take place near the ***noku***, or when, for one reason or another, supplies of freshly frozen or dried meat were exhausted. Supplies of dried meat could be stored in the ***noku*** for several years (Petri 1930: 36; Turov 1975).

The most intensive moose hunt occurred during the last days of August and in September, on the approach toward the permanent autumn/winter base camp, and also directly from the ***meneien*** itself. Hastening before the fur hunt to provide themselves and their families with meat to last them through the whole autumn and winter, hunters worked the areas closest to the ***meneien***, where the majority of the local moose population was concentrated at that time of year. Part of the procured meat, either dry or frozen (once sub-zero temperatures arrived), was left at the kill site, while the rest was removed to the ***meneien***. Here, as in spring, the hunter's job was to catch the prey, butcher the carcass, and cache it in a temporary ***telgokon*** *labaz*. As usual, removing the meat to camp was delegated to the women. This division of responsibilities between men, who focused on hunting moose without being interrupted by other tasks, and women, who handled the transportation of the kill, meant that any family owning a herd of 10–15 reindeer could, within a relatively short period of time (2–3 weeks of intensive hunting), fully supply themselves with enough meat for both autumn and winter.

3.6 Other aspects of Evenki and Orochon reindeer husbandry subtypes

The employment of reindeer for transportation purposes by groups of mobile hunters in Central Siberia described above essentially matches the Evenki type of reindeer husbandry as defined by G. M. Vasilevich, which is characterized mainly by the absence of a continuous use of reindeer for riding (Vasilevich 1964, 1969). On the other hand, the adaptation of pack saddles for riding, the usage by women of a special cane (*tievun*) for support while riding reindeer, as well as the widespread use among mobile Evenkis of the term ***uchak*** 'riding reindeer' (***uguchak, ukchak***; TMS-2: 243) evidently indicate the beginning of a transition by these groups toward the continuous use of reindeer *pod verkh* 'for riding'.

The practice of adding reindeer milk to tea, or condensing it in a rennet bag to the consistency of thick cream and mixing it with berries, observed in the diet of all Evenki groups, evidently suggests that mobile Evenkis had been familiar for a relatively long time with milking a *vazhenka* 'cow deer' [Photo 6]. It seems that what is different about the Orochen type of reindeer husbandry in this case is not so much the quantity of reindeer milk consumed but rather the variety of milk products prepared from it, as noted by Vasilevich (1969: 77; [Photo27]). At the same time, it is quite obvious that reindeer husbandry in the hunting groups of Central Siberia at the turn of the 20th century continued to serve predominantly as a means of facilitating the Evenki hunting economy and the summer nomadizing that went along with it, as well as moving the goods involved in these activities. In other words, the use of reindeer for transportation by mobile hunters was second only to firearms as the most important economic means of facilitating the intensive exploitation of taiga animal meat and fur resources during the autumn hunting season, and a more efficient means compared to hunters without reindeer (Karlov 1982: 116–18).

Characterizing the Evenki type of transport-reindeer husbandry among the Evenkis of Central Siberia, G. M. Vasilevich noted that their year-round nomadizing was caused primarily by the demands of hunting and fishing, rather than by the requirements of reindeer husbandry per se as a branch of the economy (1969: 75–7). However, the data cited by Vasilevich, as well as those collected by us, also indicate that the observed relationship between the various procurement strategies employed in the economy and the transport-reindeer husbandry involved in these strategies, and their combined role in the formation of the mobile lifestyle, is in reality a lot more complex and needs dedicated examination.

This [further examination] is all the more necessary because several authors of investigations into the economy of Evenki groups in the Podkamennaia Tunguska, North Baikal, Upper Lena, and Lower Tunguska river regions—whose reindeer husbandry was also classified by Vasilevich as Evenki type—claim the exact opposite (Grigorovskii 1890; Kharuzina 1928; Petri 1930; Suslov 1927; Tugolukov 1969). Two conclusions about the link between mobile lifestyle and reindeer husbandry are the most interesting in this regard. Suslov, whose research focused on the hunting economy of Podkamennaia Tunguska Evenkis, wrote the following:

> "... as the hunting season proceeds, the Tunguses continuously roam with a *chum* and their entire family throughout the hunting area, selecting forest tracts where not only squirrel but also reindeer forage can be found... If there is no food for reindeer, the Tunguses are sometimes forced to abandon a tract even if it has an abundance of squirrel" (Suslov 1927: 45).

Characterizing the role of reindeer in Evenki lives, V. A. Tugolukov noted:

"Regardless of their uncomplaining nature, reindeer demand a lot from humans, namely, mobility... The nomadic lifestyle of Evenkis not only protected the precious *iagel'niki* 'reindeer moss pastures' but also promoted the rational exploitation of [productive] lands" (Tugolukov 1969: 52).

Of course, behind each of these opinions about the link between mobile lifestyle and reindeer husbandry in the economy of nomadic hunters stand specific objective observations and specific realities. It cannot be refuted that hunting and fishing, as the leading branches of the Evenki economy, ensured the maximum possible amount of vital foodstuffs, and indeed determined the essence of their nomadic lifestyle. In the same way, the association between the described viewpoints requires a comprehensive analysis of reindeer maintenance methods and usage of reindeer pastures, both characteristics of the Evenki type of transport-reindeer husbandry.

3.7 Winter: free-ranging

First, it must be noted that the snowy winter season is not a part of the annual nomadic cycle of hunting–reindeer herding groups. During this time, mobile Evenki groups stopped the hunt and lived settled lives, leaving their permanent winter base camps only for short periods to barter furs at trading posts (Vasilevich 1969: 45–50). Meanwhile, all the domesticated reindeer ranged freely within deep, narrow, and snowy taiga river valleys, rich in reindeer moss, that had been selected back in autumn. All families living in a winter **meneien** combined their reindeer for the entire snowy period into one large herd (Vasilevich 1962: 105); according to our data, such herds could sometimes number up to 300 head. It is known that in Evenki-type reindeer husbandry, free-ranging herds suffered quite significant annual losses, either falling prey to wolves or due to simple disappearance. In comparison, among the Orochen Evenkis, who periodically monitored their herds and moved them far away when wolves appeared, reindeer enjoyed more favourable conditions (Vasilevich 1969: 77).

At the same time, we suggest that given the level of economic development in taiga hunter–reindeer herders, winter free-ranging practices, as long as they complied with the well-defined requirements, were justified and actually, in our view, very rarely led to substantial losses in the herd. A large volume of biological research shows that reindeer husbandry among peoples of Northern Eurasia did not affect, for all practical purposes, the natural biological fundamentals of domesticated reindeer and moreover left unchanged not only the morphological and genetic features of wild reindeer but also their main ecological and behavioural characteristics (Baskin 1970: 3; Semenov-Tian-Shanskii 1977: 8–10, 37). It is a well-known fact that Evenkis had remarkably detailed empirical knowledge of reindeer ecology, obtained from their multi-generational practice of hunting the species. Their knowledge of the wild reindeer could likely have served as a foundation for developing methods of domesticated reindeer husbandry, including daily care and pasturing methods. In this regard, data on reindeer ecology obtained from the literature do indeed illustrate the depth of practical knowledge accumulated by taiga hunter–reindeer herders on this subject.

Reindeer herds owned by mobile hunters were obviously exposed to basic natural conditions during their time ranging freely in snowy valleys [...]. From the second half of December through March, the diet of both wild and domesticated reindeer consisted more or less completely of *iagel'* 'reindeer moss'. Proceeding from the daily requirements of reindeer and the average moss supply per land unit, we can calculate approximately the area of winter ranges into which Evenkis moved their [domesticated herds] for free pasturing once deep snow cover was established. According to the calculations of biologists, one reindeer consuming about 6 kg of reindeer moss per day during winter required about 8–16 ha of fenced pasture, or about 20 ha when foraging freely in the forest (Karelov 1979: 166–7; Kriuchkov 1979: 93). Observations on reindeer maintenance methods among tundra and forest peoples reveal that in the latter zone, reindeer populations are more sedentary. In deep snowy valleys, sheltered from wind and rich in reindeer moss and ramal (shrubby) forage, where the snow remains loose and does not hinder reindeer browsing during most of the winter, herds stay sedentary for several weeks at a time even without movement-limiting factors, until the forage is fully consumed (Baskin 1970: 52).

Woodland reindeer typically browse individually; therefore, even after being gathered in one location, reindeer disperse quite quickly. According to our data, this characteristic behaviour was partially suppressed when the herds were kept in snowy valleys because deep loose snow sharply decreases reindeer mobility and keeps them confined to a limited local area for the whole snowy period, although their regular browsing. Thus the reindeer were allowed to range freely, and with the approach of warm spring spells and before the first patches of thawed snow, the Evenkis rounded up the herd and drove it closer to the base camp. Delays in driving a herd to winter base camp led to losses of some reindeer, mainly pregnant cows and young bulls. It seems, however, that even if Evenkis could not gather together all the reindeer before the snow melted, it did not mean the ultimate loss of such individuals. First, Evenkis were well aware that woodland reindeer scattered throughout a broad territory of regional pastures and grazing grounds split up before the start of summer into small groups but nevertheless would not leave the boundaries of their relatively narrow area. In this case, even if the reindeer that disappeared from winter pastures could not be found, they inevitably appeared in one of the adjacent herds belonging to relatives or to neighbouring Evenki families (the same happened during "mushrooming season," when reindeer could also be lost). Hence, if Evenkis lost their reindeer in spring, it was possible to recover them at any time from their neighbours, because as a rule, each family marked their reindeer (Vasilevich 1969: 73). We frequently had the opportunity to observe the exchange of stray reindeer in spring and in autumn among Evenkis maintaining separate nomadic households. Anyone who found someone else's reindeer (families were perfectly familiar with the marks of neighbours' herds) considered it an obligation to return the animals to their owners as soon as possible. According to Evenkis, stealing or not returning a stray reindeer was extremely rare and, although it did not cause inter-clan skirmishes as in the 17th–18th centuries, the thieves would be condemned severely by their kinsmen.

Second, the hierarchical structure of both wild and domesticated reindeer populations dictated that mature pregnant cows became herd leaders. Therefore, in the event of losing a reindeer herd that dispersed in spring, Evenkis could usually expect that by the time of calving practically all would arrive at their traditional permanent calving grounds.

Third, even in the event that Evenkis could not, for whatever reason, find their reindeer, the owners were fully confident, and not without reason, that all the animals would show up at the smudges when the mosquitoes appeared (Petri 1930: 88). Seasonal migrations of reindeer, although not as extensive as in the tundra, evidently followed certain traditional routes; thus, Evenkis were also able to retrieve their lost reindeer while travelling along their known migration routes. This is confirmed by frequent accounts describing the relatively higher level of domestication of the woodland reindeer belonging to Evenkis as compared to the tundra reindeer, which were kept [by their herders] under constant supervision (Baskin 1970: 53; Popov 1948: 56; Prokof'eva 1976: 141).

It is widely known that the practice of free-ranging reindeer in winter involves a relatively high percentage of loss. Overall, the death of reindeer in domesticated herds during winter continues to be a problem even today (Karelov 1979: 157). The winter free-ranging of reindeer, as observed in groups of mobile Evenkis at the turn of the 20th century, apparently took into account that, as in herds of wild reindeer, the majority of losses in domesticated herds occurred during the period of snow crust and early thaw, which were accompanied by sharp temperature drops and formation of ice patches on the ground. These obstacles to accessing forage had the most critical effect on sick and weak animals, including yearlings from late litters, old animals, and breeding bulls exhausted after the mating season (Baskin 1970, 1976, 1978; Semenov-Tian-Shanskii 1977).

Another factor to be considered is the possibility of spring losses in herds of domesticated reindeer due to predators such as the wolf and wolverine. Biologists and informant accounts testify that nearly all such losses can be attributed to these two predator species; however, wolverine predation pressure should be considered negligible. It has been noted, for example, that wolverines are not even capable of killing a reindeer debilitated by sickness, not to mention chasing down a healthy animal (Semenov-Tian-Shanskii 1977: 78–80). Moreover, it has been found that in summer a healthy reindeer can run for extended time intervals at a speed of 80 km per hour, while a wolf can pursue at such a speed for no longer than 3–5 minutes, after which it slows down abruptly and gives up the chase (Kriuchkov 1979: 18). During all seasons, including winter, the hunting tactics of wolves are based on testing the reindeer's endurance, which ultimately leads to the elimination of weak and sick individuals from the herd. On the other hand, wolves could not successfully pursue reindeer spending the winter in valleys with loose snow cover, where reindeer had enough time to spot approaching predators from a sufficient distance and (as long as they were healthy) run away from the danger without difficulty.

The most significant losses in domesticated reindeer herds took place during years with early and prolonged thawing at the end of winter. The appearance of snow-ice after these thaws, especially if hard and extensive in the open valleys, doomed many reindeer to starvation or becoming an easy prey for wolves. Naturally, the strongest reindeer were in a relatively better position to survive. During such years wolves, keeping close to the herd, played the role of "forest health inspectors," eliminating weak and sick reindeer that were likely to die anyway. It is also known that sick animals, or those barely surviving the winter, would later become disease carriers in the crowded domesticated herds in summer, and would produce weak offspring, thus reducing the overall physical status [biological health] of the herd (Kriuchkov 1979: 19; Mowat 1981: 66–7). We can definitely say, then, that wolves carried out a sort of selection process, thus actively facilitating the improved health of domesticated reindeer herds. For that very reason, the majority of northern peoples who hunted wild reindeer or engaged in reindeer husbandry (including Evenkis, of course) widely professed respect for this predator [the wolf], which was directly linked with the stability of their herds and the health of both wild and domesticated reindeer (Chernolusskii 1972: 102; Mowat 1981: 66). It may be conjectured that this is why Evenkis perceive the wolf as a hunter equal to man, with "his own trail" that one should not cross. In this regard, it is significant that the generally passive attitude toward wolves attacking domesticated reindeer is simultaneously contrasted with the active hunting attitude toward another natural enemy of reindeer, the bear.

The Evenki believe that a wolf "… won't scare a reindeer for nothing; he checks, and targets the weakest ones." The bear, though, "… is a very menacing animal, scares off reindeer a lot; the reindeer run very far away, no way to gather them together" [Turov field notes]. To some degree, this characterizes the reaction of the reindeer themselves to particular predators. All this gives us reason to believe that contemporary conjectures about winter losses in free-ranging reindeer herds being caused by wolves are unnecessarily dramatized. The herd instinct of reindeer and their defensive reactions have provided them with reliable means of protection against predators and facilitated the preservation of a high population density (Semenov-Tian-Shanskii 1977: 7). Moreover, deep snow cover in the winter limited predator mobility to a greater degree than that of the reindeer, which also contributed to minimized losses. Taking refuge for winter grazing in deep snow-covered valleys was probably a conscious action on the part of Evenkis that provided reindeer with adequate protection from wolves (Petri 1930: 87). Thus, summing up the conditions and consequences of the practice of winter free-ranging of reindeer as described above, characteristic of groups of mobile hunters employing the Evenki type of transport-reindeer husbandry, we can formulate the following generalizations:

1. The conditions of reindeer husbandry aligned with the conditions of the sedentary winter lifestyle of the hunters;

2. The conditions of reindeer husbandry provided herds with proper forage and shelter (from the perspective of reindeer's inherent nature);

3. Given the capacity of reindeer for quick demographic recovery thanks to their high fertility rate, even the unavoidable losses from disease, malnourishment, or predators did not frequently cause catastrophic declines in reindeer population size (Baskin 1978: 184).

It seems thus, that these factors combined assured the stability of the size of domesticated reindeer herds. Moreover, under favourable circumstances—including a decreased wolf population resulting from extensive culling (such as the one which occurred at the end of the 19th century), good forage, absence of disease, and good health of the reproductive segment of the herd—a moderate growth of the reindeer population could have occurred. Finally, the biological characteristics and species-specific forms of reindeer behaviour also served as reliable protection of the healthy segment of the herd against predators (Semenov Tian-Shanskii 1977: 7).

3.8 Spring: calving and the start of the annual round

The settled period of life at the *meneien* winter base camps, during which the reindeer herds owned by groups of mobile hunters stayed within the small winter foraging sites [*kormozashchitnye stantsii*], came to an end with the appearance of the snow crust and start of the spring ungulate hunt. At the beginning of April (*turan* 'arrival of crows'), the 8-month-long nomadizing circuit [*tsikl*] commenced. As documented, this season in the economy of Evenkis in Central Siberia was associated with the fundamental task of maintaining and looking after the herds of transport reindeer (Vasilevich 1969: 76). We are interested in this period because of the question about the extent to which the requirements of reindeer husbandry were compatible with the migration routes of individual Evenki groups, as well as the nature of these migrations.

Before the calving season, as mentioned above, nomadizing during the hunt on snow crust maximized the extent of the spring fur hunt and the massive spring stockpiling of ungulate meat. It seems, however, that for mobile hunting groups in the forest zone of Central Siberia the coincidence of spring travel and hunting does not itself necessarily imply that this travel period was defined exclusively by the demands and conditions of squirrel and ungulate hunting. At the same time, it is obvious that the requirements of spring husbandry and methods of looking after transport reindeer were directly linked to the distance and rhythm of travel. Rather, they were determined by the natural availability of fur-bearing animals and the volume of transport loads generated by the fur hunt.

This was also partly determined by the requirements of spring stocking of moose meat and hides. We note that the most difficult period for reindeer is the beginning of spring, marked by the formation of the *nast* 'hard snow crust', and sometimes ice, after the March thaws. By this time, the supply of mineral salts and fat stored in reindeer organism since autumn is exhausted and, consequently, the animals suffer a sharp weight reduction. It is no coincidence that the highest percentage of losses in both domesticated and wild reindeer herds takes place before thawed patches appear, the sap starts to flow in trees, andespecially nutritious new shoots spring up (Semenov-Tian-Shanskii 1977: 69). We should also point out that in May and the first ten days of June, the main reindeer forage in the northern regions of Central Siberia consists of reindeer moss and wood lichen. Obviously, therefore, hunters concerned to maintain the size of their herds were forced to choose between the following two options: either allow the reindeer to free-range (which in fact did happen during years with [good] harvests of local squirrel, when hunters could stay within the bounds of their winter base camps and reindeer moved on their own into the southern slopes of valleys, where pineries were less snowy); or select routes, while travelling in search of squirrel and moose, that traversed places known to abound at this time of the year in reindeer moss and fresh shoots.

In general, reindeer husbandry conditions and the nature of transport-reindeer usage, assessed over a period of several years based on materials furnished by informants, revealed certain changes related to new developments in the exploitation of fur and meat game. During the first two years that featured high-density squirrel population in areas close to the winter base camp, hunters' mobility, as mentioned above, stayed at a minimum. Accordingly, the reindeer herds were left to their own devices. Pregnant reindeer cows, almost immediately after the rut, and especially before calving, established themselves as herd leaders controlling, the rhythm of daily activities and selecting the direction of travel to look for areas rich in reindeer moss. At the same time, the herd maintained an overall travel direction toward the permanent calving locations known to Evenkis. In the following years, when the population size of "local" squirrel decreased and extensive migration took place of the remaining population to new foraging areas, the resulting increased mobility of hunting groups was accompanied by the active use of reindeer for transport during the fur hunt. Moreover, just as during the autumn squirrel hunt, the travel routes of the hunting groups, according to Evenkis themselves, were selected in consideration of both squirrel concentrations and availability of forage for the reindeer. Thus, according to our observations and various published works (Petri 1930 and others), spring travel routes followed the southern slopes of valleys, these being the first to thaw, pineries with a southern aspect and loose snow cover, and other elevated areas of the inhabited territory that were rich in forage and easy for reindeer to move through. Once the ungulate hunt started, neither the purpose of nomadizing nor the direction of travel changed. In some years, when the Evenkis did not manage to stock the necessary amounts of meat and furs before calving, hunting and the associated movement of hunting groups continued even after the beginning of the calving season. Here, according to informant survey data, the heaviest loads were transported by single bulls and barren cows, as well as by cows that had mated at the end of the rut and thus were expected to calve late. Using pregnant cows to carry packs often caused miscarriages. However, such a practice was not the rule, and was probably employed only as an exception in Evenki households holding very few reindeer, where each working animal counted and the family was running out of time to hunt ungulates.

The pregnant cows used during hunting were monitored in order to take notice of the start of calving in time and not to allow the *vazhenki* 'cow deer' to roam far from the stop-over camp (during calving the cows, especially those calving for the first time, tried to isolate themselves [from the rest of the herd]). When born on the road, a calf was carried in [a person's] arms for the first few hours until it gained strength. If a cow did manage to escape during calving, Evenkis did not consider her to be lost; they knew she and her calf would doubtlessly return to the previous camp. According to informants, in some cases Evenkis did not go looking for a lost cow at all if they knew they would be traversing that region again in the near future (within the next 1–2 weeks). They expected to find such reindeer cows nearby one of the camps visited during that season.

Most often, however, according to Evenkis, nomadizing groups stopped the hunt when the first calves were born and moved to one of the spring base camps. Calving locations, not surprisingly, were found in permanent tracts of well sunlit pine forest, where large snow-free glades formed at the start of the calving season. The selection of sites for spring base camps apparently took into account the natural preference of reindeer cows for snow-free ground ("Reindeer won't calve on snow," Evenkis said), as well as the bonds they develop with the area where they calved for the first time. Such behaviour is characteristic of older cows, whereas those calving for the first time must be watched, led by the reins when moving between camps, and tethered at camps so they do not get lost (Petri 1930: 86; Semenov-Tian-Shanskii 1977: 55–6; Vasilevich 1969: 72).

Upon arrival at the calving site, families that had nomadized independently joined up together to form one base camp (***nengnerkit***), where they lived until the mosquitoes appeared, i.e., until mid-June, according to the traditional calendar, which is when most of the pregnant cows had already calved. Interestingly, the traditional Evenki calendar has a special name for the calving month (***shonkan-sonkan***), as well as for the month of the first green shoots and grasses, which become the main reindeer food at the beginning of summer (Baskin 1976: 87; Vasilevich 1969).

Tending reindeer during the period of settled life at spring base camp consisted of the following main measures. First, the old **kure** fences (corrals) had to be repaired, or new ones built, in order to pen for some time the reindeer cows with their newborn calves. Otherwise, reindeer cows that calved farther off could not be watched and their calves usually fell prey to [terrestrial] predators or crows. According to biologists, the latter could cause extensive losses of newborns during the calving season (Baskin 1970: 77). On the other hand, the fact that Evenkis kept cows about to calve under observation in specially fenced enclosures for approximately half a day during calving may well have also been a means of accustoming calves to humans, albeit not a fully conscious practice. Evenkis have noted, according to our data, that calves born farther off proved later to be wilder and harder to train. Indeed, biologists have noted that the surroundings in which reindeer calves find themselves in the first minutes of their lives have a great impact on the shaping of their characteristic behaviour. Thus, calves taken away from the mother, or abandoned by her, and exposed to humans in the first hours after birth undergo imprinting and follow humans for the rest of their lives. Later on, keeping calves tied up and penned helps develop their reaction toward humans as a friendly element within the inhabited environment, or "one of their own" (Baskin 1970: 15–16, 133). Taking this into consideration, we may suppose that the Evenkis' practices of keeping calving cows penned and tethering the calves were deliberate measures, apart from the effort to protect the newborns, to ensure that the calves were tamed from the first hours of their lives.

With the snow melting, the appearance of new shoots, and the swelling of tree buds (May to mid-June), the mobility of reindeer herds increased. During the daylight hours as well as after dark, reindeer spent most of the day searching for green forage, sometimes relatively far away from base camp.

Herds belonging to individual families split up into 2–3 separate groups, led by older reindeer cows that had calved five or more times. The permanent, well-bonded core of the group consisted of the old cow and her offspring, including sometimes 2–3-year-olds, joined by other reindeer, including cows with their first calves. In fact, this core determined the intra-group behaviour, their level of activity, the direction of movement to look for sheltered foraging sites, and the extent and frequency of those micro-migrations of the group that were not regulated by humans. Hence, controlling the groups, and in general the whole herd, entailed in controlling their core leaders. For example, in order to keep the herd near base camp, Evenkis tethered the reindeer cows during the night, but during the day they were set loose to browse while their newborn calves were tethered instead. Because cows maintained a strong bond with their calves until the beginning of the mating period next autumn, they remained nearby the base camp at all times. This way, the whole herd preserved its integrity and all reindeer remained under the continuous watch of their owners.

Among the other activities involved in caring for reindeer, we should also mention the practices of regular feeding with salt, and of tying up of all dogs, the latter due to the fact that even a non-hunting *laika* 'husky' could not, according to Evenkis, resist the temptation of such easy prey as a calf. The salt for supplementing the reindeer diet was kept in leather pouches. Beads carved from bone, or the *kopyttsa* 'dew claws' [vestigial hooves], removed from the back of the hind legs above the main hooves of moose or reindeer, were tied to these leather bags. When Evenkis wished to feed their reindeer, and at the same time to draw them to the camp, they shook the salt pouches, and at the sound of the rattling beads, reindeer would come out from all directions to get the treat. [See also Photo 36.]

3.9 Summer: nomadizing, smudges, and pasturing

When the mosquitoes appeared, which Evenkis marked as the beginning of summer, families left the spring base camp territories and began their summer nomadizing within their entire exploitation territory [Photo 14]. As already described in the above section, families travelling from river to river along dry watersheds and through pine and larch forests would arrive at small taiga rivers in order to harvest a wide variety of game, fish, and plant resources throughout the summer season.

At first glance, the impression emerges that the entire nature of summer nomadizing, its direction and extent, and the type of routes chosen, were in response to the requirements of comprehensive exploitation taiga resources. It seems to us, however, that these variables were to no lesser a degree determined by the requirements of reindeer husbandry. From the above accounts, it becomes evident that for the traditional branches of the Evenki economy—meat hunting and fishing, which during the period under study could satisfy virtually all the needs of Evenki families with regard to basic foodstuffs and materials for domestic production—there was no direct need for such expansive or lengthy nomadizing as was actually observed. Before the advent of commercial hunting, the staple taiga resources utilized by Evenkis within their relatively limited territories were sufficient enough to support their small, seasonally settled groups for virtually as long as necessary.

From this point of view, the size and density of mobile or seasonally settled hunter-fisher groups, regulated as they were by the inhabited environment (Gromov 1981: 332; Kabo 1979: 92–3), did not differ from each other on average. The ease with which mobile Evenkis were able to switch to a settled way of life after losing their reindeer also comes as no surprise, particularly because the two main types of traditional subsistence activity—hunting and fishing—still retained, as before, their fundamental place in the subsistence culture of the ethnos (Grigorovskii 1980; Vasilevich 1969). Essentially, changes were observed only in the transition, among Evenkis without reindeer, to a more settled way of life, including the reduction in size of annual exploitation territory and a decrease in fur hunting activity. Moreover, a notable development among Evenkis in the Podkamennaia Tunguska area, who preserved the seasonally settled lifestyle and practiced, as the other groups did, ungulate hunting and fishing, finally had to hire herdsmen from among their relatives to look after their reindeer. In summer, these herdsmen roamed the taiga along with the reindeer, just as the nomadic hunter–reindeer herders did (Anisimov 1936; Vasilevich 1969: 77). According to our data, the Chuna group of Evenkis switched to this mode of life after losing their reindeer. This leads to the conclusion that summer nomadizing was probably determined to a large degree by the requirements of summer reindeer husbandry and availability of pastures. In this regard, it would be particularly interesting to study the behaviour and summer diet of wild reindeer, comparing them with the corresponding methods of summer husbandry and pasturing of domesticated reindeer.

Throughout the entire summer nomadizing period, the main reindeer forage consists of various grasses that grow in abundance along the banks of water bodies, as well as shrubs, the most important of which are almost all species of willow-leaf plants (Baskin 1970: 87; Semenov-Tian-Shanskii 1977: 46–8). These factors are directly linked to the distribution of summer reindeer pastures; of fundamental importance among them, due to their high protective qualities, were the taiga river valleys with adjacent parcels of thin, wind-swept pineries (Baskin 1970: 95). Concentrated in such locations are supplies of forage (twigs, leaves, and young shoots of willow-leaf plants) that contain the highest percentages of the vegetable proteins, vitamins, and mineral ingredients required by reindeer. This is why willow-leaf plants are the dominant ingredient of the reindeer summer diet. Biologists believe that browsing on tiny leaves supports such important functions of the reindeer organism as shedding, antler growth, onset of rut periods (delayed or accelerated), percentage of barrenness, and the health of offspring and of adult reindeer (deficiency or low quality of green forage promotes mange). According to biologists, these benefits of green forage are the main factors contributing to the winter survival of reindeer, reindeer moss serving only as [winter] "maintenance forage" (Baskin 1970: 92, 95, 99, 105, 107; Semenov-Tian-Shanskii 1977: 69).

There can be little doubt that Evenkis at the end of the 19th century possessed the entire body of knowledge related to the technology of reindeer pasturing. Moreover, in all probability they were quite aware of the most obvious effects of reindeer summer browsing on factors such as weight gain, survival under harsh winter conditions, and cow fertility. Therefore, we may assume that Evenkis were concerned about the condition of summer pastures at least as much as they were concerned about winter pastures. As a result of their practical considerations regarding summer pastures, Evenkis established a principle of pasture rotation and rules for effective pasture usage. Also, in accordance with their practical knowledge, Evenkis evidently tried not to overuse the pastures. This would occur when reindeer, kept for a long time in one place, consumed too much of the foliage of shrubs and trees; according to experts, this unfavourably affected plant regenerative capacities (Baskin 1970: 108).

The traditional summer methods of using taiga resources were concentrated within the zone of riverbanks and adjacent peat bogs; thus, the summer nomadizing routes were chosen purposely to assure the effective use of hunting and fishing grounds, in addition to providing high-quality reindeer diets that consisted of various twigs and grasses. In choosing routes for summer travel and stop-over camp locations, Evenkis obviously also took into consideration the requirements of proper reindeer care. Our own field observations, together with ethnographic data provided by a number of previous studies (Petri 1930; Poltoradnev 1932; Rychkov 1917; Vasilevich 1969; and others), reveal the following main principles of summer reindeer husbandry and pasturing by nomadic hunting groups. In general, these are in accord with the optimal requirements described above.

From the second half of June, with the appearance of a large number of biting insects, there was no further necessity to keep reindeer tethered. From that time until the end of August to mid-September (before the daytime activity of biting insects diminished and appearance of first mushrooms),

> "... the reindeer are quiet," Evenkis say. "Early morning, at daybreak, sun rises over forest, we start the smudges. Reindeer smell smoke, run as one toward the *chumy*, right into middle of smudge. All day they stay near the smoke. In the evening, sun setting down, reindeer go out to forage, again roam the forest on their own till morning. Our only task in summer—keep the smudges going. No smoke, reindeer will run far to avoid mosquitoes. Main thing is to fire up the smudges early, reindeer will come to the smoke on their own" [Turov field notes].

For the reindeer smudge [Russ. *dymokur*], Evenkis tried to select dry pine logs about 40–60 cm thick, debarked and with not too much sap. Resinous trunks usually fire up into flames, and with the reindeer trying to get away from the *gnus* 'biting insects' and forcing their way into the very middle of the smudge, they could injure their hooves. Thus, smudges were usually enclosed by debarked pine stakes 6–8 cm thick and up to 2 m high, driven into the ground in a circle of 1.5–2 m diameter. With the top ends of the stakes interlocking [in the centre], the whole structure of the smudge enclosure was reminiscent of a chum frame of lodgepoles [Photo 30]. Inside this enclosure, the logs were arranged in a star-like formation, and their ends covered with damp moss or grass ("so the smoke is thicker"). Most of the summer camps were located in pineries, partly due to the need to have firewood at hand for the smudges. When the supply of naturally dried-out trees was insufficient, Evenkis debarked the bottoms of pine trunks at an opportune time at the beginning of summer; then the trees took 1–2 years to dry out.

As noted above, in choosing camp locations, besides access to convenient fishing spots, an important factor was the availability of fresh foliage on willow-leaf trees and riverbank sedges. In the opening and closing periods of summer nomadizing, locating camps in thin, dry, and windblown pineries was also desirable because mosquitoes were less abundant there. According to Evenkis, the need arose to change camps only after the reindeer had gradually consumed all the forage available in pastures at that location.

> "Should not live too long in one place, if the reindeer trample the pastures a lot, then next year you got to move far away; that's why the *chumovishche* 'camp' gets hauled from place to place all summer long" [Turov field notes].

Also of some significance in this regard was the fact that in congested herds of domesticated reindeer, around twice the size of wild woodland reindeer herds, the animals suffered more from biting insects.

"Stay at one place too long," Evenkis explain, "lots of mosquitoes appear. Reindeer run all over the forest, bring mosquitoes back to the *chumovishche*. Too many mosquitoes, time to move. Fresh place (i.e., at a new camp—*Auth.*), less *gnus*" [Turov field notes].

Among the other reasons for changing camps were sanitary-hygienic considerations:

"All day, reindeer stamps down [*iskopytit*] the ground around smudges; it gets completely bare. Rain wets the ground, stays muddy a long time. Reindeer don't like mud, get sick from it; sometimes they get hoof-worm from the mud. When the reindeer trample the *chumovishche* (i.e., camp site as a whole—*Auth.*) to the ground, have to move again" [Turov field notes].

The travel areas and the tempo of migration both changed with the arrival of the hottest time of the year—the second half of July and first half of August—and the appearance of gadflies, which deposit their larvae in the reindeer organism. During this time, camps were mostly located in the valleys of large taiga rivers with shaded and windy stretches of shoreline, where the reindeer could find sufficient amounts of forage as well as shelter from the gadflies. Gadflies are heliotropic insects, and thus, during the hottest noontime hours the only escape for reindeer (smudges did not help) was in the shade of leafy parts of riverside groves. To escape gadflies, reindeer often took to the water in broad, relatively shallow pools where the current was slow. Within the shoreline zone, biting insects typically pestered both reindeer and humans in the morning (until 10 or 11) and evening (after 5 or 6 o'clock), at which times Evenkis actively stoked the smudges. Besides the fact that reindeer could deplete any pasture quite rapidly, camps had to move frequently also because this period coincided with the pupation of gadfly larvae coming out of reindeer flesh. A lengthy stay in one place would thus lead to infestation of the entire area with gadfly larvae, and camping at that location the following year would be impossible. Our field data make note of several such recent sites related to the period of transition by a group of Erbogachen Evenkis to the autumn/spring fence method of reindeer husbandry. According to our Russian guide, Evenkis had used these camps in springtime several years ago, but then abandoned them. Even after several years, the insect concentration at those locations was still much higher than in adjacent parts of the taiga. In addition to these considerations, it was obvious to Evenkis that changing camp frequently provided the reindeer diet with more young shoots of shrubbery and shoreline grasses, as well as better sanitary-hygienic conditions of reindeer husbandry.

3.10 Autumn: the rut and preparation for the fur hunt

Starting in the second half of August and especially by the beginning of September, "… the *pauty* (*ovody* 'gadflies'—*Auth.*) flew away, mosquitoes and other insects eased up, and reindeer did not need the smudges anymore" (Petri

1930: 85). As the reindeer rut approached, bulls scraped their antlers and the mating rituals began. The siring bulls (***khor***) took charge of small "harems" of reindeer cows. Since the ***khory*** would try to take their harems farther away from the castrated bulls, which stayed closer to humans, it became increasingly hard to keep the reindeer near camp at this time. Keeping reindeer in a single herd during years with a good crop of mushrooms was especially difficult. At such times, typically at the beginning of summer, Evenkis would tie up the cows during the day or keep them in small pens. They allowed the cows out to browse only at night, and tethered the calves instead. In the morning, without fail the cows would return to their calves, and since the bulls stayed close to the females, the whole herd was thus kept near the base camp.

The following nomadic cycle, prompted primarily by the fur hunt, started around October 15–20, usually after the first, non-permanent, snowfall and the appearance of the "decked-out" squirrel (after the change from summer to winter coat). Nomadizing started from autumn base camps [Photo 25], normally located around the area of permanent reindeer mating grounds. It should be mentioned that biologists associate the permanent mating locations of wild and domesticated reindeer with the permanent mating grounds of wood grouse (Semenov-Tian-Shanskii 1977: 64). This was another reason why, before the start of the fur hunt, travelling groups strove to move early toward the winter ***meneien*** base camp, where domesticated reindeer traditionally mated every year. The peak reindeer rut starts around the first autumn frosts, and usually ends by mid-October, before the onset of permanent snow cover and continuous sub-zero temperatures (Baskin 1970: 121, 124). In Central Siberia, based on many years of environmental and climatic data, these events occur in late October and early November. In the regions examined in this study and inhabited by nomadic Evenkis, continuous sub-zero temperatures and stable snow cover occur between October 10 and 20 at the earliest (GUGK 1962: 57–8). In any case, by the start of the fur hunt the reindeer rut basically comes to an end. Squirrel change their summer coats for winter fur usually around the same time as the first snowfalls. Thus, by and large, the appearance of the "decked-out" squirrel and the start of the fur hunt usually coincided with the rut period of most of the reindeer herd. Only a few reindeer that had not gained enough weight in time would be late with the rut; therefore, by the start of the Evenki autumn/winter subsistence circuit, the reindeer, having finished the rut, formed again one compact herd that was relatively easy to manage.

Despite the fact that the main purpose for the migration of hunting groups at this time was to facilitate the fur hunt, there is no reason to believe that concern about reindeer pastures ranked lowest [on the Evenki priority list] to such an extent that hunters practically did not concern themselves with the matter at all. Starting approximately from September (after 20 September in northern regions), reindeer moss and winter greens (shoots and foliage covered by snow) became the main forage for reindeer; this was characteristic for both wild and domesticated reindeer, as the ecology and behaviour of the latter, for all practical purposes, was no different from that of the wild woodland reindeer (Baskin 1970: 87). For most of the Central Siberian territories, reindeer moss patches are typically sparse albeit extensive in thin pine groves, where the snow cover at this time (no deeper than 50–60 cm during practically the whole autumn/winter period) is the lowest in comparison with other areas of the taiga. This is unquestionably the reason why nomadic routes during the autumn squirrel hunt were almost the same as in summer, traversing pure pineries, rich in reindeer moss patches. It is worth noting that the direction of these migrations did not conflict with the conditions of the fur hunt, because squirrel still lived in the pineries until the advent of severe cold and major snowfalls, which covered the ground forage (mushrooms, fallen pinecones, berries, etc.) and limited access to it. Thus, I. M. Suslov was most likely correct in asserting that Evenkis, in their concern to provide their reindeer with adequate conditions, would even leave areas rich in squirrel if there was not enough forage for the reindeer (1927: 44).

Reindeer husbandry during the autumn fur-hunting season was less laborious, for there was no longer a need to build smudges. In daytime, reindeer were used to transport loads or allowed to browse freely nearby the hunting camp. But by the end of summer, the bonds between cows and yearlings weaken considerably, so during extended stays at one camp it was necessary to somehow keep the herd together. In such cases, a reindeer *bashmak* 'shoe' (***khelmegukon***) was used to limit reindeer movement. Alternatively, a collar was put on the reindeer's neck, with a short stick tied to a strap attached to the collar that could be lowered until it reached the reindeer's knees, thus limiting its mobility. We must say, however, that these measures simply served to further restrict its already typically low mobility. Namely, unlike tundra reindeer, woodland reindeer could be left in a herd to browse freely for a day or more. Moreover, watching the herd at night was practically unnecessary, because reindeer foraged in one place, using small patches at a time, provided there was enough pasture available near the camp (Baskin 1970: 53). Thus, reindeer required additional care only at the stop-over camps on the way to a new hunting area. In such cases, having decided on the location of the stop-over camp, hunters packed lightly and left camp, delegating to the women of the household [*khoziaiki*] the tasks of gathering the reindeer together around the *chumy*, moving to the new location, and setting up temporary dwellings (Petri 1930: 35–6). [...]

It is well documented that regardless of the intensive use of transport reindeer by Central Siberian Evenkis in their hunting operations, the essence of the hunts for meat and fur consisted in on-foot methods of tracking and capturing prey. Insufficient numbers of transport reindeer per individual household must have been a factor in preserving on-foot hunting methods and associated means of transporting loads. At the same time, in the contemporary "nomadic" economy of Evenkis in the area of the Lower Tunguska River, where reindeer are actively used for riding and in sledge teams, we have observed a limited use of reindeer in hunting, due to a variety of environmental and climatic factors. One of these is the depth of snow cover, which, as already mentioned, limits the use of transport reindeer to less snowy periods at the beginning of winter and in late spring. Clearly, only by shifting their packs from reindeer to sledges were contemporary mobile Evenki groups in the Erbogachen area able to use reindeer in the fur hunt for almost the entire winter (except for the ***otkiinkire*** 'deep freeze', i.e., second half of December through first half of January).

As with fur hunting, the amount of snow cover during the ungulate hunt *po nastu* 'on the snow crust' did not allow for the use of reindeer, either to help with the hunt itself or to transport the harvest. For the latter, Evenkis used traditional on-foot transportation methods such as the ***kel'che*** 'toboggan' (Fig. 4), the ***irivun*** hand-pulled hunting sledge (Fig. 5), and sometimes even the hide of the animal itself, wrapped around the dressed out and frozen meat (the term *iru* 'to drag, to carry, to cart', used in some Evenki dialects, refers to a sledge made of a frozen animal skin; TMS-1: 323).

The same materials on the Erbogachen Evenki group indicate that the use of reindeer in the ungulate hunt also creates a significant hindrance during other seasons.

> "On a *chernotropa* 'lit. black trail' [i.e., bare ground, before it snows], reindeer are just a bother," Evenkis say. "Riding your ***uchak***, see tracks, got to dismount to take a good look, old or fresh. Leading reindeer by the reins is no better; they get pestered by insects, or they figure to forage right there, and all the way you're practically dragging them by force. Besides, can't take reindeer where moose likes to go. Before snowfall, he (the moose—Auth.) always lives in the brush; brush or no brush, to him it's all the same. Walking, with his antlers and hoofs he can bring down *lesiny* 'trees' thick as your arm; once a moose starts crashing through, no brush will slow him down. But reindeer won't go through brush; got to make a path for them. Before the path is ready, moose has made a beeline out of there [*priamkom*

*Figure 4. The **kel'che** toboggan.*

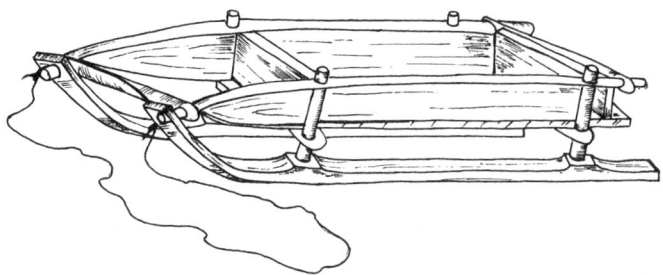

*Figure 5. The **irivun** hand-pulled hunting sledge.*

uidet], and you got to look for fresh tracks again. So, when Evenkis find tracks, let the dogs loose, skirt the brush and go through passable forest, listening for the dogs [baying]. As soon as you hear the dogs, drop the reindeer and walk fast, stalk quietly upwind. No, in the old days everybody moose-hunted [*sokhatili*] mostly on foot. Now, all the youth somehow got lazy; always want to ride" [Turov field notes].

Thus, retention of the traditional use of hand-pulled sledges, skin drags, and toboggans in *peshaia okhota* 'on-foot hunting', as well as overall retention of this type of hunting, appear to be justified.

3.11 Summary

In general, materials considered in this section reveal the following characteristics of the Evenki type of reindeer husbandry that complement in some aspects the classification developed by G. M. Vasilevich:

First, we note the significant intensifying effect that using reindeer for transportation had on the hunting economy as a whole. As mentioned above, the use of reindeer in fur hunting made it possible to expand the size of hunting territories, which in turn increased the overall yields of harvested fur-bearing animals. [Second,] in the hunt for large game animals, the use of reindeer to transport the kill led to an even clearer division of labour between males and females in the hunting group than before. The subsequent, even narrower specialization of men, and their focused involvement in hunting and fishing, established the conditions not only for providing their families with short-term food supplies and raw materials, but also for securing long-term supplies. [Third,] the highly important role of reindeer transportation in facilitating efficient and comprehensive procurement of various natural food resources and raw materials prompted hunting groups to strive to maintain the size of the reindeer herds they owned. At that particular level of development of the reindeer husbandry economy, this goal was achieved by observing the basic norms and requirements dictated by reindeer biology regarding the care and use of these animals. To this end, a key factor was the nomadic aspect of reindeer husbandry, which ensured the systematic and ecologically sustainable use of pastures for the herds, as well as the necessary rotation of *zashchitnye stantsii* 'sheltered pastures' and compliance with basic sanitary-hygienic norms.

It should be noted that changing the *zashchitnye stantsii* was in all probability no less important than keeping the reindeer fed and preventing disease. Unfortunately, this matter has yet to be fully investigated by biologists. However, one feature that is acknowledged by all experts is the extreme lack of adaptation of reindeer—and, for that matter, of all taiga ungulates—to sharp temperature fluctuations. For reindeer as well as moose, optimal temperature is within the range of $+15$ to $-30°$ C. Thus, it is quite likely that on the hottest summer days, Evenkis purposely moved their herds to bodies of water and into breezy pineries, in order to provide the reindeer with conditions closer to that temperature range. In winter, the herds were moved to deep sheltered valleys, surrounded by dense young forests that offered protection against the winter winds. To some degree, these measures preserved the internal resources of energy in these animals and provided them with relatively favourable conditions to survive the winter.

Thus, during the period covered by this study, the nomadic mode of Evenki life in the taiga zone of Central Siberia was of critical importance in facilitating the effective functioning of two key elements of their economy: [food and fur] procurement and reindeer husbandry.

Chapter 4. Economic territory, rhythm, and general principles governing the exploitation of taiga resources

This chapter rounds out our study of land use methods characteristic of Evenkis at the turn of the 20th century. To a certain extent, the methods of managing the Evenki economy that we have reconstructed describe only the most general organizational principles and dynamics of taiga land use by hunter–reindeer herder groups, which are mobile throughout most of the year. In particular, this reconstruction did not take into consideration the territorially limited local or group-specific features of land use by Evenkis. Therefore, we shall concern ourselves only with the general principles of the subject matter. Together with the methods for managing game hunting and reindeer husbandry examined in previous chapters, an important place in describing the economic system is held by the methods of managing the economic territories and the general rhythm of hunter–reindeer herder labour activities.

In our understanding, an economic territory encompasses the whole complex of hunting, fishing, pasturing, and other resources that are used throughout a lengthy period by a distinct group of mobile Evenkis. Such a delimited territory is the locus of a system of camps typical for taiga conditions, including the various dwellings and other household structures associated with those conditions. In turn, the rhythm of Evenki labour activities is viewed as an aggregate of various forms of regulating the rhythm of exploitation of the economic territory, nomadizing rhythms, and shifting between mobile and settled lifestyles.

In the ethnographic literature on Siberian hunter–reindeer herders, the rhythm of economic activity, as well as the rhythm of life in general, is usually considered within the timeframe of a complete calendar year, most often referred to as an "economic year" or "annual economic cycle."

In the conventional Evenki chronological system, the notion of an "economic year" is commonly projected onto the traditional folk calendar as lasting either 13 or 12 months (depending on which records one consults). Even G. M. Vasilevich noted the artificiality of both the very notion of the "annual economic cycle" and its expression through the traditional calendar (1969: 42–4). We cannot disagree with this, if only for the reason that the notion of the "economic year—economic cycle," being automatically associated with a closed process of production as well as with production cycles that can be divided into a number of separate sequential operations (ostensibly reflected in the names of the months), is entirely inadequate for representing the actual process of exploiting taiga resources. The materials discussed in previous chapters does not give us grounds to see a "clearly marked seasonal character" of economic activity, with a seasonally alternating sequence of hunting and fishing, as noted by A. A. Popov (ALIE 14/1/167 ff 11–12). Rather, the subsistence and economic resource exploitation patterns (excluding commercial fur hunting) practiced by mobile Evenkis in Central Siberia—at the turn of the 20th century, at least—appear to make up a continuous long-term process of integrated, multifaceted use of the entire complex of hunting, fishing, and pasture resources. At the same time, we cannot ignore the fact that the rhythm of transitions in environmental and climatic cycles reflected in the traditional calendar had a definite organizational impact on the overall rhythm and character of Evenki labour activities. To resolve this contradiction, it seems advisable to investigate in more detail the essence of the traditional Evenki calendar, including its links to the hunting–reindeer herding economy.

4.1 The traditional Evenki calendar

Comparative studies of folk calendars of pre-class societies indicate that, irrespective of the type of economy, they reflect the system of beliefs characteristic of the given society, with due attention to the rhythmic recurrence of natural processes. Practical observations of the rhythmic sequence of natural phenomena, converted into temporal categories and divided into distinct daily, monthly, and annual cycles, were conceptualized none other than "through labour, while natural rhythms were taken into consideration only to the extent of their influence on the organization of the labour process" (Iordanskii 1982: 58, 82).

As documented, the most well-defined divisions of a calendar year, based on astronomic observations, are found in the calendars of peoples whose economy has a definite agricultural orientation. Such detailed time divisions were necessitated by the demands of the agricultural economy itself, with its carefully planned labour rhythms and a systematic schedule of consecutive closed cycles of agricultural production (Iordanskii 1982: 83). Without the need for scrupulous scheduling or recording the rhythm of labour activity, and shifting during certain seasons to hunting and fishing as the predominant activity, such agricultural societies would also switch to a different system of annual time-keeping. Rather than recording the changes and cyclical sequences of non-agricultural economic activities, they recorded in their calendars the transition periods of environmental/climatic conditions, whose timing varied from year to year. This shows that, unlike farmers, hunter-fisher societies adjust their labour activities only to seasonally changing natural conditions. Accordingly, the calendars of these societies, which are in essence phenological, reflect basically a sequence of transitions in factors that condition the exploitation of natural resources. Just as with all chronological systems, the phenological calendar simultaneously reflects as much the general rhythm of the life of hunter–reindeer herders as the rhythm of their economic activities during any given season of the year (Iordanskii 1982: 84).

The above considerations are essentially the key to understanding the traditional calendar of mobile Evenkis. Our comparative analysis of the Evenki traditional calendar, based on records dating back to the period between the mid-19th and early 20th century, reveals the following.

In the earliest editions, the Evenki 13-lunar-month calendar corresponds to the Russian 12-month calendar (Krivoshapkin 1863: 74; Orlov 1857: 182–3; Tretiakov 1869: 291–2). This being the case, the monthly divisions of the Evenki calendar obviously are shifted in comparison to the Russian one; every month in the Evenki calendar consists of four weeks, each straddling two weeks of each of the two adjacent months in the Russian calendar (e.g., *kaniakich* 'month of digging coral lily' corresponds to the second half of June and first half of July). In addition, the Evenki concept of a year is divided into two separate periods—the summer period *diugani* (lit. 'summer'), comprising six months, and the winter period *an'iani* (lit. 'year'), including seven lunar months. According to Tretiakov's notes, Evenkis viewed summer as one whole period, not divisible into monthly cycles (1869: 289). Unsurprisingly, the records of the 13–lunar month, including its later 12-month editions that retain traditional Evenki terminology, as well as data in the comparative Tungus-Manchurian dictionary (TMS-1, TMS-2), indicate that most Russian translations of Evenki names of months identify seasonal changes in the environment. For example, *muchun* refers to 'greening of the larch, appearance of the first grass, and opening of tree buds', *irkin* denotes 'mosquitoes disappearing, reindeer scraping their antlers', and *ektenkire* means 'time of snow on the boughs', etc.

Obviously, every natural-climatic cycle defined in the calendar associates in the Evenki consciousness with some of the most important transitions in their lives. Thus, the month *turan* (lit. 'arrival of crows' in late April or early May), which among Northern Baikal and Barguzin Evenkis has the very specific name of *dukun* 'lean time', was undoubtedly related not only to the idea of the ongoing animal hunt *po nastu* 'on the snow crust' but also to the beginning of spring and the end of a severe long winter, as well as the appearance of new and more diverse sources of subsistence.

Discussing the annual diet of Central Siberian Evenki groups in previous chapters of this work, we have demonstrated that various plant and animal food products received priority, depending on the season and on [what was considered] the most efficient use of various resources. The month names of the Evenki calendar mark such changes: *kaniakich* 'month of digging coral lily', *charulin* 'month of collecting tree juice', *giraun* 'month of hunting on snow crust', etc. At the same time, it should be emphasized once again that identification of the periods most conducive to berry picking, digging *sarana* 'coral lily', and even hunting on snow crust in the Evenki calendar should not be taken directly to mean that other economic activities were not carried out during those months, nor that other economic activities were of lesser importance at the time. Indeed, Evenkis fished and hunted throughout the entire summer. During the month of intensive stocking of coral lily roots, an important plant food, Evenkis tended to their reindeer. Meanwhile, during the period of hunting on the snow crust, important household activities such as curing hides and sewing summer and fall clothes continued, as did fur hunting and preparations for the forthcoming calving season. Basically, in no season was there a single economic activity to which all the work time was dedicated on a daily basis—as is the case, for instance, with farmers during sowing, harvesting, etc. The integrated nature of the communal economy [*obshchestvennoe proizvodstvo*], the absence of a clear professional division of labour other than by sex and age, and finally the phenological (rather than economic) nature of the Evenki calendar itself convince us of the absence of a clear-cut seasonal cycle in their economic activities. Perceived intuitively, the rhythm of environmental changes expressed in the calendar most likely reflected the fluctuating intensity of using various resources or increased activity within any given individual branch of the subsistence economy. In all probability, such activities were carried out not throughout the entire month in question but during a much shorter period of time.

We may conjecture that the above-defined division of the astronomic year into two parts identifies in these calendars two different phases in the lives of mobile hunters. One of them, characterized by the descriptive names of lunar months and which encompasses the whole summer season (***diugani***) and parts of the spring and fall seasons (***an'iani***), is aligned with the predominant travelling lifestyle. In the calendar, this part includes six summer months, starting with ***muchun*** 'month of the first greenery' and ending with ***sirudian*** 'month of the reindeer rut'. In addition, it includes two spring months, ***ektenkire*** 'month of snow thawing' and ***turan*** 'arrival of crows', and a fall month, ***ugun*** 'flooding'.

In turn, the names of the ***tugeni*** 'winter' months, the second phase [of the calendar] defined by Central Siberian Evenkis, comprise a special group related, in our opinion, to a particular system of keeping track of time. Among these names in the Evenki winter calendar are ***mire*** 'lit. shoulder, reindeer scapula' and ***giraun*** 'lit. striding time', i.e., transition from one year to the next. It should also be noted that among the names of months documented for the Aian group of Evenkis are ***bilan*** or ***began*** 'wrist month', ***ichan began*** 'elbow month', ***oron-khoron*** 'crown of the head', and ***sonaia*** 'smoke hole in a *chum*'; these names existed in the Aian group alongside the calendar names commonly used by all Evenki groups (Vasilevich 1969: 44). We suggest that in the recent past there existed a special system of keeping track of time, common to all Evenki groups, which corresponded to the ***tugeni*** period. Names were given to the months in accordance with actual observations of the position of the North Star, e.g., ***Buga sangarin*** 'lit. heavenly hole' or the *Ursa Major* constellation, representing the mythical hunter Kheglen, who took to the skies in pursuit of a moose. The position of constellations in the firmament was observed relative to human body parts, which in turn was reflected in the traditional calendar (Vasilevich 1969: 185, 186, 210). It may very well be that, in contrast to the summer period of nomadism, which did not require precise time-keeping, the settled winter period among all Evenki groups had once been fine-tuned into more exact monthly periods. We might also suggest that the division of the astronomic year into two parts—***diugani*** and ***an'iani***—reflected, in all probability, the ancient perception of active (nomadic) light and dark (settled) periods. In the latter, economic activity gradually subsided and reached a minimum level during winter, as if imitating falling into a slow-moving, sleepy state, and the subsequent awakening of all nature in spring. Later, the lengthening of the mobile period due to the autumn and spring squirrel hunts resulted in shortening of the fine-tuned count of winter months to the three-month *tugeni* period.

When converted to the Russian 12-month calendar, the traditional Evenki calendar retained the conventional descriptive names of the summer months but preserved the precise traditional chronology for only a few winter months of the settled lifestyle. At the same time, the adjustments to the calendar did not affect its main overall purpose. In our opinion, it continued to be above all a reflection of the general rhythm of life of Central Siberian hunter–reindeer herders, albeit recognizing the successive transitions between travelling (nomadic) vs. sedentary lifeways. Their economic activities and patterns of taiga land use were only related to the annual round to the extent that migration (nomadism) existed at that time as a natural form of comprehensive and efficient use of the whole complex of taiga resources. We feel it would be justified to assert that the "annual economic cycle" was no more than an arbitrarily defined part of a multi-year continuous production process aimed to take advantage of all available taiga resources. In fact, this long-term round was not divided by Evenkis into separate production cycles, as was the case, for example, with Evens, whose calendar identified 6–8 intervals of pasture rotation (Popova 1981: 60–2). Instead, it seems to us that the traditional Evenki calendar represents regular transitions between nomadic and settled periods (i.e., intervals of mobile and sedentary life) fixed in the folklore tradition. The calendar's spring-summer and autumn monthly intervals divide the entire mobile period into separate parts, relative to the rotation of camping areas, rotation of the comprehensively used subsistence territories, as well as to the intensified exploitation of one specific resource. By and large, the rhythm of the calendar, and the cycles of rotational land use reflected therein, are determined by the rhythm of environmental and climatic changes.

4.2 Land use [*osvoeniia ugodii*]

"The pre-Revolutionary administration classified Evenkis based on their lifestyle, as 'itinerant trappers'. It was believed that the Tunguses wandered around the taiga wherever their whim took them, following only their own hunting caprice" (Tugolukov 1969: 16).

This was commonly linked to the absence of land ownership rights among Evenkis and to the lack of a clear delineation of clan and family territories. Although the question of the form of land use by Evenkis remains a subject of discussion even to this day, it can be considered an established fact that at the turn of the 20th century land ownership rights for individual families were extended only to areas where these families set up their fur hunting traps (Levin and Potapov 1956; Petri 1930; Suslov 1927; Vasilevich 1972). However, this largely theoretical question is of interest to us only to the extent to which the Evenki mobile approach to the procurement of taiga resources was connected with the permanency of economic territory used by an individual family or a group of neighbouring families within the [longer] period of several generations.

An interesting characteristic feature common to all hunter-fishers is the existence of an economic link between any territorial aggregation and specific permanent territories. The latter include the whole complex of taiga resources, which supplied the required food and raw materials for household needs, as well as water, fuel, camp site and dwelling protection, and optimal life conditions for people and their household animals (Gromov 1981: 332; Kabo 1968: 254–6, 1979: 92–3). The interest of the production group in retaining the historically formed balance between group size and availability of resources within an inhabited territory is most often noted as the underlying cause explaining the connection between a society, its subsistence economy, and the environment (Cotlow 1960: 62–3; Davidson 1975: 40; Weiner 1979: 493, 588). It is clear that this pattern was also characteristic of Evenki groups inhabiting the Central Siberian taiga at the turn of the 20th century. This proposition is supported by the examples reported in Evenki ethnographic sources of both communal land ownership (Anisimov 1936: 164–6; Grigorovskii 1890: 15–17; Levin and Potapov 1956: 725; Petri 1930: 69; Suslov 1927: 47–8) and ongoing exploitation of resources by several generations of a given hunting group (Vasilevich 1972: 166).

It is also possible to suggest that there was nothing disorderly or spontaneous in the movement of Evenki groups, nor disorderly in the "wanderings" of hunter-fisher societies in general. Any hunting collective, very well familiar with the seasonal locations of the animals they hunted, naturally planned out their "procurement" of natural resources and, thus, also planned their organized migrations throughout the territory (Alimurzaev 1981: 159–63). As demonstrated by the discussion in the previous chapter, order was also imposed, to a certain extent, on mobile Evenki hunting–reindeer herding groups in Central Siberia by the conditions of a new branch of the economy, i.e., reindeer husbandry. When selecting travel routes, Evenkis assigned as much importance to the [long-term] stability of reindeer calving and mating places, summer pastures, availability of wood for smudges, convenience of routes for travelling with reindeer, and other factors as to the actual hunting and fishing considerations. Our data, as well as data collected by a number of other researchers, provide direct evidence that these "wanderings" took place along well-defined routes (Georgi 1799; Petri 1930; Rychkov 1917). The permanency of annual travel routes of hunting groups was determined by their attachment to universally convenient (i.e., from the perspective of the needs of reindeer husbandry, hunting, and fishing) nomadic trails that the Evenkis called *tsentral'nye dorogi* 'primary roads' (Petri 1930: 33). According to our field observations, a *tsentral'naia doroga* would pass in summer through elevated dry areas (along mountain ridges and southern mountain slopes) and in autumn and early spring through lowlands, close to riverside and lakeside spruce groves, representing a closed-loop round that divided the territory of any given group into two parts.

In the field, such a route looked like an elongated ellipsoid, with long and short axes of 150–250 km and 25–30 km in length, respectively. Such *tsentral'nye dorogi* formed the core of an organized and purposeful system of managing hunting-fishing and pasture resources. The *tsentral'nye dorogi* also formed the core of corresponding permanent base camps and stop-over camps, along with their respective permanent and temporary dwelling and household structures. In other words, the very orderly organization of economic exploitation of taiga resources, and the Evenki nomadizing lifestyle within the boundaries of those resources, together determined the well-documented orderly organization of the economic territory [...]. Our own interview data and direct observations reveal the following.

Given the lack of complete and accurately documented evidence, we can only approximately estimate the size of an economic territory exploited jointly by a group of related or neighbouring Evenki families. However, Evenkis themselves are still able, with more or less confidence, to name the rivers and adjoining taiga parcels where the nomadic routes of their families and neighbours once used to run. In all probability, it may be conjectured that, having only a vague idea about land ownership rights, territorially adjacent groups naturally established closed and relatively non-overlapping areas of taiga for their use, with a "no man's land" between them. Data supporting this hypothesis can be found in the accounts of various travellers, who consistently observed that the practical geographic knowledge of taiga inhabitants was mostly limited to the territories where their entire lives were spent. We also found that any ethnos, comprised of separate groups living in relative isolation from one another, had a characteristic fear or some discomfort with regard to territories considered "not ours." Hunters usually refused to accompany [foreign] expeditions to taiga lands "belonging to others," giving as their excuse not so much their unfamiliarity with the route as their fear of unknown "bad" [*khudye*] places, [believed to be] inhabited by "strange, evil forces." In general, it is possible to say that independent but territorially adjacent Evenki communities—the main type of social organization among Evenkis at the end of the 19th century (Gurvich et al. 1970; Levin and Potapov 1956; Tugolukov 1970)—were characterized by a well-formed understanding of "own" and "alien" territories, including the absence of land ownership rights. Accordingly, their planned, annually recurring migrations took place within the closed boundaries of each community's permanent hunting, fishing, and pasture lands.

4.3 Selection of camp location

Within a territory jointly exploited by a group of neighbours, our data permitted us to document the following structure of the various camps and associated dwelling and household structures. First, we identified two areas with concentrations of base camps and camp sites occupied every year. These concentrations are located at two "polar" opposite and most distant ends along the seasonal migration route of an Evenki territorial group.

As a rule, the first area was located in low-lying wooded parts of the taiga belonging to the watershed of either [1] two adjoining larger tributaries of the Lena, Angara, Podkamennaia Tunguska, or Lower Tunguska rivers or [2] the watershed zones dividing two other main river systems. In such areas, at a short distance from each other (no more than 4–5 km), three base camps were situated—a ***meneien*** for winter, ***nengnerkit*** for spring, and **khigolorkit** for autumn—inhabited every year and for several years in a row. As noted in previous chapters, these areas usually adjoined the permanent calving and mating places, winter pastures of domesticated reindeer, and winter foraging sites of game ungulates.

Our data show that the second area, usually found along a riverbank, comprised a series of short-term ***diuvorkit*** summer camps, inhabited for one to two weeks at a time [Photo 29]. As was the case with the first area, the territory of the summer camps was inhabited continuously for two, three, or more generations of Evenki families. As pointed out above, the time at the ***diuvorkit*** was spent on intensive fishing, occasional hunting, and summer husbandry of reindeer in favourable forage and safety conditions.

According to our data, individual families, or temporarily combined groups of households with few reindeer, would travel annually along their "primary roads" and stop at a series of **urikit** "micro-regions" located a distance of one short daylight passage from one another (about 10–12 km; Fig. 6). Each **urikit** comprised a cluster of stop-over camps dating back to various years, used for a period between [a minimum] of 5 days and [a maximum of] 1.5–2 weeks. These camps were used during the summer (June–August) and autumn (second half of October–November) nomadizing periods and also during the use of hunting and fishing grounds located in the valleys of taiga rivers, lakes, marshy tundra, and mossy bogs.

Apart from the described categories of short-term camps and long-term base camps associated with the permanent seasonal distribution areas of mobile hunter–reindeer herders at the turn of the 20th century, Central Siberian Evenkis also had numerous temporary camps scattered through the territory exploited by a given group. Camps of this kind were used, as a rule, during the ungulate and fur-hunting seasons, and were most often occupied by one or two hunters for overnight stops or short stays (no more than 2 days). Such camps were also used by fishermen traveling with overnight stops to bodies of water nearby the main camp. In general, we interpret the aggregate of all categories of camps and base camps characteristic of the 19th and early 20th

*Figure 6. The **urikit** short-term summer camp.*

centuries as representing a historically formed and well-ordered system associated with both the annual nomadizing round and resource exploitation practices in the Central Siberian taiga by mobile groups of Evenkis.

In general, it can be said that a particular characteristic of camps of all different categories was that they shared a few common features and the standardized construction of dwelling and household structures. It has also been recognized that, in typological terms, Evenki architecture displays numerous analogies with that of a number of Siberian peoples (Levin and Potapov 1956, 1961). Several Evenki ethnographic studies discuss these cultural traits in extensive detail (e.g., Vasilevich 1969: 107–21). As such, it has been established that both the assortment of employed dwelling and household structures and construction elements varied depending on the natural-climatic conditions as well as the length of time spent at camps.

In this context, it will be useful to provide a more detailed description of the various types of camps and related architectural structures using our own field materials which supplement, to a certain extent, the previous knowledge available from earlier Tungus studies. From our point of view, it will be also practical to include in this description a brief explanation of the nomadizing sequence and the main kinds of activities associated with each group of camps. This will allow us to explore the general character and dynamics of the mobile lifestyle of Evenki hunter–reindeer herding groups in the Central Siberian taiga.

4.4 Camp layout and structures

As demonstrated, the general migrations of Evenki families with their reindeer commenced after the majority of reindeer cows had finished calving.

However, the second season of squirrel hunting, starting already in mid-February with the appearance of a solid snow cover, would "rouse" both hunters and dogs. While the families continued to live a settled life at the ***meneien*** base camps and prepared to move to the calving areas, or (during years with a poor squirrel harvest) to nomadize in fur-hunting areas, the hunters set out on lone day-trips to explore the lands around the ***meneien***. Any necessary overnight stops in this period were made at stop-over camps, with a hearth built of long (2–3 m) logs burning all night. As shelter from the wind, he set up a barrier made of fir boughs, which also served as a screen reflecting the heat toward the back of the sleeping hunter. If his trip away from the base camp lasted more than a day, he lay down a carpet of spruce or pine boughs near the hearth (***guluvun***) at the temporary camp and set up a half-*chum* tent (***kaltamni***) as a windscreen. The frame of the ***kaltamni***, as with an ordinary *chum*, was built of three main and several auxiliary poles (***seran***), set up on the leeward side and then covered with the lower half of the regular *chum*'s coverings, made of *rovduga* 'suede' [Photo 28]. For a hunter, such a temporary camp served as a kind of interim base from which to search for animals without having to contact the base camp. Except for the spring fur hunt, such camps were characteristic of all types of individual search trips undertaken during all seasons.

In April (***turan***), ungulate hunting began with the appearance of the snow crust, as described above. At this time, some of the territorially neighbouring groups' elderly members, adolescents, and nursing women continued to live in the ***meneien***. The rest formed separate hunting parties, consisting of a few closely related families, and exploited the lands nearby the ***meneien***. Since moose and wild reindeer, at that time, were still at the winter *kormozashchitnye stantsii* 'sheltered foraging sites', the procurement territory did not extend for more than 40–60 km away from the winter base camp (Vasilevich 1969: 46–50), and on average the hunters did not travel [from camp to camp] more than 5–6 km at a time.

Upon arrival at a stop-over camp, the reindeer were unloaded and belongings were placed on a ground-level platform made of 3–4 poles laid on top of short, thick logs—the structure was called [generically] a *labaz* (Krivoshapkin 1963: 69) or ***nemnga*** 'mobile *labaz*' (TMS-1: 587). Then the Evenkis started a ***guluvun*** 'campfire' to make tea; setting up the *chum* and unpacking their belongings commenced only after tea. It is interesting to note that we also observed this approach to the camp set-up during other nomadic seasons. In cases when the current camp was located in the same spot as during previous years (camps were usually re-visited no earlier than after 4–5 years), a new place for the *chum* was be selected on flat ground, a few metres away from the old *chumovishche*; this rule of proximity was also applied to the placement of the ***guluvun***.

[To build the *chum*,] Evenkis tamped the snow down in a circular area in the chosen spot, 4–6.5 m in diameter, depending on the number of people living in the *chum*. In general, we confirmed that the method of erecting a *chum*, its frame structure, and coverings observed by us did not differ from the traditional ones described by G. M. Vasilevich (1969: 109–11) and in the historical-ethnographic atlas of Siberia (Levin and Potapov 1961: 142, 204–5; Table VII, fig. 10–15; Table VIII, fig. 1–3). At same time, we recorded the detailed sequence of steps involved in erecting a *chum*, which had never been fully described in earlier publications, as well as some of its structural elements (see Photos 7–9). Having selected and prepared the ground for the *chum*, Evenkis started to erect its frame. Interviewees informed us that the three main poles *turgu* always had to come from the frames of previous years' *chumy*, and not be mixed with other poles. New *turgu* poles were made only when the old ones became entirely useless. The three *turgu* were joined together at the top (*duo*) in such a way that two poles forming one side of the triangle faced the direction and the trail by which they arrived at the camp. On this side, two more *turgu* poles were placed against the tripod's top end to form a doorway. Then, the remaining frame poles *kheran* were set up, working around the *chum* perimeter "*po solntsu*" (in the direction of the sun), at approximately the same distance from the centre of the *chum*. Some of these poles were part of the old frame, but some were made new. The *chum* coverings were made of tanned moose hides (*rovduga*) and consisted of four **niuk** pieces, divided into two half-coverings, the upper **uneken** and the bottom **elbenel**. The mounting of **niuk** coverings started with the lower half, **elbenel**. It was tightly pulled over the lodgepoles from left to right ("following the sun," explained Evenkis). The two lower coverings, stretched over the frame one after another, were tied to the **kheranil** [pl. of **kheran**] using straps sewn onto the upper corners. Here, the left edge of the second **niuk** was slipped under the right edge [of the first]. The upper part of the *chum* was covered in the same order, except for the smoke hole; in bad weather it was closed with a separate piece of *rovduga* or *bercsta* 'birch bark'. The upper corners of the **uneken**, made of two **niuk** pieces stitched together, had loops sewn on, through which poles with a fork at the top were passed. Two people, lifting the **uneken** with poles, would throw it over and pull it around the lodgepoles, overlapping the **elbenel** by 60–80 cm from above and lapping the right edge of the **uneken** over the left one. To finish, the entire covering was secured in place with several thick poles [laid on top], and the bottom of the *chum* was first lined with pine or spruce boughs (*lapnik*) and then covered with snow to keep warmth in. Inside the *chum*, dense flooring (*khokhto*) was made of cut pine boughs laid along the walls, on which the bedding was laid. The fireplace in the central part of the *chum*, the **aran**, was framed by a U-shaped log enclosure (*uvo*), open to the doorway. As the last step, after the *chum* was set up, a fire was started in the centre using embers from the **guluvun**, and a special pole, the **chimka**, was placed to the left or right of the entrance (next to the sleeping places). A horizontal pole, the *ikeptun*, was tied to the **chimka** and the main lodgepole, the *turgu*, positioned opposite the entrance from which to hang a cauldron, the **olloun**, suspended from wooden or iron hooks. At this point, the camp set-up was essentially complete.

Among the other household structures, although not directly related to the base camp itself, are the *labaz* stores **iumgulo** and **noku dzeptyleruk**, which, as described in previous chapters, were actively used during ungulate hunting on the snow crust. The first of them, the **iumgulo**, was a kind of log-house built of round (not debarked) logs and raised above the ground on short posts (60–80 cm high). The corners of the **iumgulo** were rounded, and the total height of the log-house did not, as a rule, exceed 1–1.5 m (Photo 10). Thick and heavy logs were placed in one row [next to each other] on top of the log-house. At that time, the game meat was usually not moved to the stop-over camp; instead, the whole family would go to the **iumgulo**. However, if a moose was shot too far away from the stop-over camp, then only part of the hunting group moved to the **iumgulo**, while the rest continued their way along the *tsentral'naia doroga* 'primary road', continuing their procuring as they went. In either case, having reached the site where harvested meat was stored, the families set up camp.

> "When there was meat in spring, we lived long and happily. We dried and cured the meat, and ate as much fresh meat as we wanted. Lived like that for up to a week," described the Evenkis [Turov field notes].

Most of the dried and cured meat was loaded into packs and brought along; part of it was also moved to the **noku dzeptyleruk** nearest the "primary road" where, as mentioned above, it was stored till summer, or sometimes for up to two years.

By external appearance and construction methods, these *labazy* are generally similar to all other stores on posts known to us, including those used for storing food as well as those used for storing clothes (**noku totyeldu**) and hunting gear and household items (**noku seleruk**). As a rule, frequently used stationary stores of this type—except the "**noku** of the primary road" [**dzeptyleruk**]—were found in the areas commonly used for permanent autumn, winter, and spring base camps. Some of these structures which we documented, and the nature of their use, were discussed by the author of this work in a separate article (Turov 1975). It was noted there that while these structures undoubtedly preserved the traditional Evenki principles, they incorporated a few elements apparently borrowed from Russian settlers from the European North, including, very likely, the hewn-plank storage structure (Photo 11) and the method of hanging doors on wooden hinges. It is possible that the design of a pitched roof of the "male" type (Photos 12 and 13), which replaced the traditional shed roof, was borrowed from Russian settlers. In sum, it seems that various borrowings and variations in the use of stationary **noku** caches (individual, group, long-term, etc.) resulted in a greater diversity of simultaneously used household structures.

In general, the **noku** on posts can be divided into two typologically different groups: the individual **noku** cache belonging to one family and a **noku** used by 2–3 related families. We observed the latter in areas where territorially neighbouring groups lived a settled lifestyle during the autumn/spring season. Essentially, the former category of *noku* differed from the latter in the size of the storage space and in the number of rooms in one structure (we saw two- and three-room stores and two-storey caches). Overall, all permanent *noku* were commonly erected on high posts (2–3.5 m tall), built of trees cut down at the appropriate height and debarked all the way to the butt. For the erection of a *noku* store, a dry place was selected, such as a hillock ("so [its] feet don't rot"), surrounded by creeks or marshy sloughs ("so that fire doesn't come near").

Measuring 2.5×3.0 m to 3.5×7.0 m, such a log or plank house was erected on four to six posts (*khalgn* 'leg'; *baksa, bakshi, bakcha* 'post'; TMS-1: 67). An entrance opening was built in one of the long walls, facing the side that was least exposed to probable precipitation. The entrance (*urke*) was closed with a door made of 3–4 hewn planks secured to each other by two cleats. For climbing up to the store, a ladder was made of a log with steps chopped out of it [Photos 11, 12, 21]. Nowadays, according to our observations, the roof of such loghouses can be made of a great variety of materials, including even *ruberoid* 'tar-paper'. A pitched roof covered with the bark of larch trees (*uldaksa*) would be considered the most traditional kind [Photo 17]. It is worth noting that in order to ensure structural durability of all the different types of permanent *noku* stores, larch was the basic material of choice for posts, flooring, and crossbeams. All the logs in the structure were debarked. Inside the store, rack-poles were inserted through [openings in] the end and side walls of the *noku*, on which birch-bark pouches were hung with food reserves, clothes, and other family belongings.

Describing the main types of economic activity during the period of hunting ungulates on the snow crust, it should also be noted that the women took advantage of the increasing daylight hours and, in addition to processing and transporting meat, kept themselves busy with the preliminary treatment of skins and hides, scraping off residual fat, meat, and scud and drying them stretched on frames or stretchers made of sticks. As mentioned above, this pattern of nomadizing was employed by hunting groups only during the first two years of [a period] particularly abundant in squirrel staple forage.

With the appearance of patches of thawed ground and compacting snow at the end of March and beginning of April, families left the winter base camp to travel separately until the beginning of the calving season, exploiting practically their entire territories and covering the greatest distances from the base camp (sometimes as far as 200–250 km or more). Nevertheless, the nature of nomadizing and moving camp remained the same as described above. Only the rhythm of the nomadic movements changed, that is, the length of the daily treks, and duration of stay at any one place.

With the calving season approaching in the herds of domesticated reindeer, Evenkis strove to wrap up the ungulate hunt and arrive in the area of their spring base camp. In the past, the Evenki groups that we studied had two or three permanent long-term *nengnerkit* base camps, used by several generations of a given group. As explained in the preceding chapter, this permanency of the ***nengnerkit*** and the calving grounds associated with them was predicated by the biological characteristics of domesticated reindeer. At the same time, the specific location of the ***nengnerkit*** for a given year was determined, according to Evenkis, by "... where the squirrel hunting was. Where the calving finds us, there we spend the spring" (the term ***nengnerkit*** derives from ***nengneni*** 'spring' [TMS-1: 653]). Our data show that all the examined spring camps (both old and recent camps used by families leading a mobile life to this day) were concentrated in the areas described below.

In years abundant in squirrel, families had enough time to return to the area of their winter base camp before the beginning of the calving season and, therefore, the first ***nengnerkit*** was located no more than 5–6 km away from their ***meneien***. The second ***nengnerkit***, used in the 3rd or 4th year after a year of good squirrel forage, was located about midway between the ***meneien*** and the summering places. The third, associated with years poor in squirrel forage, was located at a maximum distance from the areas of the winter base camp; spatially, these locations coincided with the series of summer camps, at times located as far as 200 km from the ***meneien***. In fact, the camps of the third type of ***nengnerkit*** are usually located either directly on a family's "primary road" of summer nomadizing or no more than 10–12 km away from it.

Incidentally, it useful to note that in the Evenki understanding, '***nengnerkit***' relates only to the camp associated with the reindeer calving season. Other camps, set up in spring or other seasons and occupied for a period of no more than one week, were named ***urikit*** in the Evenki lexicon (derived from ***urin*** 'to make a stop' [TMS-2: 285]). In fact, the beginning of the calving season in a domesticated reindeer herd, along with setting up the ***nengnerkit***, marks the end of the first stage [of the annual Evenki calendar]—the spring ***malaia khod'ba*** 'small walking' (according to Vasilevich 1969: 46) which gradually included the entire population of the ***meneien***, consisting of all the members of a single territorial community.

At the ***nengnerkit***, families lived a settled life for the whole of May and first half of June, until the end of the reindeer calving season and arrival of the mosquitoes. Naturally, the length of stay at one place would itself, in many ways, affect the character of the ***nengnerkit***, the justification of its setup, and some specifics of its spatial planning. The central place in the base camp was usually occupied by a large pen for calving reindeer cows and cows about to calve. It is interesting to note that today, in some Evenki families that nomadize individually with their households and, for the most part, preserve the traditional mobile way of life and activity rhythm, the term ***kure*** (*zabor* or *izgorod* 'fence', *ograda* 'enclosure', *ogorozhennoe mesto* 'fenced place', *zagon dlia olenei* 'pen for reindeer'), referring in the past to a proper fence for the calving reindeer cows, extends now to the entire enclosed part of the base camp [Photo 32]. The very tradition of fencing spring and autumn base camps evidently appeared quite recently, possibly as a result of borrowing from neighbouring peoples the tradition of penning their entire reindeer herd (Spevakovskii 1984: 125). Owing to this, it seems, the camps of contemporary Evenkis, who use this method of keeping reindeer in spring and autumn, retain to this day the traditional names of *vesennii* 'spring' and *osennii* 'autumn' *ogorod* 'yard' (Fig. 7; [Photo 25]). With their entrances facing the **kure**, skin *chumy* were setup around the reindeer-pen, which housed all the cows from the reindeer herds of the several families living jointly in the **nengnerkit**. In addition, each of the dwellings in turn was encircled by a separate fence enclosing an area 10–15 m in diameter […], which, besides the *chum*, contained a fireplace for cooking food and a low deck (*delken* 'platform on posts') for belongings. According to the Evenkis, these fences were set up in order to keep bulls and calves, wandering through the base camp, away from the *chumy* and belongings [on the **delken**].

*Figure 7. The **khigolorkit** fall camp, adjacent to the spring **nengnerkit**.*

At some distance from the living quarters of the base camp, there was a permanent *noku* for storing food supplies and equipment, both meant to be used, as a rule, by one or two related families (Photos 15 and 16). Based on their construction and usage particulars, such structures combining storage of food and goods, including clothes, hides and skins, hunting gear, and equipment, were analogous to the *noku* described above. Also, this is where at the start of summer nomadizing all unnecessary belongings were left. We may assume that at the turn of the 20th century, most Evenki families having reindeer herds of 25 or more head developed a tradition of fencing in the whole territory of the spring base camp. Besides these observations, G. M. Vasilevich also noted the same principle governing *nengnerkit* organization among the mobile Evenkis of Central Siberia (1969: 72, 76). Today, the lack of accurate data allows us to make only approximate estimates of the size of territory enclosed by a group of families living together in a *nengnerkit*. Evenkis themselves comment on the above as follows: "Fences used to be big; you'd walk along a fence all day, wouldn't get halfway round."

According to our observations, contemporary spring enclosures of individual Evenki families keeping up to 50 reindeer could reach a diameter of 7 km. It should be emphasized that, in our opinion, fencing of the entire territory of spring base camps was not a characteristic of all categories of *nengnerkit*, but rather only of those located in the vicinity of the *meneien*. Usually, nearly all the families that lived at one *meneien* in winter would gather together at the same *nengnerkit*, which allowed the expenditure of the great volume of work necessary to fence in a huge territory. It also appears that in the remaining cases, Evenkis limited themselves to building only pens for calving reindeer cows. This was not merely because fencing the whole base camp would be too hard a job for one family, but mainly because it was not necessary, due to the fact that a small family's reindeer herd stayed near their living quarters on account of the herd leaders, i.e., the pregnant cows, being penned in. In big herds, however, there is a more pronounced tendency to disperse and break up the entire flock into smaller reindeer groups, which forage in their own local patches of pasture.

Since the settled life in the *nengnerkit* lasted for over a month, the pasture patches adjoining the base camp were indeed heavily trampled over such a long time. Consequently, every year the Evenkis had to move their spring base camps some distance away, thus allowing the trampled pastures to regenerate. On their regular visits to the *nengnerkit* near their winter camp, the Evenkis added new fence to the existing old enclosure [Photos 33, 34]. According to their own words, fencing a new pasture could add an area of up to one-third of the total fenced *nengnerkit* territory.

As already mentioned earlier, besides taking care of the reindeer, the economic activities of Evenkis during calving season included preparations for summer nomadizing, continuation of the moose hunt, repairing equipment and old summer clothing, making new clothes, processing hides and skins, and fishing; all the adults of the *nengnerkit* who were not involved in tending reindeer participated in these activities. In general, Evenkis tried to complete all these very time-consuming domestic chores before the beginning of summer travel. The women preferred to have only small manual jobs left for the summer, such as clothes repairs and processing small skins. Once processed, the large moose and reindeer hides, which were used for *chum* coverings, bedding, and outer clothing, were stored in the ***noku*** utilized during both the autumn and summer seasons of settled life.

With the arrival of mosquitoes and the end of calving in most pregnant cows, groups living in a single camp split into families that travelled separately, sometimes joined by relatives. According to our data, such nomadizing groups retained a stable composition for several years. Each group, after leaving their spare belongings in a ***noku*** cache (Vasilevich 1969: 116), travelled along its "primary road" toward riverbanks. According to our materials and the evidence of a number of authors (Anisimov 1936; Georgi 1799; Polevoi 1965; Rychkov 1917; Vasilevich 1962, 1969), the final destination of nomadizing during the first half of summer was, as mentioned above, the cluster of ***diuvorkit*** summer base camps. Very likely, exactly such base camps were observed by N. Spafarii in his time, who recorded them every 2–3 km along the banks of the Angara River (1882: 88, 91, 97–100).

As already mentioned in previous sections, the purpose of nomadizing, its tempo, and the nature of camps were determined by a number of factors that together ensured a comprehensive and multifaceted exploitation of hunting, fishing, and pasture resources. Judging by the fact that already by the beginning of July, having covered a distance of 150–200 km, nomadizing groups arrived in the areas of these base camps, the tempo of travel was relatively high. Moving along the banks of small taiga rivers crossed by the "primary road," they stopped for 2 or 3 days. For their base camps, they selected dry, elevated places along riverbanks, with supplies of firewood for smudges and with holes in the river for fishing. Evenkis stayed at the same camp for a longer period, up to 2 weeks, only if they happened to harvest a moose. Upon reaching the area of the series of ***diuvorkit***, the tempo of travel decreased sharply, and stays at these camps became longer. The banks of large rivers swept by strong winds provided the domesticated reindeer with protection against mosquitoes, and the Evenkis with places rich in fish. In these summering areas, groups moved a maximum of 2–3 times. The decision to change camp location, as usual, took into consideration as much the need to conserve pastures as the Evenki notion that one must not stop at the old *chum* sites every year.

According to Evenki interview data, the short-term nature of base camps located consistently along the "primary roads" of the nomadic travel necessitated the relative simplicity of their layout and absence of any auxiliary household structures. The central place within a ***diuvorkit*** was assumed by a birch bark *chum* (Fig. 8-1), set up with the entrance facing the trail in the direction of the previous camp. Food preparation and all household activities were carried out outside the dwelling, near the ***guluvun*** 'campfire', as a rule,

*Figure 8. Types of dwelling and household structures of Central Siberian Evenkis: 1–birch **dziu** lodge; 2–**ugdama dziu** fixed bark housing used at the beginning of winter; 3–part of a "fall enclosure" fence with a reindeer passage **khonngo**.*

above which a ***khonan*** 'tripod' was set up [Photo 35]. In some cases, in order to provide protection against mosquitoes for people involved in some minor woodworking or in women's manual tasks, camp inhabitants set up a small smudge in a spot convenient for such chores. Similar smudges were set up in the middle of a *chum* at dusk, to smoke out mosquitoes from the living quarters. The number of *chumy* [set up] at a ***diuvorkit*** camp normally corresponded to the number of families migrating together, although sometimes two small, related families (e.g., young [couple] and their parents) lived together in the same *chum*. Smudges for reindeer were placed between the *chumy*, usually in a ratio of one smudge per 5–6 reindeer (see Photo 5). It is interesting to note that the head woman's spot inside the *chum* was where she could keep an eye on reindeer at the smudges without stepping outside.

On the whole, the smudges (***khammin***) were an effective means of keeping reindeer near the camps; however, they required from the Evenkis a lot of effort to stock enough wood for them. According to our observations, a reindeer herd of 40–50 required an average of ten to fifteen pine logs per day, each 4–5 m long and at least 25 cm in diameter. Among the auxiliary household structures utilize at this time, our data show that a ***delken*** 'store on piles' was used to cache the transported supplies of food, saddles, belongings, and equipment. Structurally, the ***delken*** consisted of a platform made of 4–5 logs of average width, arranged in a row across logs resting on four to six posts 1 m above the ground [Photo 4].

At the end of July and beginning of August (***khunmin, irkin***), with the appearance of a greater number of gadflies and plant bugs, the nomadic groups left the ***diuvorkit*** camps and led their reindeer into shaded pastures located along the banks of small taiga rivers. They traveled along the "primary road," which at this time passed though lowlands, up to 25–30 km away from the route taken during the first half of summer. The general direction of nomadizing was toward the autumn base camp, while the rhythm of movement and duration of stays at stop-over camps was equivalent to those before the arrival at the series of ***diuvorkit*** summer camps. The same is true of the layout of these autumn base camps, and the number of dwelling and household structures set up there. Because in the deep, practically windless parts of the taiga the menace of *gnus* 'biting insects' was greater than on the banks of large rivers, smudges were made for the reindeer not only during the stop-overs. In order to keep reindeer together while traveling, and to ensure that "reindeer don't get mixed up in a caravan," Evenkis used a special kind of traveling smudge, a ***tonku***. The traveling smudge, according to descriptions of older-generation Evenkis who explained its old usage, consisted of a clay pot (later replaced by metal vessels) with narrow neck and holes in the side walls. The traveling smudge was kindled using pieces of rotted wood or cones that had been lit by the camp smudges. During travel, these smudges were carried on a thong in front of each group of reindeer in a caravan. Both the loaded reindeer and those running with calves alongside found themselves within the winding tail of the smoke. Apart from our data, evidence of the usage of similar smudges is found in the materials of a number of investigations (Georgi 1799: 48; Vasilevich 1969: 76; Vitsen 1705: 60). It is also interesting that A. P. Okladnikov reports such pots found among the materials from settlements of the Neolithic Age (1950: 237).

Around the middle of August, the tempo of travel slowed down somewhat, and the duration of stays at one camp increased, sometimes up to between one and two weeks. This change was linked mainly to the commencement of Evenkis' purposeful search for moose. As mentioned earlier [Chapter

2.1], hunters left their kill on a *telgokon* 'temporary platform cache' (Fig. 3). While simple, the construction of the *telgokon* still retained the structural elements common to all stores. Consequently, we suggested earlier that this was, in all probability, the most ancient type of *labaz* (Turov 1975). The kill was laid down on the platform and lifted 2–3 m off the ground, which ensured protection of the meat from rodents and small vermin. To scare bears and wolverines away from the meat, a "long" smudge or a hunter's smoke-saturated clothing were left under the platform. Depending on how far from base camp the animal was captured, either in the same or the opposite direction relative to the main travel route of the family, the families either moved "to the meat" or moved the meat to the base camp, packed on reindeer. In any case, they would "live with the meat in one place for a long time," drying it on a rack called a *teliun*, lattice made of willow twigs, secured to 4–6 stakes driven into the ground. Part of the dried meat was taken along, and part was moved to one of the nearest ***noku dzeptyleruk*** stores along the "primary road" (Fig. 3.2, 4).

In the second half of August and beginning of September (***irkin-sirudian***), the pace of nomadizing increased sharply and so did the distance of daily travel between stop-over camps. During this time, Evenkis strived, by accelerated travel, to reach the areas of autumn base camps located in the vicinity of permanent reindeer mating places. While travelling toward the autumn base camps, hunters set out individually in various directions off the "primary road" in search of moose. These searches did not last more than 2–3 days, whereupon the travel resumed. When their hunt was successful, the dried meat, as in the situation mentioned earlier, was partly taken along, and partly stored in a ***noku*** along the "primary road."

In the second half of September, families usually reached the *osennie ogorody* 'autumn enclosures' in which, joined by a few families, they lived a settled life until mid-October, i.e., until the beginning of the fur hunt. The main types of economic activity during this period comprised reindeer care and mending of clothing and equipment needed for squirrel hunting.

While the majority of a base camp's residents lived a settled life, hunters set out individually to hunt nearby the base camp, with the goal of stocking up on autumn moose meat and hides, considered [at this time of year] to be the most valuable in terms of nutrition and raw materials. Sometimes, hunters searching for prey foraged as far as up to 30–40 km away from the base camp; however, they would not remain out of touch with their families for more than 2–3 days at a time. As mentioned above, the obtained meat was either be taken to a ***noku*** at a winter base camp or left in a ***iumgulo*** cache at the kill site.

Autumn base camps formed a single territorial unit with the winter ***meneien*** base camps, located a distance of no more than 4–5 km away and in the direct vicinity of the spring base camps. The second [Evenki] name for the autumn enclosure, ***khigolorkit***, appears to derive from ***sigelkehe*** or ***sigeleseni*** ('lit. late autumn', 'in autumn when snow falls'; TMS-2: 78–9), although the Evenki dictionary definition does not include a direct translation of the term as "autumn camp." In our opinion, the term "autumn enclosure" defines more precisely the nature of this camp. As a matter of fact, "autumn enclosure" represented a fenced section of the same terrace of a taiga river where one of the "spring enclosures" (i.e., *nengnerkit* camp) was located. Quite often, the "autumn enclosure" was actually more like an extension of the "spring enclosure."

In sum, construction of the autumn fence did not differ from that of a spring one, except for one detail. The **kure** 'autumn fence' had a special gate, the **khonngo**, designed to allow reindeer lagging behind on the approach to camp to enter the enclosed area and join the main herd [Photo 26]. Structurally, the **khonngo** was a 2–3-m gap in the fence (Fig. 6-3). Two auxiliary fences about 30–40 m long were built perpendicular to the entrance, fanning out in the direction away from the fence and coming together on the inside of the fence so that, having entered the enclosure, following the reindeer already driven through it, via the **khonngo** and once inside the reindeer could not get out again.

In general terms, the layout of an autumn base camp (Fig. 5) resembled that of a spring ***nengnerkit***. Moreover, the ***noku*** for food and other things were common to both categories of base camp. Places for *chumy* were selected keeping in mind that the old spots occupied during previous years were considered "unclean." As at the ***nengnerkit***, the moose-hide *chumy* of the "autumn enclosure" were fenced in [Photo 32], along with a ***delkokon*** platform store for travel equipment. With the arrival of cold and inclement weather, in addition to the outdoor ***guluvun*** 'campfire', which was still used to cook food during the midday hours, an iron stove, if available, was set up inside the *chum*, but more often than not a hearth was built. Three sides of the hearth were lined with logs, and an additional pole called the ***chimka***, with the ***ikeptun*** tied to it, was placed inside the dwelling in front of the entrance. While used mostly for heating, food too was cooked on such a fireplace in the morning and evening.

After the snow fell, the families moved into bark *chumy* (Photo 18), built in the same way as the ***golomo*** dwellings documented by G. M. Vasilevich (1969: 112) and similar to the bark *chumy* described in the overview of Evenki dwelling structures [published] in the historical-ethnographic atlas of Siberia (Levin and Potapov 1961: 184–5; Fig. 6, 2). The main frame of the bark *chumy*, as documented by us at base camps of the Erbogachen and Chuna Evenkis, consisted of four thick ***turgu*** poles, with their forks connected at the top. On all four poles, at a distance of 60–70 cm from the top, small forks were left in order to support short horizontal bracket-poles, ***tolboko***. The rest of the frame poles—logs split lengthwise in half [halfrounds—*Ed.*]—were placed next to each other loosely resting against the ***tolboko***, thus creating a round living area with a diameter of 4–6 m. Similarly to an ordinary portable *chum*, two additional ***turgu*** were used to create the ***urkkhe*** 'entrance opening'. Inside the ***golomo***, a ***chimka*** pole was placed to the right or left of the entrance, in the same fashion as in any stationary or long-term dwelling used during the cold season. The frame of the *golomo* was covered with rows of diagonally laid sheets of larch bark, removed in early autumn from trees near the base camp.

It should be noted that our data document two types of *golomo* structures, both described also by G. M. Vasilevich (1969: 112). At camps of the Erbogachen group of Evenkis, we observed personally a *golomo* with an earth-and-sod roof, while in other groups such a construction was preserved only in their memory. According to the available data, in the past this type of *golomo* was the traditional winter dwelling built at the *meneien*; this assertion is in part supported by its second name, *tugedzek* 'wintering site, winter camp, winter dwelling' [Russ. *zimov'e, zimnaia stoianka, zimnik*] (TMS-2: 204; Vasilevich 1969: 112). Among the Evenkis on the Podkamennaia Tunguska, D. A. Cherniak, a student in the Faculty of History at Irkutsk State University, recorded the term *tugedzen* 'wintering at places rich with reindeer moss'.

It is interesting to note that among the Chuna Evenkis we recorded yet another name for a bark *chum*, *dziu irektime* (possibly derived from *irekte* 'larch'). Moreover, when talking to Evenkis, they often referred to the same type of bark *chum* as either *golomo* or *ugdama dziu* [Photo 18]. For example, in the transcription of conversations with the older generation of the Kaplin family (Pangarakai clan, Erbogachen group of Evenkis), their head, V. P. Kaplin, insists on the name *golomo*, explaining that the bark *chum* used to be constructed as a true *golomo*, a quadrangular semi-dugout dwelling; we did encounter such a structure in decayed condition at one of the base camps, now abandoned. At the same time, his wife, M. P. Egorchenok, insisted on the name *ugdama dziu*, explaining that all structures covered with bark were formerly called *ugdama*. The Tungus-Manchurian dictionary (TMS[-2]: 244) includes the terms *uldaksa, ogdan*, and *urdaksa* for the bark of coniferous trees, while G. M. Vasilevich provides a description of a summer bark-covered hut called *ugdama* (1961: 30–9, 1969: 113). The term *golomo* itself is of interest, seeming to consist of two separate words: *golo* (*brevno* 'log', *plakha* 'block', *churka* 'log', *koloda* 'chock'; TMS-1: 159–60) and *mo* (*derevo* 'tree', *zherd'* 'pole', *palka* 'stick', *brevno* 'log', *stolb* 'trunk'; TMS-1: 540–1). All in all, these are only guesses about the origin of this word. At the same time, the data described above allow us to suggest that at the turn of the 20th century, Evenki groups in Central Siberia were familiar with both types of dwelling.

With the onset of continuous freezing daytime temperatures and the first snowfall, which in the Central Siberian taiga occurred in early October, the season of *bol'shaia khod'ba* "long walking" related to the fur hunt began (Vasilevich 1969: 48). However, the nomadizing did not include the entire community living at the base camp, but only those individuals who were directly involved in the squirrel hunt (hunters and their wives). This was recorded in our field observations as well as in the materials of other researchers (e.g., Petri 1930; Suslov 1927; Vasilevich 1962, 1969). B. E. Petri wrote that

8–15 reindeer were enough to meet fully the transportation needs of hunters during the fur-hunting period (1930: 35). Thus, a hunting party, most often consisting of members of one family, set out on the "primary road" in the direction of the areas farthest away from base camp with only some of the reindeer kept by the household. At the same time, members of the territorially adjacent group that were not involved in the hunt shifted to a fully settled life in the permanent winter base camp, after moving the remaining reindeer into pastures rich in reindeer moss. Typically, only the elderly and children unable to participate in the hunt stayed at the ***meneien***; even nursing children were included with their mothers participating in the hunt.

Around the end of November and into early December, after driving their reindeer into deep, snow-covered valleys, the communities in their entirety shifted to a fully settled life in the ***meneien***. With the arrival of the "deep freeze" (***otki***), including all of January (***giraun***), the fur hunt was not carried out. Living the settled life, Evenkis did not, however, entirely cease their subsistence activities; they were only reduced to a minimum. As documented, during this time the Evenkis travelled to trading posts to barter furs, and occasionally they set out on short-term hunting trips into the taiga in search of large game. And by the end of January, during warmer days when squirrel left their nests for brief excursions in search of forage, Evenkis would make short trips on skis to track them down in their nests and stock up on furs for spring trading. In sum, then, while the annual cycle of nomadizing ended upon arrival at the ***meneien*** and driving the reindeer into heavily snow-covered valleys abundant in reindeer moss, subsistence activities aimed at the exploitation of necessary resources available on a seasonal basis continued.

4.5 The Evenki mobile lifestyle

In sum, the materials presented in this chapter suggest that the notion of *brodiazhnichestvo* 'wandering', i.e., a process of spontaneous and uncontrolled exploitation of the inhabited environment by taiga hunter–reindeer herders, should be viewed merely as a convention. [Rather, we assert that] changes in living conditions that were independent of humans but controlled by nature itself, as well as accommodations in timing made by communities to allow the most efficient exploitation of various natural resources of livelihood, permitted the Evenkis of Central Siberia to develop a principled and very orderly system of resource exploitation, which was documented at the turn of the 20th century. Based on the evidence presented above, this system involved the following principal foundations:

- regulation via natural cycles of the annual nomadic lifestyle, during which taiga resources were comprehensively exploited;
- annually recurring transitions between patterns of mobile and settled vital activity (livelihood); and

- nomadizing within a permanent territory along "primary roads" established by several generations, passing through permanent areas of seasonal settlements and associated hunting, fishing, and pasture resources.

In our opinion, some of the perceived *besporiadochnost'* 'disorganization' and spontaneity were introduced in the mobility of taiga hunter–reindeer herders by the commercial fur hunt. Namely, depending on the conditions of the fur hunt, Evenkis were frequently forced to abandon their permanent subsistence territories and exploit new areas; however, they always returned to the old *chumovishcha* '*chum* sites' (Vasilevich 1969: 6, 42; 1972: 166). This circumstance, combined with the Evenkis' pattern of continuous nomadizing and the custom of never returning to an old camp sooner than 2–3 years after leaving it, is the likely reason for the appearance of the term *brodiachie* 'wandering' Tungusy in the literature of the past century [i.e., 19th century—*Ed.*]. The establishment of fur hunting as a commercial activity and its intensive development at the turn of the 20th century stimulated not only the expansion of economic territories and their ensuing assignment to individual owners, but also, increased inevitably the degree of mobility of hunting groups. This happened due to the fact that the autumn and spring travel seasons, both of which were related to the search for fur-bearing animals, were added to the traditional period of summer nomadizing. The same reason accounts for the increased role of transport reindeer and the growing size of the herds managed by individual households (Karlov 1982; Poltoradnev 1934; Suslov 1930).

A comparison between the principles of economic exploitation of resources in the cultural tradition of Central Siberian Evenkis and other typologically similar economic systems of the taiga zone would allow us to place the Evenki economic strategy within the typological series of *foraging economies of Northern Eurasian hunter-fishers that use relatively small herds of domesticated reindeer for transportation*. However, this is a task for separate and rather extensive research; regardless of the large body of comparative data already available, in our opinion, it would require an investigation into the resource exploitation patterns practiced by other ethnic groups. With regard to its extent and nature, such a comparative ethnographic approach would be [generally] akin to the work completed by Iu. B. Simchenko based on materials describing the culture of wild reindeer hunters (1976). Clearly, this research would also need to include an examination of both general patterns of development and the evolution of a given cultural economy system as well as its specific ethno-cultural expressions, for example, in Western and Eastern Siberia, the Amur basin, and the Pacific Far East. We are not convinced that an attempt to identify regional variants of economic exploitation of resources within relatively homogeneous environmental zones would be justified, although such an exercise seems to suggest itself. Here we once again draw attention to the well-known analogies between economy and material culture which, at one time, provided foundations for the formulation of a cultural economy model, and which, even under preliminary comparison, reveal stadial [evolutionary] commonalities.

We purposely refrain from comparing the results of this research with data on other regional groups of Evenkis or other peoples genetically related to them. Based on an assessment of numerous relevant publications (Grigorovskii 1890; Gurvich 1977; Popova 1981; Radde 1857; Tugolukov 1969, 1970; Spevakovskii 1984; Vasilevich 1969; etc.), it is clear that Trans-Baikal Evenkis, Evens, or northern reindeer herding Iakuts, despite some specific differences explicable in terms of ecological particularities of the inhabited territories, are characterized by the same general principles of resource exploitation [as the Central Siberian Evenkis]. Apart from ethnic features of a genetic character, the cultures of all these peoples are united by a common calendar of seasonal transitions between mobile and settled lifestyle, by a link between nomadism and multifaceted exploitation of natural resources, and by the genetically common nature of transport-reindeer husbandry [Photo 19]. According to the author's personal communication with A. I. Arbatskii, an employee of the Laboratory of Archaeology and Ethnography at Irkutsk State University, who spent a great amount of time working among Trans-Baikal Orochens, their culture shows patterns of economic territorial organization, methods of choosing camp and base camp locations, as well as principles of seasonal travel and rhythm of household and subsistence activities that are all identical to those observed by us [among the Evenkis of the Central Siberian taiga].

Of much greater interest are the analogies identified in the cultural tradition of hunter-fishers in Northern Eurasia, who are not genetically related to the Evenkis of Central Siberia. Primarily, these analogies refer to the common characteristics of reindeer husbandry that have been repeatedly observed by both early researchers (Bogoraz-Tan 1933; Maksimov 1928) and contemporary authors (Krupnik 1977; Shnirel'man 1977, 1980; Vainshtein 1960, 1970, 1971; etc.). Among these analogies, in our opinion, it is particularly important to point out the exclusive use of domesticated reindeer for transportation, the relatively small size of individual herds, an increase in the number of reindeer per household concomitant with the development of commercial fur hunting, and the practice of keeping reindeer unconfined in winter and near smudges in summer (Alekseenko 1967; Gemuev and Pelikh 1974; Khomich 1972, 1984, 1986; Koviazin 1936; Kozmin 1981; Lukina 1973, 1984, 1986; Lukina et al. 1975; Pelikh 1981; Prokof'eva 1976; Vainshtein 1972). Also of interest is the simultaneous appearance here, in a pattern similar to the Evenkis of Central Siberia, of reindeer husbandry and changes in the rhythm and intensity of hunting activities (Gogolev et al. 1975; Gurvich and Dolgikh 1970; Petri 1928; Popova 1981). In sum, the similarities in methods of reindeer use for transportation and in methods of herd maintenance are [quite] numerous and symptomatic. At the same time, unlike the Evenki type of reindeer-transport husbandry, the Western Siberian [Samoed], Sayan, and to some extent the Ket models characteristically used sunshades for reindeer in summer. The origin of this custom, perhaps, is related to the differences between the economic orientation of Evenkis and the other ethnic groups. In this regard, it is also symptomatic that in summer the Khanty, Selkups, Forest Nenets, and Kets left their reindeer under the care of herdsmen specially designated by the community, while Evenki families traveled the whole summer together with their reindeer.

Equally interesting is the comparison of traditional folk calendars. Similar to the Evenki culture, the calendars of Iukagir forest groups (Kreinovich 1972), Nanaitsy and Udekhes (Smoliak 1984), Kets (Alekseenko 1967), and Forest Nenets (Khomich 1974), which are phenological by nature, are divided into two semantically different parts: the summer "year" and winter "year." It is important not to overlook the fact that the 13-month calendar, widespread among the cultures of hunter-fishers, is based on a practical knowledge of recurring and seasonally changing environmental-climatic cycles which, like the Evenki culture, were entwined with the overall character of their economy and daily life, and the more general lifestyle (sedentism, seasonal sedentism, nomadism). The grounds for such an assumption are inherent in the formulation *cultural economy* itself. One might suppose that similar environmental characteristics of the taiga zone contributed to the formation of models of spatial organization of subsistence activities and daily life, in the culture of the peoples inhabiting it, that were analogous to those existing in the past. This was apparently expressed in the same methods of establishing seasonal base camps, and in the alternating seasonal exploitation of various patches of "communal" resources.

It is interesting to note that certain organizational elements of the hunting–reindeer herding economy of Central Siberian Evenkis reach beyond the boundaries of ethnic cultures. For example, the Nganasans have a similarly divided calendar year into summer and winter cycles (Popov 1948: 15–16). Furthermore, the Saami and Nganasan methods of reindeer husbandry entail, in particular, a continued rotation of pastures, similar to the Evenki method (Chernolusskii 1972: 102, 206–7, 214–15; Popov 1948: 26–7).

Extending the scope of comparison to the cultures classified as *upper type of foraging economy*, including its subtypes of *peshie* 'on-foot' and *konnye* 'horse-riding' hunters of the temperate and northern (taiga) zones (Markov 1979), we can identify intriguing similarities in the cultures of North American Indians. For instance, in the past, the Montana and Naskapi, Cree, Kauchodin, Tlingit, Blackfoot, Kyowa, Pawnee, and other tribes employed various combinations of an integrated hunting-fishing-gathering economy. In a fashion similar to the Evenkis of Central Siberia, the economy of these tribes focused on the most economically efficient seasonal exploitation of food resources. Common to all of them was the practice of preparing supplies of meat for the future and caching these provisions in stores. In a manner also similar to the Evenkis, their subsistence lifestyle, particularly the hunting and transportation of loads, employed small herds of horses (15–20 head) that, once introduced, invariably brought about a number of changes in the structure of their nomadizing, their settlements, and degree of mobility of the sometimes unmounted hunters (Averkieva 1974: 90, 257–9, 265, 268, 279–80; Helm and Leacock 1978: 363–5, 375; Veltfish 1978: 196–9; Ziber 1937: 20–4). It is also useful to note that the rhythm of nomadic economic activity among North American Indians has previously been observed to be similar to that of the Evenkis, as have the layout and types of settlements, their territorial distribution and function (Averkieva 1974: 48, 56–7; Helm and Leacock 1978: 385–6; Ziber 1937: 20–1). Based on these characteristics, the lifestyle of the temperate and northern (taiga) hunters has been commonly classified recently as "sedentary–mobile" type, characterized by "mobile modes of subsistence" (Andrianov 1978: 124; Markov 1979: 180, 1981: 84–5; Semenov 1973: 53–7).

Apart from those mentioned above, there are also well-known analogies in the material culture: tools, hunting equipment, dwelling and household structures, and household items. Among them, we would like to point out the portable *chum* 'conical dwelling structures' that were extremely widespread in the cultures of Siberian hunter-fishers and hunter–reindeer herders, and the even more widely encountered and structurally standard (built on posts) stores for food and belongings. The latter are of interest not only due to the similarities in their design. Indeed, we discovered in the Erbogachen group of Evenkis that a great number of grave surface structures dating from the late 19th century till the 1950s bear a remarkably strong structural resemblance to the household *labaz* stores on posts as described above (Photos 20–23). This is all the more interesting in the context of the widespread aerial disposal of the dead among the cultures of Siberian peoples, as well as the ritual *ambarchyk* 'little cache' of the Khanty, the latter being structurally similar to some of the household structures discussed here and to dwellings in the cultures of Amur peoples (Kreinovich 1973). Stores on posts, known essentially among all hunter-fisher groups of Northern Eurasia, display territorial associations with specific types of permanent base camps and seasonally used camps that are practically identical to those documented among the Evenkis (Alekseenko 1974; Dolgikh 1971; Konakov 1983; Khomich 1972, 1984; Kreinovich 1972; Larkin 1964; Sokolova 1963; Taksami 1961; Vdovin 1973; etc.). Considered to be one of the most important elements of the traditional culture, and shaping and organizing to a known extent the environment inhabited by hunter-fishers (Sem 1983), the stationary and lightweight portable dwellings and household structures on posts quite likely played an important role in the spatial organization of their economic activities.

On the whole, we view the existence of analogies among indigenous cultures of Siberia, including those listed above as well as a number of others, as being justified. Evidently, they are the combined result of similarly unfolding adaptive processes acting on societies at the same cultural stage and within a similar natural environment, as well as the product of common (at least initially) patterns of economic exploitation of that environment.

Conclusions

The initial objective of the research described here was to reconstruct the most general and important aspects of the culture of mobile hunter–reindeer herders, specifically, in the Evenkis of Central Siberia at the turn of the 20th century, with a particular focus on their methods of economic exploitation of taiga resources. Clearly, each territorially distinct group developed its own locally specific solutions to achieve the desired economic goals, in response to the characteristic features of the exploited environment. Undoubtedly, of great importance in this regard were the intensity and permanency of Evenki contacts with Russian farmers and traders, as well as with Buriat {check} and Iakut cattle herders, and also the extent to which Evenkis were integrated into the economic structure of the Russian state. Local factors such as number of reindeer per household, number of people in a family and its composition, income derived from the fur trade, and others were of great importance in the development of regional economic particularities. This is why we regard the reconstructed process of economic exploitation of taiga resources as a general model in which it is possible to identifiy the following patterns common to all Evenkis of Central Siberia:

1. For the most part, economic exploitation of resources was a long-term (multi-year) process combining hunting, fishing, and reindeer herding activities, all facilitated by the ecological characteristics of the environment. The effective and rational exploitation of natural resources by Evenkis was ensured by the specific rhythm of economic and subsistence activities, as well as by the focus of procurement activities, which shifted seasonally between various food resources.

2. The "mobile–settled" character of subsistence activities should be considered the key element of the ecologically motivated comprehensive exploitation of taiga resources. Moreover, mobility as a means of organizing the seasonally variable exploitation of a series of hunting, fishing, and pasturing resources appears to have been the optimal strategy available at that time to meet all the needs of a given community.

3. The mobile strategy of exploitation of taiga resources was integrated with a schedule of migrations implemented within the boundaries of a permanent economic territory and along permanent routes, themselves associated with a structure and spatial distribution of base and short-term camps of all categories. In this context, *brodiazhnichestvo* 'wandering, mobility' should be viewed as a means of planned and efficient exploitation of natural resources.

This model, which emerged around the turn of the 20th century, integrated the traditional natural aspects of the economy (i.e., large game hunting, fishing, transport-reindeer husbandry, and gathering) with a new commercial element (i.e., fur hunting), which led to changes in Evenkis' organization and implementation of economic activities. This trend is best seen in the increased role of transport reindeer, a slight increase in the number of reindeer per household herd, and increase in the mobility of Evenki hunting–reindeer herding groups forced to reckon with the requirements of reindeer husbandry during summer nomadizing. Another consequence of the increased role of fur hunting in the overall economic system of Evenkis in Central Siberia involved extension of the season and distance of annual migrations, both related to the autumn and spring fur hunts. Moreover, we believe that the development of commercial fur hunting is linked to the establishment of the tradition of preparing supplies of meat and other foodstuffs for long-term storage, as well as the tradition of concentrated caching of these supplies in ground-level and elevated stores. Serving as intermediate supply bases for hunters during the procurement seasons, the stores preserved their overall traditional construction details and were located along the primary roads [*tsentral'nye dorogi*] of the mobile hunters, in the neighbourhood of upcoming fur hunts.

Our study represents essentially the first attempt at systematic generalization of various materials on Evenki economy. This publication of a large body of new data broadens and, to a certain extent, frames and gives order to the existing knowledge about the traditional economy of these taiga hunter-fishers. This work also has useful value in that it systemizes the materials about Evenkis' historically accumulated practical experience of interacting with their environment. Further examination of this topic remains one of the most pressing tasks in [Russian] ethnography. We also hope that the general model reconstructed here will be useful for retrospective research on earlier forms and methods of economic exploitation of resources by Evenki hunting groups. These expectations are based on our understanding, as revealed by this study, that the principles governing the organization and implementation of Evenki economic activity did not emerge out of nowhere; indeed, they developed and improved upon much older principles.

Examination of the historically acquired experience regarding the use of nature by the peoples of Siberia has become a significant and multifaceted research objective, giving impetus for a new field of *ethnogeography* to develop within the existing discipline of *historical geography* [in Russian scholarship].

Today, this is a topic of national importance due to the fact that, in the Siberian context, many government economic projects, implemented without taking into account the historical experience of indigenous peoples, have often led to unjustified harm. In this respect, dedicated ethnographic and interdisciplinary ethnogeographic and ethnosociological research would seem to be particularly relevant. Thus, the work undertaken by us may be considered the beginning of an exploration of this new direction, and its results and main conclusions will doubtless be subject to verification via future studies.

Glossary

compiled by K. Maryniak

Proper names and administrative units are in roman type (Enisei, oblast). Russian-language terms, some of which are non-standard, are in italics (*belka*), except those that have entered the English language (artel, shaman). Evenki terms are in the nominative singular and are listed in an italicized bold font (***delken***), with a virgule separating dialectal variations.[14]

Term	Definition
amaka	bear
amanat	hostages
ambarchyk	dim. of *ambar* 'cache, storehouse'; cf. *labaz*
an'iani / anngani	lit. 'year', winter season
aran / kharan	fireplace in a *chum*
artel	here, a co-operative team; the term is taken from the name for Russian and early Soviet associations of workers or peasants for collective effort
bagdaka	occasional hunting for woodland reindeer
baksa / baksha / bakcha / bakshi	posts supporting a storage platform
belka	squirrel; *belkovka* is a colloquial term for 'squirrel hunt'
beresta	birch bark; *berestianka* is a local Siberian term for a small birch bark boat with a wooden frame
bol'shaia khod'ba / bol'shoe shaganie	lit. 'long walk', a colloquial name for the fur hunt period, which lasts 4–5 of the 7 months of the autumn/winter half-year in the Evenki calendar
brodiachii	lit. 'wandering', though 'mobile' is a more current definition; *brodiazhnichestvo* 'wandering, mobile lifestyle' is interpreted by M. G. Turov as a means of methodical and frugal natural resource usage
buchivun / buchilaun / butivun	rack for drying meat over a fire; cf. ***telivun***

---

14. Additional variations are taken from the Baikal Archaeology Project's translation of A. A. Sirina's Russian monograph on Katanga Evenkis (Sirina 2006). —*Ed.*

Term	Definition
chernotropa	lit. 'black trail', a path on which the snow has melted
chimka / simka	special vertical pole in a *chum*; cf. **ikeptun**
choom	English form of *chum*
chum	among the nomadic peoples of Siberia, a conical hut, tent, or lodge of fir poles covered with skins or birch bark, latterly canvas (analogous to the North American tipi); *chumovishche* is the location where the *chum* is erected, or a colloquial term for the camp overall. See **diu**.
dedushka	dim. of *ded* 'grandfather'
delken / delkan	storage platform on posts; Russ. *labaz*
delkokon / delkekon	small storage platform for travel gear
diu / dziu	transportable conical tent or lodge covered with skins, birch-bark mats, or canvas, tipi; Russ. *chum*
diugani / diovani / diuvani	summer
diuvorkit / diovodian / diuvodian / diugadian	summer camp; cf. *stoianka*
dymokur	smudge. See **khammin**.
dzeptyleruk	"central road," the main travel route
dziu	See **diu**.
ektenkire / oktankire	"time of snow melting," March–April
elbenel / ellun	covering for the lower part of a *chum*; cf. **niuk**
giraun / giravun	"month of hunting on snow crust," January–February
gobchik / golbets	trapezoidal mortuary structure made of logs
golomo	stationary pit dwelling with a wooden frame, usu. pyramidal in form and covered with sod or bark; cf. **ugdama**
gubernia	in the Russian Empire and Soviet Union, a regional administrative-territorial unit above the uezd, okrug, or raion; province
guluvun	campfire for cooking food
iagel'	reindeer moss (*Cladonia rangiferina*), also Icelandic moss (*Cetraria islandica*); *iagel'nik* is a lichen patch or pasture

Term	Definition
iasak	impost or tribute taken in furs for the imperial Russian crown
ikeptun / *ikepten*	vertical post in a *chum*, or a horizontal pole for the **olloun** hearth-hook
irkin	"fattening time for animals," around the second half of August and early September, when there are fewer biting insects
iumgulo	a type of meat cache
kaltamni / *kaltan* / *kaltar* / *kaltala*	half-lodge used in summer travel; cf. ***diu***
kamys / *kamus*	leather made of reindeer or moose leg skins
kel'che	toboggan; Russ. *volokusha*
khammin / *sammin* / *samngin*	smoky fire, esp. for driving away mosquitoes, smudge; Russ. *dymokur*
kharan	See ***aran.***
kheran / *seran*	secondary frame pole in a *chum*; cf. ***turgu***
khokto / *khokhto* / *khoktokon*	flooring in a *chum*, usu. of pine branches; also, a pack trail
khona / *sona* / *suona*	1. north; 2. frame pole in a *chum*; 3. smoke hole in a *chum*
khonan	trivet tripod above the ***guluvun*** cooking fire
khonngo	one-way gate in a ***kure*** reindeer fence
kiramki	leister, fish spear
kochevoi	nomadic; cf. *brodiachii*
konnyi	mounted, or horse-drawn
korennoi	indigenous; cf. *tuzemnyi, inorodnyi*
kormozashchitnaia stantsiia	lit. 'forage-and-protective station', a term used to refer to sheltered feeding ranges used by moose or deer in the taiga
koto	bear spear; Russ. *pal'ma*
kraevedenie	lit. 'territory studies', usu. translated in Russia as 'local lore'; the closest normal English equivalent is 'regional studies'

Term	Definition
krai	territory, more specifically, an administrative-territorial unit in the late Imperial period, the Soviet period, and in the Russian Federation; above the raion and the okrug, the krai is roughly equivalent jurisdictionally to a gubernia or oblast, but is much larger in area
kure / kurekan	fence enclosing an autumn or spring camp
labaz	generic term for various kinds of storage structures; specifically, a storage platform on posts. See **delken**, **noku**.
laika	a local breed of hunting dog, Siberian Husky
lapnik	pine or spruce branches
lenok	*Brachymystax lenok*, of the Salmonidae family
lodoshnyi	using boats
los'	moose. See *sokhatit'*.
malaia khod'ba	spring travel or nomadizing
malochislennye narody	lit. 'unnumerous' or 'numerically small' peoples, a Russian statistical and demographic category for minorities with a population of less than 30,000; also sometimes officially referred to as *malye narody* 'small peoples'
miagkaia rukhliad', miagkoe zoloto	lit. 'soft stuff, soft gold'—fur as a commodity
muchun	"month of the first greenery," early spring
nalim	burbot
nast	thin crust of ice over snow
meneien / meneen	winter camp
niuk	*chum* covering made of *rovduga*; cf. **elbenel, uneken**
noku / neku	cache or store on posts; Russ. *labaz*
oblast	in the USSR and FSU countries, an administrative-territorial unit above the county-level raion; province

Term	Definition
okrug	during the 1920s, an administrative-territorial unit within a krai; sometimes translated as 'national area', they are latterly established for numerically small peoples of the Far North and Far East who inhabit large and sparsely populated areas
oktankire / *oktiinkire*	See *ektenkire*.
olenevodstvo	reindeer husbandry
olenii mokh	reindeer moss. See *iagel'*.
olennyi	using reindeer, reindeer-herding
olenukha	cow reindeer; cf. *vazhenka*
olloun / *oldoun* / *ollan*	hook for *khonan* cooking tripod
pal'ma	bear spear. See *koto*.
pektyrevun / *pykteraun*	wooden block on a rope hung around the neck of a restive reindeer to restrict its movement
peshii	unmounted, on foot
ponage	board-frame backpack; Russified as *poniaga*
rovduga	suede, usually of reindeer, caribou, or moose hides (M. G. Turov defines it only as moose hide); cf. *kamys*
rybolovstvo	fishing, harvesting fish
samngin	See *khammin.*
sarana	coral lily (*Lilium pumilum*)
seran	See *kheran*.
shaman	person who acts as an intermediary between the natural and supernatural worlds, using magic to cure illness, foretell the future, control spiritual forces, etc.
sig	whitefish
sidiachii	lit. 'sitting', settled; cf. *lodoshnyi, brodiachii*
sirudian	"month of the reindeer rut," late August and early September
sobachii	using dogs; cf. *konnyi, olennyi, peshii*
sokhatit'	hunt moose; from *sokhatyi,* a local name for moose (Russ. *los'*)
stoianka	stop-over camp. See ***urikit***.
stoibishche	long-term base camp

Term	Definition
taimen'	a large salmonid fish, *Hucho taimen*, native to the lakes and rivers of Siberia
telgokon / telgekon	a type of platform cache for meat
teliun / telivun / taliun / talivun	net made of twigs on which meat and fish are cured over the fire or in the sun; cf. ***buchivun***
tipi	North American name for a choom or *chum*
tungusy / tunguzy / tangusy / tongusy	Iakut name for the Evenki people, known by them to live on the Tungus River
tungusovedenie	Tungus (Evenki) studies
tugeni	winter
turan	"month of the return of the crows," April
turgu / tur	main pole in a *chum*; cf. ***kheran***
tuzemnyi	native, aboriginal; cf. *korennoi, inorodnyi*
uchak / uguchak / ukchak	reindeer used for carrying people; a riding reindeer
ugdama / ugdan	stationary dwelling with a rectangular base, a frame covered with bark, and a flat roof; cf. ***golomo***
ukikit	fishing enclosure, fishing spot
uldaksa / ugdaksa	bark covering for a cache
uneken / unokon	covering for upper part of a *chum*; cf. ***niuk***
uprava	in the Russian Empire at the end of the 19th century, a lower-level administrative district for non-Russian minorities; cf. *okrug*
urikit	short-term camp, from ***urikit*** 'to stop'; Russ. *stoianka*
urke	entrance to a *chum*; gateway in a ***kure*** reindeer fence
uvo / ugo	U-shaped log or wood block enclosure around the fireplace in a *chum*
vazhenka	reindeer dam; cf. *olenukha*
volokusha	toboggan. See ***kel'che***.
Yakut	common spelling of Iakut
Yenisei	common spelling of Enisei
zimov'e, zimnik	winter camp, wintering site

References

ALIE [Archive of the Leningrad Chapter of the USSR Academy of Sciences' Institute of Ethnography]. St. Petersburg.

ALIE. 14/1/167.* A.A. Popov manuscript materials [field notes] on hunting equipment of Siberian peoples in the 19th century and until 1925 (1951).

ALIE. 22/1/37. G.M. Vasilevich manuscript materials [field notes] on Evenki language and folklore.

ALIE. K-V/1/139–142. Russian translation by V.G. Trisman of the chapter on Siberia from N.C. Witsen's *Noord en Oost Tartaryen,* 2nd edn. Amsterdam 1705.

Alekseenko, E.A. 1967. *Kety: Istoriko-etnograficheskie ocherki.* Leningrad.

———. 1974. Narodnye znaniia ketov. In *Sotsial'naia organizatsiia i kul'tura narodov Severa* 218–30. Moscow.

———. 1976. Sredstva peredvizheniia ketov. *Sibirskii etnograficheskii sbornik* 64, no. 3: 64–97.

———. 1986. Promyslovaia kul'tura naseleniia Turukhanskogo regiona. In *Kul'turnye traditsii narodov Sibiri* 57–94. Leningrad.

Alimurzaev, G.N. 1981. Osobennosti pervobytnogo obshchestva i ego sviazi s okruzhaiushchei sredoi. In M.P. Kim (ed.) *Obshchestvo i priroda: Istoricheskie etapy i formy vzaimodeistviia* 159–63. Moscow: Nauka.

Andrianov, B.V. 1978. Neosedloe naselenie mira i opyt ego kartografirovaniia. In *Problemy etnicheskoi geografii i kartografii* 119–40. Moscow.

Andrianov, B.V., and N.N. Cheboksarov. 1972. Khoziaistvenno-kul'turnye tipy i problema ikh kartografirovaniia. *Sovetskaia etnografiia,* no. 2: 3–16.

Anisimov, A.F. 1936. *Rodovoe obshchestvo evenkov.* Leningrad.

Antropova, V.V. 1952. Iz istorii transporta u narodov Sibiri. *Kratkie soobshcheniia Instituta etnografii* 15:23–26.

Arutiunov, S.A. 1981. Obychai, ritual, traditsiia. *Sovetskaia etnografiia,* no. 2: 97–99.

---

* Numbering indicates *fond* 'collection' / *opis* 'accession' / *delo* 'file'.

———. 1982. Printsipy i zakonomernosti vkhozhdeniia innovatsii v kul'turu etnosa. *Sovetskaia etnografiia,* no. 1: 8–21.

Averkieva, Iu.P. 1974. *Indeitsy Severnoi Ameriki.* Moscow.

Bakhrushin, S.V. 1955. Ostiatskie i vogul'skie kniazhestva v XVI–XVII vv. *Sbornik izbrannykh trudov po istorii Sibiri XVI–XVII vv.* 3:86–152.

Bakhta, V.M., and T.V. Seniuta. 1972. Lokal'naia gruppa, sem'ia i uzy rodstva v obshchestve aborigenov Avstralii. In *Okhotniki, sobirateli, rybolovy* 68–90. Leningrad.

Bannikov, A.G. 1965. O promysle losia. In *Biologiia i promysel losia* 3–8. Moscow.

Bannikov, A.G., and V.P. Teplov. 1964. *Dvizhenie chislennosti i plotnosti losia v RSFSR.* Moscow.

Baskin, L.M. 1970. *Severnyi olen': Ekologiia i povedenie.* Moscow.

———. 1976. *Povedenie kopytnykh zhivotnykh.* Moscow.

———. 1978. Severnyi olen'. In *Krupnye khishchniki i kopytnye zveri: Les i ego obitateli* 160–90. Moscow.

Bogoraz-Tan, V.G. 1928. *Rasprostranenie kul'tury na zemle.* Moscow.

———. 1933. Olenevodstvo: Vozniknovenie, razvitie i perspektivy. *Izvestiia AN SSSR* (Moscow: Laboratory of Genetics), pp. 219–251.

Bromlei, Iu.V. 1973. *Etnos i etnografiia.* Moscow.

———. 1981a. Kul'tura i etnicheskie aspekty ekologii. In M.P. Kim (ed.) *Obshchestvo i priroda: Istoricheskie etapy i formy vzaimodeistviia* 85–95. Moscow: Nauka.

———. 1981b. *Sovremennye problemy etnografii: Ocherki istorii i teorii.* Moscow.

———. 1983. *Ocherki teorii etnosa.* Moscow.

Butinov, N.A. 1968. Pervobytno-obshchinnyi stroi (osnovnye etapy i lokal'nye varianty). In *Problemy istorii dokapitalisticheskikh obshchestv.* Moscow.

———. 1977. O spetsifike proizvodstvennykh otnoshenii obshchinno-rodovoi formatsii. *Sovetskaia etnografiia,* no. 3: 47–58.

Chernolusskii, V.V. 1972. *V kraiu letuchego kamnia: Zapiski etnografa.* Moscow.

Chesnov, Ia.V. 1982. *Ob etnicheskoi spetsifike khoziaistvenno-kul'turnykh tipov.* Moscow.

Clark, P. [Klark, P.] 1863. Ocheul'skie i Tuturskie tungusy Verkholenskoi okrugi. *Zap. SORGO* 6:87–96.

Cotlow, L. [Kotlou, L.] 1960. *Zanzabuku: Opasnoe puteshestvie.* Moscow. [Russian translation of *Zanzabuku: Dangerous Safari.* New York: Rinehart 1956]

Danilova, L.V. 1968. Diskussionnye problemy teorii dokapitalisticheskikh obshchestv. In *Problemy istorii dokapitalisticheskikh obshchestv* 27–66. Moscow.

———. 1981. Prirodnye i sotsial'nye factory proizvoditel'nykh sil na dokapitalisticheskikh stadiiakh obshchestvennogo razvitiia. In M.P. Kim (ed.) *Obshchestvo i priroda: Istoricheskie etapy i formy vzaimodeistviia* 109–24. Moscow: Nauka.

Davidson, B. [Devidson, B.] 1975. *Afrikantsy: Vvedenie v istoriiu kul'tury.* Moscow. [Russian translation of *The Africans: An Entry to Cultural History.* London: Longmans 1969]

Dolgikh, B.O. Starinnye zemlianki ketov na reke Podkamennoi Tunguske. *Sovetskaia etnografiia,* no. 2: 156–65.

———. 1960. *Rodovoi i plemennoi sostav narodov Sibiri v XVII v.* Moscow.

Dolgikh, T.B. 1971. Traditsionnoe zhilishche lesnykh nentsev r. Pur. *Sovetskaia etnografiia,* no. 4: 93–103.

Dorogstaiskii, B. 1925. *Pushnye i promyslovye zveri Pribaikal'ia i ikh ekonomicheskoe znachenie.* Irkutsk.

Dulov, A.V. 1983. *Geograficheskaia sreda i istoriia Rossii, konets XV–seredina XIX v.* Moscow.

Engels, F. n.d. Proiskhozhdenie sem'i, chastnoi sobstvennosti i gosudarstva [Origins of the Family, Private Property, and the State]. In K. Marks and F. Engels. *Sochineniia* 23–178, 2nd edn., vol. 21.

———. n.d.-a. Rol' truda v protsesse prevrashcheniia obez'iany v cheloveka [The Part Played by Labor in the Transition from Ape to Man]. In K. Marks and F. Engels. *Sochineniia* 486–99, 2nd edn., vol. 20.

GAIO [State Archive of Irkutsk Oblast]. Irkutsk.

GAIO. 26/3/4.* On toll-taking from Tunguses by [Russians], with prohibition of toll-taking.

GAIO. 26/3/8. Data on standardized prices.

* Numbering indicates *fond* 'collection' / *opis* 'accession' / *delo* 'file'.

GAIO. 26/3/59. On markets in Orlenga volost.

GAIO. 32/4/245. Summary of food prices in the second half of August 1914.

GAIO. 32/34/31. Summary of Buriats and Tunguses leading a nomadic lifestyle.

GAIO. 150/1/27. Documents regarding allocation of hunting grounds: On issue of lead and powder on credit.

GAIO. 161/2/907. Data on markets for 1904 throughout Irkutsk gubernia.

GAIO. 161/4/409. Price schedule for goods acquired as *iasak* and sundry taxes.

GAIO. 461/2/1. On hunting grounds.

GAIO. 461/2/7. On *iasak* taxes and prices for various furs: On commercial hunting and fishing.

Gal'perin, I.S. 1977. *Fiziologiia cheloveka i zhivotnykh*. Moscow.

Gemuev, I.N., and G.I. Pelikh. 1974. Sel'kupskoe olenevodstvo. *Sovetskaia etnografiia*, no. 3: 83–95.

Georgi, I.G. 1799. *Opisanie vsekh v Rossiiskom gosudarstve obitaiushchikh narodov...*. St. Petersburg.

Girusov, E.V. 1981. Osnovnye istoricheskie etapy vzaimodeistviia obshchestva i prirody. In *Obshchestvo i priroda: Istoricheskie etapy i formy vzaimodeistviia*. Moscow.

Gogolev, E.V., I.S. Gurvich, I.M. Zolotareva, and M.N. Zhornitskaia. 1975. *Iukagiry: Istoriko-etnograficheskii ocherk*. Novosibirsk.

Gracheva, G.N. 1986. Nekotorye cherty khoziaistvennoi deiatel'nosti narodnostei severa Srednei Sibiri v proshlom i v nastoiashchem. In *Kul'turnye traditsii narodov Sibiri* 95–120. Leningrad.

Grigorovskii, N. 1890. Poezdka na Verkhniuiu Angaru." *Izvestiia VSORGO* 21, no. 2: 1–29.

Gromov, G.G. 1981. Khoziaistvennyi areal kak forma vzaimodeistviia obshchestva i prirody. In M.P. Kim (ed.) *Obshchestvo i priroda: Istoricheskie etapy i formy vzaimodeistviia* 330–8. Moscow: Nauka.

GUGK [Chief Administration for Geodesy and Cartography]. 1962. *Atlas Irkutskoi oblasti*. Moscow–Irkutsk: Ministry of Geology and Protection of Underground Resources of the USSR.

Gurvich, I.S. 1977. *Kul'tury severnykh iakutov-olenevodov*. Moscow.

Gurvich, I.S., and B.O. Dolgikh (eds.) 1970. *Obshchestvennyi stroi u narodov Severnoi Sibiri, XVII–nachalo XX v.* Moscow: Nauka.

Gurvich, I.S., B.O. Dolgikh, and A.V. Smoliak. 1970. Khoziaistvo narodov Severa v XVII–XX vv. In I.S. Gurvich and B.O. Dolgikh (eds.) *Obshchestvennyi stroi u narodov Severnoi Sibiri v XVII – nachale XX vv.* 38–70. Moscow: Nauka.

Gvozdetskii, N.A., and N.I. Mikhailov. 1978. *Fizicheskaia geografiia SSSR.* Moscow.

Helm, J., and E.B. Leacock. [Khelm, Dzh., E.B. Likok.] 1978. Okhotnich'i plemena Subarkticheskoi Kanady. In *Severoamerikanskie indeitsy* 361–97. Moscow. [Russian translation of "The Hunting Tribes of Subarctic Canada" in E.B. Leacock and N.O. Lurie (eds.) *North American Indians in Historical Perspective* 343–74. New York: Random House 1971]

Iordanskii, V.B. 1982. *Khaos i garmoniia.* Moscow.

Its, R.F. 1982. Sovremennye ekologicheskie problemy i traditsionnoe prirodopol'zovanie narodov Severa." *Vestnik AN SSSR*, no. 5: 67–71.

Iurgenson, P.B. 1964. Struktura i sostav populiatsii losia v mestnykh okhotnich'ikh ugod'iakh. In *Biologiia i promysel losia* 13–34. Moscow.

Ivanov, V.N. 1978. *Russkie uchenye o narodakh Severo-Vostoka Azii.* Iakutsk.

Jochelson, W. [Iokhel'son, V.M.] 1898. Ocherki zveropromyshlennosti i torgovli mekhami v Kolymskom okruge. *Izv. VSORGO* 10, no. 3.

Kabo, V.R. 1968. Pervobytnaia obshchina okhotnikov i sobiratelei (po avstraliiskim materialam). In *Problemy istorii dokapitalisticheskikh obshchestv* 223–65. Moscow.

———. 1979. Teoreticheskie problemy rekonstruktsii pervobytnosti. In *Etnografiia kak istochnik rekonstruktsii istorii pervobytnogo obshchestva* 60–107. Moscow.

———. 1981. Pervobytnoe obshchestvo i priroda. In M.P. Kim (ed.) *Obshchestvo i priroda: Istoricheskie etapy i formy vzaimodeistviia* 149–58. Moscow: Nauka.

———. 1982. Istoriia pervobytnogo obshchestva i etnografiia. In *Etnos v doklassovykh i ranneklassovykh obshchestvakh* 53–67. Moscow.

Kalachev, I.V. 1871. Obraz zhizni koriakov i tungusov, zhivshikh v Irkutskoi oblasti v 1766 godu. *Izv. VSORGO* 2, no. 3: 43–45.

Kaletskii, A.A. 1978. Los'. In *Krupnye khishchniki i kopytnye zveri: Les i ego obitateli* 87–128. Moscow.

Karelov, A.M. 1979. *Traditsionnyi severnyi kompleks otraslei BAMa.* Irkutsk.

Karlov, V.V. 1982. *Evenki v XVII – nachale XX v.: Khoziaistvo i sotsial'naia struktura.* Moscow.

Kharuzina, V. 1928. *Tungusy.* Moscow–Leningrad.

Khomich, L.V. 1972. Nekotorye osobennosti khoziaistva i kul'tury lesnykh nentsev. In *Okhotniki, sobirateli, rybolovy* 199–214. Leningrad.

———. 1974. Materily po narodnym znaniiam nentsev. In *Sotsial'naia organizatsiia i kul'tura narodov Severa* 231–48. Moscow.

———. 1984. Ob inoetnicheskikh elementakh v traditsionnoi kul'ture nentsev. In *Etnokul'turnye kontakty narodov Sibiri* 14–29. Leningrad.

———. 1986. Kul'turnye traditsii v trudovoi deiatel'nosti i material'noi kul'ture olenevodov severa Zapadnoi Sibiri. In *Kul'turnye traditsii narodov Sibiri* 12–41. Leningrad.

Kim, M.P. (ed.). 1981. *Obshchestvo i priroda: Istoricheskie etapy i formy vzaimodeistviia.* Moscow: Nauka.

Kim, M.P., and L.V. Danilova. 1981. Prirodnoe i sotsial'noe v istoricheskom protsesse. In M.P. Kim (ed.) *Obshchestvo i priroda: Istoricheskie etapy i formy vzaimodeistviia* 6–19. Moscow: Nauka.

Kolosov, A.M. 1980. *Zoogeografiia Dal'nego Vostoka.* Moscow.

Konakov, N.D. 1983. *Komi: Okhotniki i rybolovy vo vtoroi polovine XIX– nachale XX v.* Moscow.

Kopylov, I.P. 1928. *Tungusskoe khoziaistvo Lensko-Kirenskogo kraia: Po dannym ekspeditsii 1927 goda.* Novosibirsk.

Kopylov, I.P., A.V. Dobrovol'skii, and I.A. Shergin. 1940. *Promyslovye zveri Irkutskoi oblasti.* Irkutsk.

Kostrov, N.A. 1857. Ocherki Turukhanskogo kraia. *Zap. SORGO* (St. Petersburg) 4:61–175.

Koviazin, N.M. 1936. *Ocherki po promyslovomu khoziaistvu i olenevodstvu Krainego Severa.* Leningrad.

Koz'min, V.A. 1981. Olenevodstvo narodov Zapadnoi Sibiri v kontse XIX– nachale XX vv. (problemy proiskhozhdeniia i tipologiia. Candidate of History diss. Leningrad.

Kozlov, V.I. 1971. Etnos i territoriia. *Sovetskaia etnografiia*, no. 1: 89–100.

———. 1983. Osnovnye problemy etnicheskoi ekologii. *Sovetskaia etnografiia*, no. 1: 3–16.

Kozlov, V.I., and V.V. Pokshishevskii. 1973. Etnografiia i geografiia. *Sovetskaia etnografiia*, no. 1: 2–13.

Kozodoev, I.I. 1977. O neobkhodimom pribavochnom produkte v pervobytnoi ekonomike. *Sovetskaia etnografiia*, no. 3: 59–63.

Kreinovich, E.A. 1972. Iz zhizni iukagirov na rubezhe XIX i XX vv. *Strany i narody Vostoka* (Moscow) 13:56–92, *Strany i narody basseina Tikhogo okeana*.

———. 1973. *Nivkhgu*. Moscow.

Kriuchkov, V.V. 1979. *Sever: Priroda i chelovek, perspektivy osvoeniia*. Leningrad.

Krivoshapkin, M.F. 1863. Ob ostiakakh, tungusakh i prochikh inorodtsakh Eniseiskogo okruga. *Zap. SORGO* 6: 39–86.

Krupnik, I.I. 1975. Prirodnaia sreda i evoliutsiia tundrovogo olenevodstva. In *Karta, skhema i chislo v etnicheskoi geografii* 26–43. Moscow.

———. 1977. Faktory ustoichivosti i razvitiia traditsionnogo khoziaistva narodov Severa. Abstract from Candidate of History diss. Moscow.

Lar'kin, V.G. 1964. *Orochi*. Moscow.

Lashov, B.V., and O.P. Litovka. 1982. *Sotsial'no-ekonomicheskie problemy razvitiia narodnostei Krainego Severa*. Leningrad.

Lashuk, L.P. 1970. O nekotorykh aspektakh traktovki pervichnoi formatsii. *Sovetskaia etnografiia*, no. 5: 72–83.

Levin, M.G. 1936. Evenki severnogo Pribaikal'ia. *Sovetskaia etnografiia*, no. 2: 71–78.

Levin, M.G., and N.N. Cheboksarov. 1955. Khoziaistvenno-kul'turnye tipy i istoriko-etnograficheskie oblasti. *Sovetskaia etnografiia*, no. 4.

Levin, M.G., and L.P. Potapov (eds.). 1956. *Narody Sibiri*. Moscow–Leningrad.

Levin, M.G., and L.P. Potapov (eds.). 1961. *Istoriko-etnograficheskii atlas [narodov] Sibiri*. Moscow: Izd-vo AN SSSR.

Lopatin, I.A. 1922. Gol'dy: Amurskie, ussuriiskie i sungariiskie. *Zapiski OIAK* (Vladivostok).

Lukina, N.V. 1973. Olenevodstvo Vakhovskikh khantov. In *Iz istorii Sibiri* 145–68. Tomsk.

———. 1984. Nekotorye voprosy proiskhozhdeniia olenevodstva khantov. In *Etnografiia narodov Sibiri* 10–17. Novosibirsk.

———. 1986. Kul'turnye traditsii v khoziaistvennoi deiatel'nosti khantov. In *Kul'turnye traditsii narodov Sibiri* 121–38. Leningrad.

Lukina, N.V., V.M. Kulemsin, and E.M. Titarenko. 1975. Khanty r. Agan (po materialam ekspeditsii 1972 g.). In *Iz istorii Sibiri* 130–77. Tomsk.

Mainov, I.I. 1898. Nekotorye dannye o tungusakh Iakutskogo kraia. *Trudy VSORGO* (Irkutsk), no. 2.

Maksimov, A.N. 1928. Proiskhozhdenie olenevodstva. *Uchenye zapiski RANION* 6.

Maloletko, A.M. 1983. Geograficheskie nazvaniia Khantaiskoi gidrosistemy. *Voprosy geografii Sibiri* (Tomsk) 14:103–124.

Markarian, E.S. 1981a. K ekologicheskoi kharakteristike razvitiia etnicheskikh kul'tur. In M.P. Kim (ed.) *Obshchestvo i priroda: Istoricheskie etapy i formy vzaimodeistviia* 96–109. Moscow: Nauka.

———. 1981b. Uzlovye problemy kul'turnoi traditsii. *Sovetskaia etnografiia,* no. 2: 78–96.

Markov, G.E. 1979. *Istoria khoziaistva i material'noi kul'tury.* Moscow.

———. 1981. Skotovodcheskoe khoziaistvo i kochevnichestvo. *Sovetskaia etnografiia*, no. 4: 83–94.

Marx, K. [Marks, K.] 1960. Kapital. In K. Marks and F. Engels, *Sochineniia.* 2nd edn., vol. 23. Moscow: GosPolitizdat. [English translation taken from MECW at http://www.marxists.org/archive/marx/works/1867-c1/ch07.htm, accessed 15 January 2010]

Marx [Marks], K., and F. Engels. n.d. Nemetskaia ideologiia. In K. Marks and F. Engels, *Sochineniia* 15–78. 2nd edn., vol. 3. [English translation taken from MECW at http://www.marxists.org/archive/marx/works/1845/german-ideology/ch01a.htm, accessed 15 January 2010]

Marr, N.Ia. 1926. *Sredstva peredvizheniia, orudiia samozashchity i proizvodstva v doistorii.* Leningrad.

Masson, V.M. 1971. *Ekonomika i sotsial'nyi stroi drevnikh obshchestv.* Leningrad.

Mavrodin, V.V., and Val.V. Mavrodin. 1981. *Iz istorii otechestvennogo oruzhiia: Russkaia vintovka.* Leningrad.

Middendorf, A.F. (1869–1877). *Puteshestvie na Sever i Vostok Sibiri.* Vol. 2, parts 5–6.

Miller, F.F. 1895. Tungusy, iakuty, chukchi. *Zhivopisnaia Rossiia* 12, no. 1: 279–294.

Miller, G.F. 1937. *Istoriia Sibiri.* Vol. 1. Moscow.

———. 1941. *Istoriia Sibiri.* Vol. 2. Moscow.

Mowat, F. [Mouet, F.] 1981. *Ne krichi: Volki.* Moscow. [Russian translation of Farley Mowat's *Never Cry Wolf,* undet. edn.]

Nikolaev, S.I. 1961. Timptonskie evenki. In *Sbornik statei i materialov po etnografii narodov Iakutii.* Iakutsk.

Okladnikov, A.P. 1950. *Tunguso-man'chzhurskaia problema i arkheologiia* (Moscow) 18.

———. 1968. Neolit i bronzovyi vek Prybaikal'ia. *Istoriia SSSR,* no. 6: 25–42.

Okladnikov, A.P., and V.V. Alekseev. 1981. XXVI s'ezd KPSS i zadachi gumanitarnykh issledovanii v Sibiri. In *Istoricheskii opyt khoziaistvennogo i sotsial'no-kul'turnogo razvitiia Sibiri: Materialy k konferentsii* 3–10. Novosibirsk.

Orlov, P. 1857. Bauntovskie i angarskie brodiachie tungusy. *Vestnik RGO* 6:180–92 (no. 21, part 2).

Pelikh, G.I. 1981. *Sel'kupy v XVII v.: Ocherki sotsial'no-ekonomicheskoi istorii.* Novosibirsk.

Pestov, I. 1833. *Zapiski ob Eniseiskoi gubernii 1831 goda.* Irkutsk.

Petri, B.E. 1928. Promysly karagas. *Izv. VSORGO* (Irkutsk) 53:35–67.

———. 1930. *Okhota i olenevodstvo u tuturskikh tungusov v sviazi s organizatsiei okhotokhoziaistva.* Irkutsk.

Plekhanov, G.V. 1923. *K voprosu o razvitii monisticheskogo vzgliada na istoriiu.* Vol. 7. Moscow.

Plotnikov, M. 1924. *Olenevodstvo.* Chita.

Polevoi, B.P. 1965. Zabytyi istochnik po etnografii Sibiri. *Sovetskaia etnografiia,* no. 5: 122–29.

Poltoradnev, P.G. 1932. *Olenevodstvo tungusov (r. Nizhnei Tunguski).* Moskva–Irkutsk.

Pomishin, S.B. 1971. O transportnom ispol'zovanii olenia tofalarami. *Sovetskaia etnografiia,* no. 5: 128–31.

Popov, A.A. 1948. *Nganasany: Material'naia kul'tura.* Moscow–Leningrad.

Popov, M.V. 1977. *Opredelitel' mlekopitaiushchikh Iakutii.* Novosibirsk.

Popov, N. 1926. Pishcha tungusov. *Izv. VSORGO* (Irkutsk).

Popova, U.G. 1981. *Eveny Magadanskoi oblasti: Ocherki istorii, khoziaistva i kul'tury evenov Okhotskogo poberezh'ia, 1917–1977.* Moscow: Nauka.

Problemy istorii dokapitalisticheskikh obshchestv. 1968. Moscow.

Prokof'eva, E.D. 1976. Olenevodstvo tazovskikh sel'kupov. In *Material'naia kul'tura narodov Sibiri i Severa* 139–55. Leningrad.

Radde, G. 1858. Ozero Baikal: [Razdel 2.] Etnograficheskii ocherk pribaikal'skikh buriat i tungusov. *Vestnik RGO*, pp. 137–49.

Rakita, S.A. 1983. *Priroda i khoziaistvennoe osvoenie Severa.* Moscow.

Romanova, A.V., and A.N. Myreeva. 1968. *Dialektologicheskii slovar' evenkiiskogo iazyka: Materialy govorov evenkov Iakutii.* Leningrad.

Rychkov, K.M. 1917. Eniseiskie tungusy. Part 1. *Zemlevedenie* 24. No. 1–2.

Samokhin, A.T. 1929. Tungusy Bodaibinskogo raiona. *Sibirskaia zhivaia starina* (Irkutsk: VSORGO) 8–9:5–66.

Sem, Iu.A. 1983. Nekotorye voprosy sravnitel'no-sopostavitel'nogo izucheniia material'noi kul'tury narodov Severa. In *Istoricheskaia etnografiia: Traditsii i sovremennost'* 124–30. Leningrad.

Semenov, Iu.A. 1976. O spetsifike proizvodstvennykh (sotsial'no-ekonomicheskikh) otnoshenii pervobytnogo obshchestva. *Sovetskaia etnografiia,* no. 4: 93–113.

Semenov, Iu.I. 1973. O materinskom rode i osedlosti v pozdnem paleolite. *Sovetskaia etnografiia,* no. 4: 52–65.

———. 1979. Evoliutsiia ekonomiki rannego pervobytnogo obshchestva. In *Issledovaniia po obshchei etnografii* 61–124. Moscow.

———. 1982. Kochevnichestvo i nekotorye obshchie problemy khoziaistva i obshchestva. *Sovetskaia etnografiia,* no. 2: 48–59.

Semenov-Tian-Shanskii, O.I. 1977. *Severnyi olen'.* Moscow.

Shnirel'man, V.A. 1977. Rol' domashnikh zhivotnykh v periferiinykh obshchestvakh (na primere traditsionnykh obshchestv Sibiri i Ameriki). *Sovetskaia etnografiia,* no. 2: 29–42.

———. 1980. Proiskhozhdenie i rasprostranenie olenevodstva. In *Proiskhozhdenie skotovodstva* 175–89. Moscow.

———. 1986. Pozdnepervobytnaia obshchina zemledel'tsev-skotovodov i vysshykh okhotnikov, rybolovov i sobiratelei. In *Istoriia pervobytnogo obshchestva: Epokha pervobytnoi rodovoi obshchiny* 236–426. Moscow.

Simchenko, Iu.B. 1976. *Kul'tura okhotnikov na olenei Severnoi Evrazii: Etnograficheskaia rekonstruktsiia.* Moscow.

———. 1978. Severnaia Aziia. In *Pervobytnaia periferiia klassovykh obshchestv do nachala velikikh geograficheskikh otkrytii.* Moscow.

Sirina, A.A. 2006. *Katanga Evenkis in the 20th Century and the Ordering of Their Life-world.* Northern Hunter-Gatherers Research Series 2. Edmonton: CCI Press. [English translation, with added editor's preface, glossary, and index, of *Katangskie evenki v XX veke: Rasselenie, organizatsiia sredy zhiznedeiatel'nosti,* 2nd edn. Moscow–Irkutsk: Ottisk 2002]

Smoliak, A.V. 1984. *Traditsionnoe khoziaistvo i material'naia kul'tura narodov Nizhnego Amura.* Moscow.

Sokolov, G.A. 1979. *Mlekopitaiushchie kedrovykh lesov Sibiri.* Novosibirsk.

Sokolov, M.P. 1925. Pushnoi promysel Srednesibiriskogo kraia. In *Predvaritel'nye materialy po raionirovaniiu Srednesibirskogo (Leno-Baikal'skogo) kraia* 14–27. Irkutsk.

Sokolova, E.P. 1963. Materialy po zhilishchu, khoziaistvennym i kul'tovym postroikam obskikh ugrov. *Trudy Instituta etnografii* 84.

———. 1982. *Strana Ugroiia.* Moscow.

Spevakovskii, A.B. 1984. Etnokul'turnye kontakty tungusoiazychnykh narodnostei na vostoke Sibiri (eveny i evenki). In *Etnokul'turnye kontakty narodov Sibiri* 121–31. Leningrad.

Starikovich, S.F. 1982. *Zverinets u kryl'tsa.* Moscow.

Stepanov, A.P. 1835. *Eniseiskaia guberniia.* St. Petersburg.

Stepanov, N.N. 1939. Mezhplemennoi obmen v Vostochnoi Sibiri, na Amure i na Okhotskom poberezh'e v XVII v. *Uchenye zapiski LGU* 48:53–79.

———. 1961. Khoziaistvo tungusskikh plemen Sibiri v XVII v. In *Voprosy istorii Sibiri* 209–62. Leningrad.

Suslov, I.M. 1927. Okhota u tungusov. *Okhotnik i pushnik Sibiri,* no. 1: 44–49.

———. 1930. Raschet minimal'nogo kolichestva olenei, potrebnogo dlia tuzemnogo seredniatskogo khoziaistva. *Sovetskii Sever,* no. 3: 23–35.

Taksami, Ch.M. 1961. Seleniia, zhilye i khoziaistvennye postroiki nivkhov Amura i zapadnogo poberezh'ia o. Sakhalin (seredina XIX–nachalo XX vv.). *Sibirskii etnograficheskii sbornik* (Leningrad) 3:98–166, o.s. 64.

Ter-Akopian N.B. 1977. O sotsial'no-ekonomicheskikh otnosheniiakh v pervobytnom obshchestve. *Sovetskaia etnografiia*, no. 3: 64–67.

TMS-1. 1975. *Sravnitel'nyi slovar' tunguso-man'chzhurskikh iazykov*. ed. V.I. Tsintsius. Vol. 1. Leningrad: Nauka.

TMS-2. 1977. *Sravnitel'nyi slovar' tunguso-man'chzhurskikh iazykov*. ed. V.I. Tsintsius. Vol. 2. Leningrad: Nauka.

Tolstov, S.P. 1931. Problemy dorodovogo obshchestva. *Sovetskaia etnografiia*, no. 3–4: 69–103.

———. 1946. K voprosu o periodizatsii istorii pervobytnogo obshchestva. *Sovetskaia etnografiia*, no. 1: 25–30.

———. 1961. Nekotorye problemy vsemirnoi istorii v svete dannykh sovremennoi istoricheskoi etnografii. *Voprosy istorii*, no. 11: 107–18.

Tret'iakov, P. 1869. Turukhanskii krai: Ego priroda i zhizn'. *Zapiski RGO* 2:215–530.

Tugolukov, V.A. 1962. Vitimo-olekminskie evenki. *Trudy Instituta etnografii* (Moscow) 78:67–97.

———. 1969. *Sledopyty verkhom na oleniakh*. Moscow.

———. 1970. Sotsial'naia organizatsia evenkov i evenov. In I.S. Gurvich and B.O. Dolgikh (eds.) *Obshchestvennyi stroi u narodov Severnoi Sibiri, XVII–nachalo XX v.* 214–47. Moscow: Nauka.

———. 1974. Evenki basseina reki Turukhan. In *Sotsial'naia organizatsia i kul'tura narodov Severa* 58–81. Moscow.

———. 1980. Etnicheskie korni tungusov. In *Etnogenez narodov Severa* 152–76. Moscow.

Turov, M.G. 1974. Nekotorye svedeniia ob evenkakh Chunskogo raiona. In *Drevniaia istoriia narodov iuga Vostochnoi Sibiri*. Vol. 1, pp. 237–48. Irkutsk.

———. 1975. K probleme proiskhozhdeniia i evoliutsii evenkiiskogo labaza-'noku'. *Drevniaia istoriia narodov iuga Vostochnoi Sibiri*. Vol. 3, pp. 193–209. Irkutsk.

———. 1978. K voprosu o religioznykh vozzreniiakh evenkov Angaro-Chunskogo vodorazdela. *Drevniaia istoriia narodov iuga Vostochnoi Sibiri*. Vol. 4. Irkutsk.

———. 1979. K analizu khoziaistva evenkiiskikh okhotnich'ikh grupp taezhnoi zony Sibiri (XVII nachalo XX v.). In *Tezy konferentsii: Arkheologiia, etnografiia, istochnikovedenie*. Irkutsk.

——. 1982. K probleme rekonstruktsii modeli khoziaistva grupp evenkov taezhnoi zony Srednei Sibiri (konets XIX–nachalo XX v.). In *Material'naia kul'tura drevnego naseleniia Vostochnoi Sibiri*. Irkutsk.

——. 2008. *Evenki: Osnovnye problemy etnogeneza i etnicheskoi istorii*. Irkutsk: Amtera.

Vainshtein, S.I. 1960. K voprosu o saianskom tipe olenevodstva i ego vozniknovenii. *KSIE* (Moscow) 84:54–60.

——. 1970. Problemy proiskhozhdeniia olenevodstva v Evrazii. Part 1. *Sovetskaia etnografiia*, no. 6: 3–14.

——. 1971. Problemy proiskhozhdeniia olenevodstva v Evrazii. Part 2. *Sovetskaia etnografiia*, no. 5: 37–52.

——. 1972. *Istoricheskaia etnografiia tuvintsev. Problemy kochevogo khoziaistva*. Moscow.

Vasilevich, G.M. 1936. *Materialy po evenkiiskomu (tungusskomu) fol'kloru*. Leningrad.

——. 1949. Fol'klornye materialy i plemennoi sostav evenkov (tungusov). In *Trudy II vsesoiuznogo s"ezda Geograficheskogo obshchestva*. Vol. 3, pp. 355–64. Moscow.

——. 1951. K voprosu o nachale stanovleniia tungusskikh iazykov. In *Tezy dokladov: Soveshchanie po metodologii etnogeneticheskikh issledovanii*. Moscow.

——. 1961. Ugdan — zhilishche evenkov Iablonevogo i Stanovogo khrebta. *Sbornik MAE* (Moscow), pp. 30–39.

——. 1962. Evenki Katanagskogo raiona. *Sibirskii etnograficheskii sbornik* 4, *Trudy Instituta etnografii* (Moscow), n.s., 78:98–121.

——. 1964. *Tipy olenevodstva u tungusoiazychnykh narodov (v sviazi s problemoi rasseleniia)*. Moscow.

——. 1966. *Istoricheskii fol'klor evenkov*. Leningrad.

——. 1969. *Evenki: Istoriko-etnograficheskie ocherki*. Leningrad.

——. 1972. Nekotorye voprosy plemeni i roda u evenkov. In *Okhotniki, sobirateli, rybolovy* 160–71. Leningrad.

Vasilevich, G.M., and M.G. Levin. 1951. Tipy olenevodstva i ikh proiskhozhdenie. *Sovetskaia etnografiia*, no. 1: 63–67.

Vdovin, I.S. 1973. *Ocherki etnicheskoi istorii koriakov*. Leningrad.

Veltfish, Dzh. 1978. Indeitsy stepei: Ikh preemstvennost' v istorii i indeanizm. In *Severoamerikanskie indeitsy* 193–219. Moscow.

Vereshchagin, N.K., and O.S. Rusakov. 1979. *Kopytnye Severo-Zapada SSSR: Istoriia, obraz zhizni i khoziaistvennoe ispol'zovanie.* Leningrad.

Vinogradov, G.M. 1926. Etnograficheskie izucheniia Vostochno-sibirskogo otdela Russkogo geograficheskogo obshchestva. *Izvestiia VSORGO* (Irkutsk) 50, no. 6: 3–37.

Voilochnikov, A.T. 1977. Belka. In *Okhota na pushnykh: Ekologicheskie osnovy promysla* 179–215. Moscow.

Vorob'ev, N.N. 1926. Naselenie Prichunskogo raiona. *Sbornik MAE* (Moscow) 33, no. 2–3: 59–112.

Weiner, J.S. [Uainer, Dzh.] 1979. Ekologiia cheloveka. In *Biologiia cheloveka* 472–596. Moscow: Mir. [Russian translation of "Human Ecology" in G.A. Harrison, J.S. Weiner, J.M. Tanner, and N.A. Barnicot's *Human Biology: An Introduction to Human Evolution, Variation, and Growth* 399–508. London: Oxford University Press 1964]*

Zhekulin, V.S. 1982. *Istoricheskaia etnografiia: Predmet i metody.* Leningrad.

Ziber, N.N. 1937. *Ocherki pervobytnoi ekonomicheskoi kul'tury.* Moscow.

Zinner, F. P. 1968. *Sibir' v izvestiiakh zapadnoevropeiskikh puteshestvennikov i uchenykh XVIII v.* Irkutsk.

---

*Author's citation of Weiner on p. 18 in this volume is actually a quotation in Weiner's chapter of the cited reference of Le Gros Clark F. 1951. The Malthusian Heritage. In F. Le Gros Clark and N. W. Pirie (eds.) *Four Thousand Million Mouths: Scientific Humanism and the Shadow of World Hunger.* London: Oxford University Press, p. 17. —*Ed.*

Appendix: Selected photographs

All photographs are by the author unless otherwise indicated. Included here are several more photographs than in the original Russian edition. Some of the numbering has been altered, and errors in the original captions have been corrected.

Photo 1. Family of the Evenkis V. P. Kaplin (Pangarakai clan) and his wife, M. P. Egorchenok.

Photo 2. E. I. Rukosueva (Ovodyl clan) of the Chuna Evenki group.

*Photo 3. Permanent **noku-delken** food cache at an autumn base camp [osennii ogorod 'autumn garden'] of the Katanga Evenki group.*

*Photo 4. Permanent **noku-delken** food cache or labaz near the summer migration route of some Trans-Baikal Evenkis. Photo by A. I. Arbatskii.*

Photo 5. Reindeer in smudges at a summer stop-over camp.

Photo 6. Milking reindeer cows in a smudge; summer camp of V. P. Kaplin. Lower Tunguska Evenkis.

*Photo 7. Starting point in the process of erecting a chum at a summer stopover camp. The three **turgu** 'main poles' have been tied together at the top, forming the skeleton frame of the dwelling.*

*Photo 8. Next stage of erecting the chum: all the lodgepoles are in place, and one of the two **elbenel** lower covers has been attached.*

*Photo 9. The 'chum **diu**' dwelling is ready.*

Photo 10. **Iumgulo** *ground-level cache or labaz, used in late autumn for storing frozen meat.*

Photo 11. **Noku dzeptyleruk** *'food cache' on three posts.*

Photo 12. Cache or labaz made of hewn planks and a pitched roof; the posts are 3.5 m tall. Chuna River Evenkis.

Photo 13. Cache (labaz) on six posts. Katanga Evenkis.

Photo 14. Reindeer loaded with packs in preparation for migration.

Photo 15. Permanent cache (labaz) for storing winter clothing and equipment, belonging to a group of related families staying together at a winter base camp. Lower Tunguska Evenkis.

*Photo 16. **Delken** food cache at the autumn base camp (stoibishche) of V. P. Kaplin. Katanga Evenki group.*

Photo 17. Old cache on one of the travel routes of the Kaplin family; photo taken in autumn during the fur hunt.

*Photo 18. Evenki woman E. I. Rukosueva beside an old **ugdama-diu** bark chum, or **golomo** lodge (Chuna Evenkis, base camp on Brodovaia R.).*

Photo 19. **Ugdama** *cache (labaz) for a small volume of food stores. Bark of Siberian larch used for the cover. Trans-Baikal Evenkis. Photo by A. I. Arbatskii.*

Photo 20. **Gobchik** *log mortuary structure on a shaman's grave. Katanga (Lower Tunguska) Evenkis.*

Photo 21. Unusual construction of a cache or labaz (collapsed in this photo): two-storied, on low posts. According to informant descriptions, the first storey was used to store equipment, and the second was used to store food. Chuna Evenkis.

Photo 22. Food cache (produktovyi labaz) on two posts up to 3 m tall. Chuna Evenkis.

Photo 23. Crushing trap for wolverines. Katanga Evenkis.

Photo 24. Hunter's snow-shoes/skis (lyzhi). Bindings visible on left ski, kamus lining (skins from the legs of a moose) on right. Chuna Evenkis.

Photo 25. Panorama of the autumn base camp of L. P. Sichogir, before the start of the fur hunting season. Katanga Evenkis.

Photo 26. Gateway for reindeer left behind, part of the fence of an autumn enclosure, facing the trail from the previous camp. Katanga Evenkis.

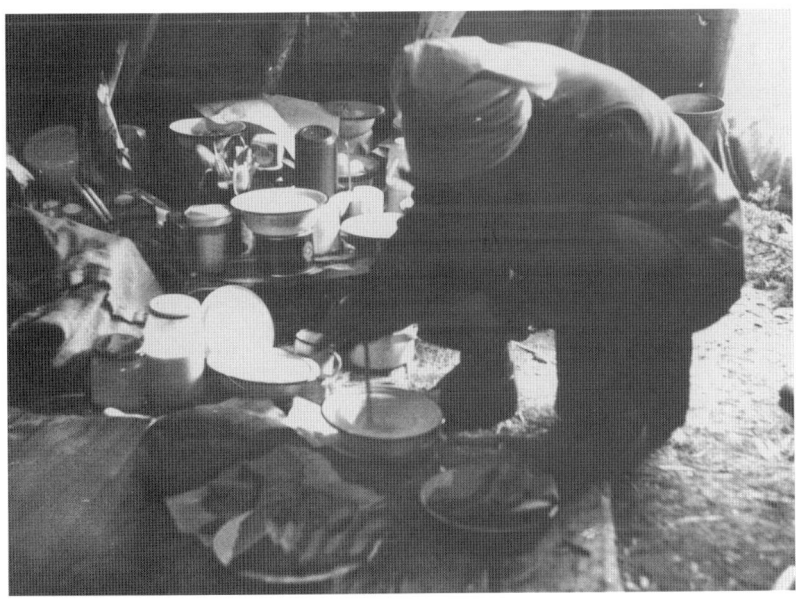

Photo 27. Churning the cream from reindeer milk. The 'mixer' is evidently a borrowing from the Russian mutovka *'whisk'—a stick with a wooden cross-piece attached.*

Photo 28. Preliminary processing of moose hide into **rovduga** suede.

Photo 29. **Diugani** summer camp in the nomadizing territory of L. P. Sichogir. Katanga Evenkis.

Photo 30. Reindeer in smudges at a summer camp. Katanga Evenkis.

Photo 31. L. P. Sichegir, master of the camp (stoibishche). Katanga Evenkis.

Photo 32. Early autumn: chum in an autumn reindeer pasture.

Photo 33. Part of an autumn pasture enclosure.

Photo 34. Close-up of fastening for autumn pasture enclosure.

Photo 35. **Guluvun** *fire (koster) for cooking food.*

Photo 36. An ancient method for keeping reindeer close to base camp in late autumn and early spring: domesticated reindeer stand near a **chiken** *trough (groove cut into a log) with human urine, which is salty and thus attractive to reindeer. Camp of L. P. Sichogir.*